EXPLORER'S GUIDE

YELLOWSTONE & GRAND TETON NATIONAL PARKS

EXPLORER'S GUIDE

YELLOWSTONE & GRAND TETON NATIONAL PARKS

FOURTH EDITION

JEFF WELSCH AND SHERRY L. MOORE

THE COUNTRYMAN PRESS
A division of W. W. Norton & Company
Independent Publishers Since 1923

For comments, suggestions, or corrections, please write to:
Explorer's Guide Editor
The Countryman Press
500 Fifth Avenue
New York, NY 10110

You can email Jeff and Sherry at gardenangelink@aol.com.
Check out our Countryman Press guidebook Facebook pages for *Explorer's Guide Yellowstone & Grand Teton National Parks*, *Backroads & Byways of Montana*, and *Oregon Wine Country: A Great Destination*.

Copyright © 2019 by Jeff Welsch and Sherry L. Moore
Interior photographs by the authors unless otherwise specified
Maps by Erin Greb Cartography © The Countryman Press

For information about permission to reproduce selections from this book, write to
Permissions, The Countryman Press, 500 Fifth Avenue, New York, NY 10110

For information about special discounts for bulk purchases, please contact
W. W. Norton Special Sales at specialsales@wwnorton.com or 800-233-4830

Library of Congress Cataloging-in-Publication Data
Names: Welsch, Jeff, author. | Moore, Sherry L., author.
Title: Explorer's guide Yellowstone & Grand Teton National Parks /
Jeff Welsch and Sherry L. Moore.
Other titles: Yellowstone & Grand Teton National Parks and Jackson Hole.
Description: Fourth edition. | New York : Countryman Press, a division of
W. W. Norton & Company, [2019] | Series: Explorer's guide | Includes bibliographical
references and index.
Identifiers: LCCN 2019014516 | ISBN 9781682683507 (pbk. : alk. paper)
Subjects: LCSH: National parks and reserves—United States—Guidebooks. |
Yellowstone National Park—Guidebooks. | Grand Teton National Park (Wyo.)—
Guidebooks. | Jackson Hole (Wyo.)—Guidebooks. | Wyoming—Guidebooks.
Classification: LCC F722 .W45 2019 | DDC 917.87/5204—dc23 LC record
available at https://lccn.loc.gov/2019014516

The Countryman Press
www.countrymanpress.com

A division of W. W. Norton & Company, Inc.
500 Fifth Avenue, New York, NY 10110
www.wwnorton.com

978-1-68268-350-7 (pbk.)

10 9 8 7 6 5 4 3 2 1

To Daisy, Cash, Cameron, and Parker,
future stewards of the Greater Yellowstone Ecosystem.

EXPLORE WITH US!

More than 4 million visitors come to the Greater Yellowstone region each year to immerse themselves in the history, geology, scenery, and wildlife of a natural and wild landscape. In our fourth edition of *Explorer's Guide Yellowstone & Grand Teton National Parks*, we strive to enhance the extraordinary.

Whether you're marveling at wolves and grizzly bears in the wild, gazing in abject wonder at mountains touching the sky, or getting acquainted with the colorful personalities of the parks' gateway communities, we give you the story behind the portrait. On these pages you'll get historical, geological, and ecological lessons you won't find in other guidebooks. You'll get easy-to-understand descriptions of the fiery world just beneath your feet and the wonders before your eyes. And you'll get the backstory on the region's charismatic megafauna: wolves, grizzly bears, bison, moose, elk, and more.

Even though Yellowstone and Grand Teton National Parks are inextricably linked in the Greater Yellowstone Ecosystem, for this edition we have further distinguished them, providing primers devoted to information pertinent to each park. Yellowstone remains separated into five chapters—one for each of the entrances with pay stations. Within each chapter you'll follow the roads inside the park that begin and fan out from those entrances. Grand Teton National Park is covered in a separate chapter in the same format.

Each chapter includes key information on gateway communities while highlighting can't-miss attractions and recreation outside the parks. We have made every attempt to organize important information so that it is easily found, understood, and current, but changes occur rapidly in these tourist destinations. Restaurants come and go, and hours and menus change, literally with the seasons. What was true last week might not be so during your visit.

WHAT'S WHERE A major change in the fourth edition is an alphabetical listing of important information to ensure you get the most from your Yellowstone and Grand Teton National Parks bucket-list vacation. It is where you'll find out how to stay safe and healthy, acquire permits and licenses, and know the best places to get a closer look at the region's colorful history.

LODGING Choosing where to lay your head at night is vital to a successful trip. We've made a point of including lodging we would recommend to our family and friends, whether you're on a budget or needn't spare any expense. We have stayed in many of the hotels, motels, lodges, cabins, and other accommodations listed, or have relied on friends, acquaintances, and others connected to businesses for further insight. Please note, none of the entries are paid listings.

We use a $ symbol to reflect average high-season (summer) rates for most rooms. Costs differ dramatically by season, and you can expect slightly lower rates in the winter unless you're in ski country. The best opportunities for bargains are in the so-called "shoulder" seasons of spring and fall. We also include icons for lodging that welcomes pets, meets ADA standards, and has a restaurant on-site.

Our lodging codes are as follows:

Best Lodging
$:   Up to $100
$$: $100–200
$$$: $200–300
$$$$: Over $300

Because of the many lodging choices in these communities, we further arranged best selections into groupings based on price. The exception to our "best of" dining and lodging criteria is inside YNP and GTNP, where we have included everything.

When you see the "Authors' favorite" star icon, you'll know these are places we consider to be the best of the best and eagerly frequent. We give them our seal of approval for a variety of reasons, starting with the quality of the experience.

Finally, we have made every attempt to determine open times for lodging, dining, and attractions, including if they close for a month in spring and fall to regroup. If facilities are open year-round, no seasons are noted.

DINING As with lodging, getting the most out of your restaurant experiences is also an important part of your journey. Dining choices abound in Greater Yellowstone, and on these pages we offer favorites based on our personal experiences and the recommendations of friends or acquaintances who live in these communities. Consideration is based on many factors: reputation, ambiance, quality and diversity of menu, and local popularity. We further organize the various options based on whether we favor them for breakfast, lunch, or dinner. Again, none of these are paid entries.

Dining codes ($) are based on the price of an average entrée. In cases where we have two sets of dollar signs separated by a slash, either most meals are in the lower range or there is a significant difference between breakfast and dinner. Generally, because menus change so frequently, we don't mention specific entrées. If we do, it's a signature dish or typical representation of the menu. Finally, each restaurant includes a "B," "L," "D," "Br," and/or "HH" to reflect whether it serves breakfast, lunch, dinner, Sunday brunch, and/or has a happy hour. Our codes are as follows:

Best Dining
$:   Up to $12
$$: $13–25
$$$: $26–39
$$$$: Over $40

KEY TO SYMBOLS
- ✪ **Authors' favorites.** Some lodging and dining have consistently stood out to us for their personality and quality. Owners who bring their A games with their unique environs earn a star.
- 🐾 **Pets.** Even though rules are strict in the parks, Greater Yellowstone generally is a dog-friendly region where it isn't uncommon to see Fido curled up behind the bar or registration counter. You'll see a lot of these symbols.
- ♿ **Meets ADA standards.** This is a primitive region, and that goes for many cabins and other lodging. Many don't have ADA approved rooms; we note those that do but suggest you call ahead to confirm.
- 🍴 **Restaurants on-site.** Some lodging includes a restaurant on the premises. For guest ranches, the symbol is included if a dining area is open to the public.

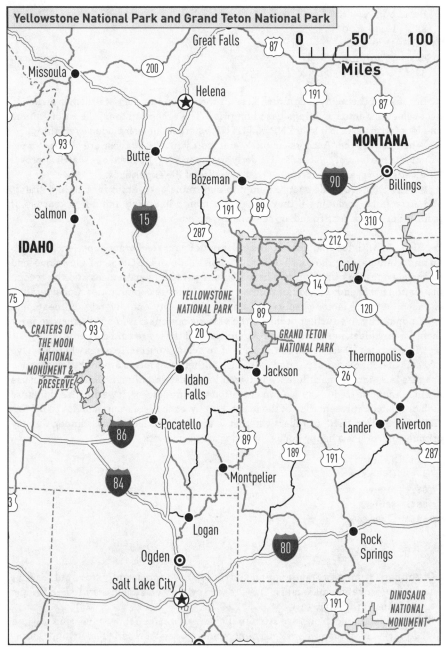

Yellowstone National Park and Grand Teton National Park

CONTENTS

MAPS

ACKNOWLEDGMENTS

We again thank the many Greater Yellowstone residents and visitors who share with us their special insights into this magnificent part of the world. We would also like to thank The Countryman Press and W. W. Norton & Co. for the opportunity to share our affection for Yellowstone and Grand Teton National Parks. Having lived in Yellowstone's backyard since 2004 and immersing ourselves in exploration—for fun, for work, and for this book—the depth of our appreciation, admiration, and respect for this wild country has increased every year. We are truly fortunate to be witnesses to one of the last great, intact, temperate ecosystems on the planet.

—Jeff Welsch and Sherry L. Moore

INTRODUCTION

If wondrous scenery, incomparable wildlife viewing, riveting geology, and the chance to witness natural processes mostly unimpeded by humans aren't enough incentive to put Yellowstone and Grand Teton National Parks at the top of your vacation list, then consider: It could all be gone tomorrow, obliterated in a cataclysmic instant.

We're not talking about a noticeably warming climate and its conspicuous consequences. Or the encroaching masses of humanity that have doubled the region's population and threaten to love Yellowstone, Grand Teton, and the surrounding wild country to death. Or pen strokes from government leaders who seem determined to unravel more than a century of conservation successes. We're not even talking about a recurrence of the dramatic 1988 fires that scorched one-third of Yellowstone's 2.2

OLD FAITHFUL PUTS ON YET ANOTHER SHOW, AS IT FAITHFULLY DOES EVERY HOUR OR SO   JIM PEACO / NPS

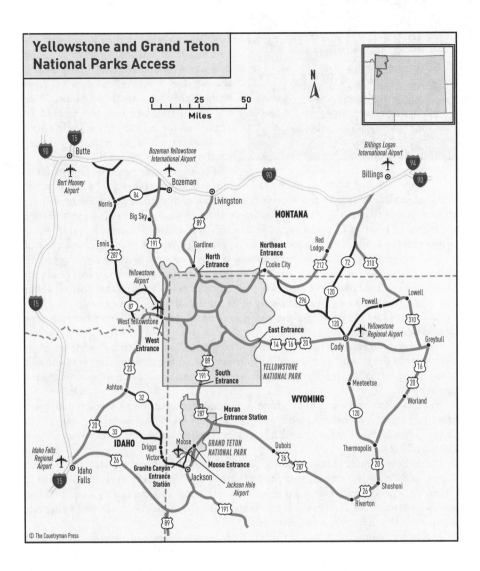

Yellowstone and Grand Teton National Parks Access

0 25 50
Miles

N

Butte
Bert Mooney Airport
Bozeman Yellowstone International Airport
Bozeman
Norris
Big Sky
Livingston
MONTANA
Billings Logan International Airport
Billings
Ennis
Gardiner
North Entrance
Northeast Entrance
Cooke City
Red Lodge
Yellowstone Airport
West Yellowstone
West Entrance
East Entrance
Cody
Powell
Lowell
Yellowstone Regional Airport
Greybull
YELLOWSTONE NATIONAL PARK
South Entrance
Meeteetse
WYOMING
Worland
Ashton
Moran Entrance Station
Moose
GRAND TETON NATIONAL PARK
Moose Entrance
Dubois
Thermopolis
Idaho Falls Regional Airport
Driggs
Victor
Granite Canyon Entrance Station
Jackson
Jackson Hole Airport
Idaho Falls
IDAHO
Shoshoni
Riverton

© The Countryman Press

million acres, from which the park has undergone an astonishing renaissance right before our eyes.

It's more ominous than that. It's megatons of pent-up geothermal fury, poised to unleash its ire on the planet much the way it did about 640,000 years ago ... and about 700,000 years before that ... and about 700,000 years before that, and ...

Detect a trend here? Maybe. Or maybe not. Scientists can't say for sure when, or if, the molten rock just beneath Yellowstone's 1,300-square-mile caldera will erupt in such a manner as to make the 1980 Mount St. Helens eruption seem like a burp. Television documentaries remind us of this specter, especially when the Greater Yellowstone region is routinely visited by earthquake "swarms." Or when a rock fissure appears seemingly overnight, as occurred in 2017. Or when a 100-foot gap suddenly opens in the Teton Range, stunning climbers and moving park officials to close a popular trail in July 2018. The usual rush to conclusion from such events—cue the brooding background music—is that a massive eruption is imminent.

Of course, such natural shock and awe wouldn't bode well for those of us living downstream—downstream being everywhere from West Yellowstone to West Philadelphia. But truth be known, this uneasy alliance between man and nature is part of the allure of the world's first national park and its majestic younger sibling 8 miles to the south.

For as you marvel at the jagged, fault-blocked Tetons rising like "granite cathedrals" above Jackson Lake to a cloudless sky, you'll contemplate the silent rumblings underfoot and realize that Mother Nature sets the ground rules here. As you admire the belching, hissing, and spewing of Yellowstone's 10,000 geothermal features, you'll respect just how alive and unpredictable this planet truly is. As you glimpse a pack of wolves systematically hunting down an ailing elk, or coyotes herding a young pronghorn for a meal, or a bison calf and its mother suffocating in a bog after plunging through ice—all scenes we've witnessed—you begin to understand that the beauty of this extraordinary ecosystem lies partly in its unvarnished natural cycles.

And that's just the point. Yellowstone and Grand Teton are not drive-through zoos or wild animal parks.

Of course, you couldn't tell it by summer "bear jams," where traffic slows to an impatient halt. Or the tales of camera-toting tourists getting too close to their subjects and being gored by elk, charged by bison, or warned with an irritated snort by a protective mother bear.

Visitors who either don't understand this concept or treat it with cavalier disregard often pay a price, sometimes with their lives. Every year, people tumble over cliffs, drown in swift rivers, fall into boiling geysers, or wind up on the wrong end of bison horns and elk antlers.

It's understandable to an extent why some might disregard nature's laws here. After all, when Yellowstone was created in 1872 with a signature from President Ulysses S. Grant, the idea was to preserve a place of natural beauty, yes, but purely FOR THE BENEFIT AND ENJOYMENT OF THE PEOPLE—the motto etched into the stones on the famed Roosevelt Arch at the North Entrance in Gardiner.

Predators deemed contrary to this vision were relentlessly eradicated to the point where wolves were exterminated and mountain lions and grizzlies were perilously close to extinction. Hunting was allowed and poaching was routine in the early days. Until the late 1960s, federal officials slaughtered elk by the thousands or rounded them up to replenish depleted herds elsewhere in the West because without predators—especially wolves—their numbers skyrocketed and they grazed plant life to the nubs. Bison were reduced from the 30 million to 60 million that once thundered across the Great Plains to about a dozen in Yellowstone's Lamar Valley. Just two generations ago, black bears routinely congregated at Yellowstone's entrances for food handouts, and bleachers were set up around dumps behind park hotels so tourists could watch grizzlies gorge every evening on steak bones, potato peels, and half-eaten vegetables.

Ever since a seismic shift resulting from the publishing of The Leopold Report in 1963, though, efforts have been made to inch Yellowstone and Grand Teton National Parks as close as humanly possible to a natural condition. Hunting is now outlawed except for an "elk reduction program" in a small portion of Grand Teton. Feeding wildlife is strictly prohibited; black bears no longer come looking for handouts at entrance stations and the dumps were shut down overnight, to great initial detriment to the grizzly. Fishing is highly regulated on most streams. Other than lake trout in Lake Yellowstone, wildlife within Yellowstone's boundaries is protected. And other than bison, which are culled outside the park every few years to protect vegetation and limit the number that disperse, animal populations are allowed to repopulate naturally. Wildlife-sensitive areas are off-limits to humans at certain times of the year. Motorized and mechanized recreation is tightly regulated.

The crowning moment of this ecosystem-first philosophy came in 1995, when 14 gray wolves from Alberta, Canada, were introduced into Yellowstone's Northern Range, followed by 17 more from British Columbia the following year. Central Idaho's Frank Church–River of No Return Wilderness received a few more at the same time. The controversial transplants brought the park's ecology full circle seven decades after a government-sponsored eradication ended with the removal of the last native wolf in 1926.

Some scientists have credited the thriving wolf packs with restoring the health of the Lamar Valley ecosystem and other parts of the park. They tout a "trophic cascade,"

OXBOW BEND ON THE SNAKE RIVER IS ALWAYS PRIMED FOR A PHOTO OPPORTUNITY NPS

DID YOU KNOW?

About 98 percent of Yellowstone tourists never go farther than 100 yards from a roadway, meaning that roughly 98 percent of the park is experienced by less than 2 percent of its visitors.

starting with the fear *Canis lupus* has reinstilled in elk, their favored prey. No longer able to casually browse, the elk instinctively became more nomadic again, allowing cottonwood, willow, and aspen to regenerate after 70 years of futility. The resulting new plant growth purportedly has led to the return of songbirds and beavers, whose dams have created improved habitat for the struggling Yellowstone cutthroat trout. In turn, newly sprouted streamside berry bushes are providing forage for an expanding population of the grizzly bear, whose existence could be jeopardized partly by beetle and fungus decimation of whitebark pines and the loss of vital protein provided by their nuts.

With wolves back on the landscape, all of the wildlife species that were here when the first Anglos arrived more than 200 years ago roam freely again. This extraordinary conservation success renders Greater Yellowstone perhaps the last great largely intact temperate ecosystem on the planet. Yet it remains a fragile and vulnerable environment, and visitors are asked to tread lightly.

Outside the parks, a rich assortment of outdoor and indoor adventures awaits on the remaining 18 million acres of the Greater Yellowstone Ecosystem, including the scenic sage-and-conifer valley known as Jackson Hole.

River runners ply the Snake River's Class III rapids south of Jackson. West Yellowstone touts itself as the snowmobile capital of the world, with Cooke City not far behind. Greater Yellowstone streams that serve as the uppermost headwaters to America's three greatest river systems—the Missouri, Columbia, and Colorado—offer the finest trout fishing on earth, with hundreds of guides eager to share their second- or third-favorite holes. Six downhill ski resorts are within 50 miles of either park. Jackson Hole is a mountain biker's mecca worthy of mention in the same breath as Moab and Whistler. Ice climbers from around the world come to Bozeman's Hyalite Canyon and Cody's South Fork of the Shoshone. And adjacent federal wilderness areas provide solitude and adventure for hunters, anglers, hikers, campers, and packers wishing to see the land much the way Jim Bridger and John Colter saw it in the early nineteenth century.

The surrounding communities of Jackson, Cody, and Dubois in Wyoming; Bozeman, Ennis, Gardiner, Red Lodge, and West Yellowstone in Montana; and Driggs, Victor, Island Park, and Ashton in Idaho offer diverse restaurant fare, comfortable lodging ranging from the provincially rustic to cowboy-luxe guest ranches, and attractions befitting this wild corner of the West.

For those wanting the full park experience, upgraded lodging and dramatically improved dining are available inside both parks, from frontier luxury at historic Old Faithful Inn and Jenny Lake Lodge to no-frills rooms at Mammoth Hot

WOLVES WERE RESTORED TO YELLOWSTONE NATIONAL PARK IN 1995 AND ABOUT 100 WOLVES ROAM THE PARK TODAY JACOB W. FRANK / NPS

CYCLISTS LUNCH AT INDIAN CREEK BRIDGE IN EARLY APRIL, WHEN ALMOST ALL YELLOWSTONE ROADS ARE CLOSED TO MOTORIZED VEHICLES

Springs and bare-bones cabins at Roosevelt Lodge. If the increased rates at Yellowstone's lodging have priced you out of the market, campgrounds are plentiful. And there's always the certainty of solitude in the backcountry.

Today, those who put Yellowstone and Grand Teton at the top of their getaway docket can still witness some of the planet's finest handiwork in northwest Wyoming, southwest Montana, and southeast Idaho. That's true whether your tastes lean toward the towering backdrop of the snowcapped Tetons or the intricate web of life spun in front of your eyes in vast Yellowstone.

And part of this allure is the understanding that what Mother Nature gives she can also take away in an instant, just as she did 640,000 years ago . . . and 700,000 years before that . . . and 700,000 years before that.

YOU NEED A HAND TO UNDERSTAND JUST HOW BIG A WOLF PAW PRINT IS

YELLOWSTONE
NATIONAL PARK

"FOR THE BENEFIT AND ENJOYMENT OF THE PEOPLE"

YELLOWSTONE NATIONAL PARK

CREATED BY ACT OF CONGRESS MARCH 1 1872

A PRIMER

✳ Geology

Relax. You won't be vaporized by a sudden explosion from the earth's most schizo-
phrenic subsurface. When the time comes, scientists believe the molten chaos beneath
the Greater Yellowstone Ecosystem will provide plenty of warning.

It's all because the earth under Yellowstone is tossing, turning, pushing, pulling,
roiling, hissing, snorting, and heaving unlike anywhere else on the planet so visible
to humans. Yellowstone's 10,000-plus geysers, hot springs, fumaroles, travertine terraces, mud pots, and paint pots comprise more geothermal activity than the rest of the
globe's landmasses combined. Some 1,000 to 3,000 earthquakes are measured annually, including occasional "swarms" like the one in February 2018 in which more than
200 temblors were recorded in one night. Since 1900, there have been 30 quakes rating
5.5 or higher on the Richter scale. And this activity offers a mere glimpse of the underground activity since the first of three major eruptions starting 2.1 million years ago.

The numbers from that initial blast are staggering. More than 600 cubic miles of
ash rode air currents to what is now the Midwest, the Gulf of Mexico, and Canada, covering thousands of square miles in minutes. The 0.026 cubic miles of ash covering 11

PETRIFIED REDWOODS ARE SCATTERED ON SPECIMEN RIDGE, ALONG WITH ENTOMBED BREADFRUIT, MANGROVE, AND
OTHER ANCIENT TREE REMAINS JACOB W. FRANK / NPS

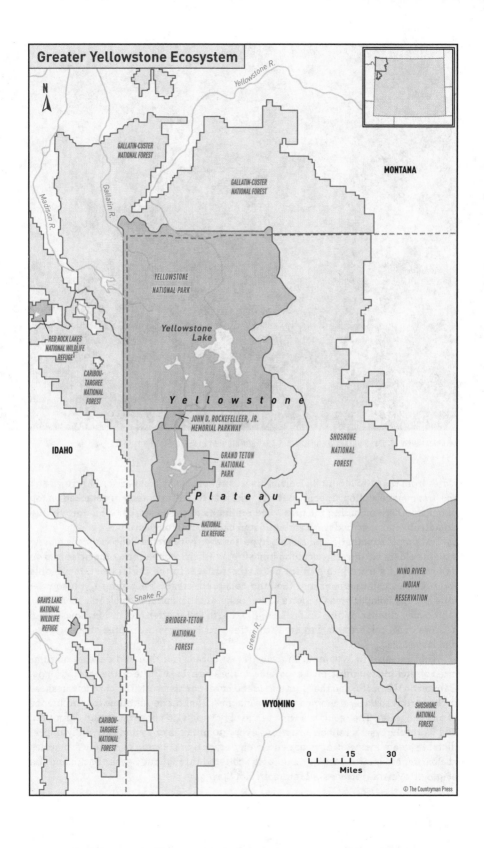

AN AERIAL VIEW OF UPPER GEYSER BASIN REVEALS THE TURMOIL JUST BENEATH EARTH'S SURFACE JIM PEACO / NPS

states from the 1980 Mount St. Helens blast is minuscule by comparison. And it wasn't the first major eruption. Specimen Ridge, where 27 fossilized forests are stacked on top of one another—including the preserved remnants of redwoods, oaks, mangrove, and breadfruit—has petrified trees carbon-dated back 50 million years.

The simple explanation for all this hyperterra activity is that Yellowstone is mostly a giant caldera sitting atop a combustible fire pit where molten rock, otherwise known as magma, is a mere 3 to 5 miles below the surface. In the initial blast, mountains were blown to smithereens and the land collapsed, creating a gaping 1,300-square-mile hole. By comparison, Oregon's Crater Lake, another collapsed volcanic mountain, is 37 times smaller. While Crater Lake filled with water after Mount Mazama caved, Yellowstone's caldera was carpeted with trees, rocks, streams, plains, steamy vents, and large lakes.

What remains in Wyoming's far northwest corner is a thin and delicate circular crust stretching roughly from Lewis Lake on the south, Lake Butte on the east to Norris, Canyon on the north, and the Montana-Idaho border on the west. The gaps and fissures in the earth's surface, combined with the magma's shallow depth, allow the confluence of fire and water. The result is a wide range of hot spots, in appearance and definition: Old Faithful geyser's reliable eruptions every 90 minutes or so and the wildly unpredictable Steamboat waiting years and even decades, the hissing of steamy fumaroles at Roaring Mountain, gurgling mud pots scattered throughout Geyser Basin, and the elegant travertine terraces of Mammoth Hot Springs.

Yellowstone's geothermal activity is also at least initially responsible for the park's most breathtaking feature: the Grand Canyon of the Yellowstone. At 20 miles long, up to 1,200 feet deep, and ranging from 1,000 to 4,000 feet across, the Grand Canyon's story begins with the arrival of glaciers whose impact would be felt as far south as the Tetons. The glaciers dammed the Yellowstone River, forming lakes. When the ice retreated, water poured forth and eroded lava rock made vulnerable by hot gases just beneath the surface. The rocks, called rhyolite, weren't so submissive to the onrushing water in two notable spots—the edge of the caldera and the junction of two different types of rhyolite.

These spectacular visual treats are now recognized as the Lower Falls (308 feet) and Upper Falls (109 feet) of the Yellowstone River. Both are favorites of the tourist's camera because of dramatic drops, the colorful hues of the canyon walls, and fine mists that create surreal light. It's no wonder the most alluring vistas are named Inspiration Point, Artist Point, and Grandview.

Also inspiring is the Northern Range, highlighted by towering mountains roughly along the northern boundary. Noteworthy is the dramatic gap in age between the Gallatin and Absaroka Mountains on the west, north, and east, and the Washburn Range and Red Mountains to the south. While both rise above the Yellowstone, Gardner, and Lamar River Valleys, the Gallatins and Absarokas are about 50 million years old. By contrast, the area between the Washburns and Reds, best seen from Dunraven Pass, is a product of Yellowstone's most recent major eruption 640,000 years ago. The hike to the top of 10,243-foot Mount Washburn provides a dramatic look at this explosive past. Rivulets of water cascade from these high peaks toward the Lamar River, which cuts across a grassy plain renowned for its wildlife.

THE GRAND CANYON OF THE YELLOWSTONE CUTS A YAWNING 20-MILE CHASM   JIM PEACO / NPS

HOT TIMES IN THE OLD PARK

Yellowstone certainly is renowned internationally for its spectacular wildlife and scenery, but its 10,000 thermal features are the reason this fiery region became the world's first national park. Here is a closer look at the four types of thermal features in the park and surrounding areas.

Geysers: The best known of Yellowstone's thermal attractions are the least common, comprising about 3 percent. Still, the 250 geysers (Icelandic for "gush forth") represent more than half of the world's total, and except perhaps for the travertine terraces at Mammoth Hot Springs, no type of thermal feature draws more tourists. Geysers are formed when water and snow seep into hot rock. As the heated water rises above the cold water and races to the surface, it expands and becomes trapped by steam bubbles in a chamber of resistant rhyolite rock. The pressure eventually forces it violently skyward. Think of your kitchen pressure cooker. Geysers even have distinctions. Fountain geysers spray water widely, while cone geysers, such as Old Faithful, are more like an uncorked fire hydrant.

GREAT FOUNTAIN GEYSER ERUPTS ABOUT EVERY 12 HOURS AND CAN LAST FOR AN HOUR OR LONGER JIM PEACO / NPS

Most of Yellowstone's geysers are distributed throughout nine basins, about half in Upper Geyser Basin, where Old Faithful's dependability has lured millions of spectators. For a geyser treat unfettered by crowds, try the 17-mile round-trip hike into Shoshone Geyser Basin near Grant's Pass.

Hot Springs: They're the same as geysers, without the drama. Most of Yellowstone's hot springs merely spill out of the ground at temperatures nearing 200 degrees, though Crested Pool has been known to explode despite having no constrictions. The Rockies and Cascade Range of Oregon and Washington are dotted with thousands of hot springs, many offering

✳ People

Imagine that you've migrated across the frozen Bering Strait, crossed the wilds of what is now Alaska and British Columbia, and ventured south into what would be called—in about 13,000 years—Montana. Along the way, you've traversed retreating glaciers from an ice age, evaded saber-toothed cats, and feasted on woolly mammoths. Suddenly you come across a trembling landscape unlike any you've ever known. Seething, spewing, gasping—all just reemerging after thousands of years trapped restlessly in icy seclusion.

a welcome respite for hikers, skiers, boaters, etc. But anyone looking for such relief in Yellowstone will be sorely disappointed. For safety reasons, the park has a blanket regulation against soaking in thermal pools, even in the backcountry. People have scalded themselves, and some springs carry potentially deadly microorganisms. Some intrepid hot-potters know of a few uncharted gems. One example is Mr. Bubbles, formerly known as Nirvana Pool, like Boiling River a junction of hot thermal waters and the chilly flow of the Ferris Fork River in the park's Bechler Region.

Fumaroles: These are geysers without the water, much of which has been vaporized by the time it reaches the surface. Fumaroles are known for their hissing sounds and rotten-egg smell of hydrogen sulfide; most notable examples are at Soda Butte in the Lamar River Valley and crossing the Yellowstone River Bridge near Tower. The appropriately named Roaring Mountain, just north of Norris, is the most prominent and visible example.

Mud Pots: Take a hot spring, add mud, and subtract a consistent water source. Presto, you've got a mud pot. Mud pots rely on snow and rain for sustenance. The bubbling, which has the look of a witch's brew, is from escaping gases. Add minerals to the recipe and you've got a colorful paint pot. Check out the Artist Paint Pots southwest of Norris, the Fountain Paint Pot Nature Trail in Lower Geyser Basin, and the West Thumb Paint Pots.

ROARING MOUNTAIN NEAR NORRIS JUNCTION IS A CLASSIC EXAMPLE OF A FUMAROLE JIM PEACO / NPS

Such was the genesis of the physical and spiritual reverence humans have held for Yellowstone. The awe continued with latter-day Indians and the first Anglos, who arrived in the eighteenth century. Food riches beckoned those first humans, known as the Folsom and Clovis cultures. If archaeologists are correct, the earliest residents used obsidian to hunt mammoth, camels, mastodons, beaver, and bighorn bison that, compared to today's descendants, would've looked as if they were on steroids. Those first inhabitants might also have used the same tools to fend off attacks from lions, bears, and wolves that also scarcely resembled the carnivores now roaming Greater Yellowstone.

After the ice departed, it probably ushered in a 2,000-year period where the land was delicate tundra. Only after gradual warming did Yellowstone begin to take on its

MOUNT WASHBURN SHIMMERS AGAINST A BRILLIANT STARRY NIGHT SKY JACOB W. FRANK / NPS

current profile, about 9,000 years ago. Lodgepole pine appeared, along with Engelmann spruce and whitebark pine, whose nuts became a favorite of the grizzly bear. Blood found on arrowheads, knives, rocks, and other tools scattered throughout the region suggests that deer, elk, rabbit, sheep, and bear were plentiful. In an ominous precursor of our current overconsumption habits, evidence also suggests these cultures pillaged their bounty. The decline of game caused dramatic social restructuring and forced a focus on smaller game and plants for food.

Today's visitors would be surprised to learn they might not be the first to complain about summer crowds, though climates were so harsh that only the Sheep Eaters—bighorn-eating ancestors of Idaho's Shoshone and Bannock tribes—made permanent homes in Yellowstone and the Grand Teton region. Hundreds of fire rings, wickiups, campsites, petroglyphs, tepee rings, obsidian points, burial grounds, and buffalo kill sites have been discovered. Researchers also believe that most evidence of those long-ago residents has been lost to harsh climes and time. The whereabouts of most existing remote religious sites remain a mystery because the Park Service guards the secrecy of their locations lest vandals, geocachers, or treasure hunters exploit them.

To the south, lack of hot springs, geysers, and other warming features apparently limited winter habitation of the Grand Teton/Jackson Hole area even more than Yellowstone because large game migrated to lower elevations. The ancestors of what would become the Crow, Bannock, Shoshone, and Blackfeet feasted on summer roots on the plateaus and then crossed the Continental Divide to wait out the deep snows of the Little Ice Age that ended in the decades just before Yellowstone was established in 1872. Other Indians would winter in the broad expanse north of what is now Gardiner, where winds scoured the Yellowstone River Valley of snow and left a paradise of native grasses and small animals. As the climate warmed over 2,000 years, large game returned and humans followed.

In general, indigenous peoples didn't live full time on the Yellowstone Plateau because hunting was better in the valleys in every direction. Indians referred to what is now the Yellowstone area as "Burning Mountains" and reputedly feared evil spirits—though today both the tribes and National Park Service dismiss the assertion as a myth perpetuated by a government reluctant to acknowledge Indians' imprint. The Bannock Indians, for instance, created a trail from what is now Targhee Pass on the Idaho-Montana border to the Clarks Fork of the Yellowstone and Shoshone Rivers near present-day Cody, Wyoming, to access hunting grounds. Many other tribes used the trail, and evidence of Indians cooking and preparing hides in the hot springs has surfaced.

It took nearly a century from the park's creation to officially recognize tribal impacts, after at first asserting that Indians saw Yellowstone as taboo. In 2001, the park began allowing free entrance to members of tribes known to inhabit the area historically, as long as they were entering for "traditional purposes."

The Europeans who first arrived in the late 1770s were French Canadian fur trappers in search of beaver pelts. They came up the Missouri River and dispersed up its tributaries—including the Yellowstone, Madison, and Gallatin Rivers, which are birthed on the Yellowstone plateau. Their legacy remains in names gracing towns, rivers, and mountains today.

The Yellowstone, known by the Indians as Elk River, was named *Rive des Roche Jaunes* ("River of Yellow Rock") by the French. It is presumed the name stems from the ocher rimrock 150 miles downstream from the park near present-day Billings, Montana, but also possibly the similarly hued outcroppings near the Yellowstone's confluence with the Missouri River in North Dakota. The French influence also is apparent in the Tetons themselves, christened *Les Trois Tetons*—"The Three Breasts"—by trappers apparently yearning for female companionship. The Shoshone called these mountains *Teewinot,* or "Many Peaks."

SHOSHONE INDIANS OFTEN CAMPED IN YELLOWSTONE AND THEIR TEPEE POLES CAN BE FOUND IN THE PARK TO THIS DAY NPS

The trappers and Indians had the woods, grasses, and rivers to themselves in a tenuous détente until the Lewis and Clark Corps of Discovery passed along the northern flank of the region in 1803, after President Thomas Jefferson ordered exploration of the Louisiana Purchase territory. Lewis and Clark never saw the Yellowstone or Teton areas, but they heard Shoshone and Nez Perce tales of rolling thunder emanating from the mystical land to the south. Lewis and Clark's reports of bountiful resources began to pique a nation's interest, and one of the trip's members, John Colter, returned to Yellowstone five years after the expedition to trap beaver.

But it wasn't until 1827 that Americans on the East Coast received their first detailed description of Yellowstone-Teton, thanks to trapper Daniel Potts's vivid accounts in a Philadelphia newspaper. Colter and Potts were just two of many fur-trapping mountain men whose tales of the Northern Rockies grew to mythical proportions. Though their era lasted only until about 1840, names such as Jim Bridger, Jedediah Smith, and the Sublette boys live on. Their legacies are perpetuated in Western art, folklore, and movies such as *Jeremiah Johnson,* named for a real-live mountain man, John Jeremiah "Liver-Eating" Johnston. For about 15 years, Anglo and Indian trappers would gather annually at rendezvous sites for whiskey-drinking, arm-wrestling, skirt-chasing, gun-dueling, poker-playing precursors to some of the tamer frontier-day festivals many small western towns stage today.

The next wave of explorers came after the Civil War. Easily the most significant was a group formed at the behest of the Northern Pacific Railroad, which sought a route across Montana and needed publicity to entice investors. In 1870, the railroad bankrolled the 19-member Washburn-Langford-Doane Expedition. The group planned to follow a route detailed a year earlier by the Folsom-Cook-Peterson expedition, whose account in a popular magazine had rekindled flagging attention. East and West Coast media stories of the Washburn expedition ensured that Yellowstone would forever be in the national consciousness. During the Civil War era, annual tourist visits began to skyrocket past the average of 500 who came to soak in Mammoth Hot Springs.

In 1872, after further attention came from the compelling images of landscape painter Thomas Moran and photographs by William Henry Jackson, Congress voted to designate Yellowstone the world's first national park. President Ulysses S. Grant signed the Yellowstone Act that year. The region was ultimately and ironically saved from development by its own ruggedness. Amid the nation's headlong rush to exploit the West's resources, Yellowstone was deemed so remote and inhospitable that protecting it couldn't possibly hinder "progress."

"Protection" was a misnomer, however. Initially, the park was under such siege from poaching, squatters, and vandalism that the US Army was called in to quell the lawlessness and land grabbing. For three more decades, the cavalry patrolled the park on horseback, first from Camp Sheridan and then from Fort Yellowstone, now the park's headquarters at Mammoth. Their role was a far cry from Yellowstone's current mission. The Army built roads and fought fires. It also protected elk and bison from poaching, and eliminated natural predators such as coyotes, wolves, and mountain lions, using poisons. The cavalry's presence ended in 1916 with the formation of the National Park Service.

The next major players in the Yellowstone region were the railroads. By the early 1880s, Jay Cooke's Northern Pacific had reached Livingston, Montana, and Averell Harriman's Union Pacific had driven its golden spike in northern Utah. Railroad spurs were built from Livingston to Gardiner and from Pocatello, Idaho, to present-day West Yellowstone, Montana. At the turn of the century, more than 80 percent of tourists arrived by train and then entered the park in carriages or on horseback. Railroad barons had grand visions of development in Yellowstone, including building a dam at the

CALVARY DRILLS AT FORT YELLOWSTONE WERE COMMON IN THE EARLY TWENTIETH CENTURY WHEN THE ARMY WAS IN CHARGE OF PROTECTING THE PARK FROM VANDALISM, SQUATTING, AND POACHING NPS

falls in the Grand Canyon of the Yellowstone River. But others adamant about keeping the park in its natural state stonewalled them.

The railroads' era lasted about as long as that of the mountain man. Construction of Grand Loop Road was finished in 1905, and the first car entered Yellowstone legally in 1915. Within a quarter century, more visitors had entered the park via car than by train, and rail service to Gardiner ended in 1960 and to West Yellowstone in 1970. Today, all that remains of the railroad's influence are the abandoned track beds and renovated stations at West Yellowstone and Gallatin Gateway. Fast forward to today: Yellowstone has 370 miles of roads and five pay-station entrances, with one, at Gardiner, open year-round to automobile traffic.

The park's mission continues to evolve, and the age-old debate over recreational values versus intrinsic values has been shifting. No longer is the prevailing sentiment "How can the park serve the people?" but rather "How can people serve the park?"

One example revolves around fire. When once park officials attempted to extinguish all accessible blazes, fire presently is viewed as essential to ecological health. One result was the controversial and misleading "let-burn" policy that made national headlines in the summer of 1988, when the media descended on the unprecedented inferno that Yellowstone had become. Images of towering

EARLY TRANSPORTATION REQUIRED REAL HORSE POWER UNTIL CARS WERE LEGALLY ALLOWED IN THE PARK IN 1915 NPS

THE CROWN FIRE RAGES NEAR THE OLD FAITHFUL AREA IN 1988, KNOWN AS THE SUMMER OF FIRE NPS

smoke, vast wastelands with the ghostly spire remnants of lodgepole pine, and flames nipping at the fringes of Grant Village, Old Faithful, and Cooke City dominated TV screens. Once the anxiety died with the last smoldering ember, and after an astonishing 800,000 acres burned, cooler heads prevailed.

Turns out the devastation was partly a function of the old Smokey Bear doctrine that the only good fire is a dead fire. Mother Nature had a system for cleansing the ecosystem of bugs, disease, and deadfall. Suppression of these natural cycles created the perfect recipe for devastation. Well before 1988, scientists recognized that burns were necessary for the health of the forest and that conflagrations were inevitable.

The hand-wringing began subsiding as early as late that summer, when the park's "recovery" was already evident in the tender shoots of wildflowers and grasses. Three decades later, the spires of 200-year-old lodgepoles stand over verdant understories that provide browse for wildlife. Wildflowers are abundant. Animals are thriving and more visible than ever. And the park is closer to a natural balance than at any time since the post–Civil War era. Research suggests burns akin to 1988 had happened before, and surely will happen again with increasing frequency regardless of human intentions. The good news is that nature heals quickly and provides an education along the way.

Other challenges remain. Limited funding has created infrastructure concerns at a time when visitation to Yellowstone surpassed 4 million for the fourth consecutive year in 2018; for context, the park didn't reach 3 million until 2003. The endangered Yellowstone cutthroat trout's future is further at risk because of warming waters and the illegal introduction of voracious lake trout into the frigid waters of Yellowstone Lake, once a stronghold for a native fish coveted by anglers and needed for sustenance by no fewer than 47 wildlife species.

Though only 1 percent is intensely developed and 90 percent of visitors limit themselves to these areas, the park is increasingly challenged by the volume of people and cars. Perhaps even greater forces are coming from outside park borders. Logging and mining isn't as prolific as it once was, but oil and gas operations blanket northern and western Wyoming, impacting wildlife corridors and water and air quality. Even more of a threat: As more people have recognized the region's quality of life, housing developments have sprouted on the fringes of both parks, compromising the wildness and isolation that lure people here in the first place.

Most concerning is the climate. In the past seven decades, the average temperature at Gardiner, Montana, has risen 3.7 degrees. Climate models suggest an even faster increase in the coming years. Results are already visible in vast swaths of dead and dying whitebark pines, helpless against pine-bark beetles now surviving relatively mild winters. High-elevation snowpack that once lasted deep into the spring in the shadows of whitebark branches now melts more rapidly. Early runoff means warmer and less water for fish, recreationists, and irrigators in the headwaters of the West's three great river systems: the Missouri, Columbia, and Colorado.

Above all, even at 2.2 million acres, Greater Yellowstone is an ecological island, cut off from endless wild country to the northwest that stretches deep into Canada and Alaska. Despite the ecosystem's ability to regenerate from fire and other natural disasters, its landscapes are fragile and its wildlife vulnerable in the face of human intrusion and intervention. And yet, Americans can take great pride in the fact that the world's first national park and the lands surrounding it continue to constitute one of Earth's last great largely intact temperate ecosystems—a place where the natural world mostly works as it was intended.

✳ Wildlife

For all the beauty, recreation, and awe-inspiring natural features of Yellowstone, wildlife viewing always ranks high for reasons to come see America's first national park. For millions, Yellowstone is where they'll glimpse their first bear, wolf, and genetically pure bison, and possibly elk, bald eagle, bighorn sheep, and mountain goat. Every day can offer a new gee-whiz moment. And happily, as one park biologist puts it, Yellowstone

FIREWEED EMERGES FROM THE ASHES JUST A FEW MONTHS AFTER THE 1988 FIRES JIM PEACO / NPS

A SMOOTH LANDING BY AN OSPREY RETURNING TO ITS NEST IN YELLOWSTONE'S GRAND CANYON JIM PEACO / NPS

is as "carnivore-rich" as it has been since the park was established in 1872.

Wildlife management has undergone dramatic changes in both parks, but especially Yellowstone. Elk were relentlessly hunted and bison nearly went extinct from wholesale slaughter until the 1894 Lacey Act prohibited hunting of wildlife within park boundaries. The law didn't prevent the concerted extirpation in the 1920s of the wolf, which as a predator was deemed a "bad" animal for its threat to "good" animals, namely elk and deer. Grizzly bear feeding shows were staged until 1941, and handouts for black bears at entrance stations were allowed until the early 1970s, perpetuating a drive-through zoo image.

Without natural predators, elk were necessarily killed by the thousands or deported to other states because they were ravaging vegetation. Controversy over the elk slaughter led to the 1963 Leopold Report, calling for more natural management. Its idealistic principles were adopted five years later, and although Yellowstone can still feel like a theme park in the summer, its evolution—climaxed by the restoration of wolves in 1995—has enhanced the wildlife experience for visitors and improved habitat. Your chances of seeing a grizzly in Yellowstone are better than at any time since the dumps were closed.

Although most people come to Yellowstone in the summer, the best time to witness wildlife is spring, with autumn running a close second. For our entrance-fee money, there's nothing quite like late May, before the high-country snows melt. Most wildlife—elk being a notable exception—have their young tailing them by mid-month. Bears have emerged from their dens with cubs, and wolf pups frolic in their new world. It isn't unusual to see all these charismatic mammals at once in a 360-degree panorama in the Lamar Valley. It has earned its nickname: the American Serengeti.

During any season, the best times to view animals are early morning and dusk, when they often feed in the open. By midafternoon, most have curled up for a nap or respite from the "heat." One tip for locating predators even when they're out of sight: Look for large groups of squawking ravens putting on an aerial circus just above the ground. It's a likely sign of a fresh carcass—which means grizzlies, wolves, coyotes, eagles, and other hungry opportunists will eventually arrive. You'll discern a decided pecking order that usually starts with a bear. If you do decide to stop anywhere, all four vehicle tires must be off the roadway to keep traffic flowing. Watch for **NO PARKING** signs intended to keep wildlife and people alike safe.

Here's a closer look at the charismatic wildlife in Yellowstone, along with optimal spots for viewing. See Chapter 7 for best viewing in and around Grand Teton National Park.

BEAR (BLACK) The black bear appears to be on solid ground, with roughly 500 roaming Yellowstone and surrounding areas. They don't inspire the same fear or awe in people as grizzlies, but respect their space. You're more likely to see a black bear near one of the roads than a grizzly, so they're show-stoppers. Like all bruins, the black bear has a strong sense of smell. In Yellowstone, they hibernate in north-facing dens beginning in November and emerge with cubs in the spring, typically in March. These newborns are known as COYs, or cubs of the year. Ever wonder how they hibernate all winter without needing a bathroom break? In short, their metabolism slows dramatically and they essentially recycle their waste internally. The time bears hibernate depends on weather and food sources. They're omnivores, which means they'll eat vegetation and meat—mostly fish, rodents, and the occasional elk calf.

Black bears aren't always easy to distinguish from grizzlies because some are cinnamon colored. The primary differences: Grizzlies have a shoulder hump, smaller ears, and concave face. The black bear's nose is flatter and ears larger.

Best viewing: Black bears cover most of the park, but a good bet is the Tower Junction area and just across the Yellowstone River Bridge—an area some naturalists christened "The Bearmuda Triangle."

BEAR (GRIZZLY) *Ursus horribilis* remains the iconic and fearsome symbol of wild Yellowstone. Hiking in grizzly country heightens the senses like few other adventures. Remarkably, four decades ago biologists feared that such experiences were destined to become a distant memory. Grizzlies were on the verge of extinction in Greater Yellowstone after food sources dried up, most notably the hotel and restaurant garbage dumps that provided evening feeding spectacles. Many grizzlies starved and some had to be euthanized because they were approaching campgrounds and community dumps, looking for food. Populations dropped perilously close to the point of no return, to less than 200.

Thanks to Endangered Species Act protections imposed in 1975, the grizzly has evolved to become one of the region's most astonishing conservation success stories.

A YOUNG BLACK BEAR EMERGES FROM THE WOODS ALONG FOUNTAIN PAINT POT ROAD

Though officially the number is just over 700, some biologists say as many as 1,000 were roaming Greater Yellowstone as of 2018—including roughly 150 within the park. Bear attacks remain exceedingly rare, and both grizzly and black bear want to avoid humans, but it's imperative to take proper precautions. Bear spray should be as much a part of a hiker's arsenal these days as good boots.

A male grizzly bear can weigh up to 700 pounds—twice that of an adult male black bear. Like the black bear, the grizzly is omnivorous, but it tends more toward meat and will inevitably show up at an elk or bison carcass.

Best viewing: The Lamar and Hayden Valleys are ideal simply for their openness. Look in the tree lines across the valleys. With elk carcasses more available thanks to wolves, it's no longer a shock to see grizzlies emerge periodically from hibernation in the middle of winter.

BIGHORN SHEEP Like many Yellowstone mammals, these muscular animals nearly lost their toehold four decades ago. Though hunting outside the park played a role, the bighorn was most challenged by a lack of nutrition due to large populations of elk disrupting their foraging patterns and limiting food supplies. Bighorns tend to live in herds or bands, so if you see one, chances are others are camouflaged on rocky cliffs or in sagebrush. Though both have horns, females (ewes) have shorter curls while males' (rams) are longer and more curved to provide built-in weapons for dominance during mating season (November and December). Consider yourself fortunate if you happen upon two males ramming each other at high speeds as if auditioning for a Discovery Channel documentary.

A MAMA GRIZ AND HER CUBS TAKE A STROLL IN THE LAMAR VALLEY JIM PEACO / NPS

LOOK FOR BIGHORN SHEEP NEAR YELLOWSTONE'S NORTH ENTRANCE AND THE YELLOWSTONE PICNIC AREA

Best viewing: Bighorn sheep like the high country and other ground far from most humans. But it isn't uncommon to glimpse some of the 250 or so residents, especially on the steep pumice near the North Entrance in the Gardner River Canyon. They also hang out across the road from the Yellowstone River Picnic Area near Tower Junction and on the cliffs above the Lamar River and Soda Butte Creek confluence.

BISON While touring Yellowstone, you're almost guaranteed to see bison by the dozens or hundreds in the valleys, though many disperse to higher ground and greener grass in the summer. At one time the American bison was reduced to a mere two dozen, all pastured at the Buffalo Ranch in the Lamar Valley. Today, the last genetically pure remnants of herds that thundered across the Great Plains by the millions generally number between 2,800 and 5,000 in the park (Grand Teton's roughly 1,000 bison contain cattle genes). They are in two herds: the northern herd, primarily concentrated in the Lamar Valley, and the central herd, about half the size and mostly in the Hayden Valley.

Few wildlife exhibitions are as pleasing as watching rust-colored bison calves run clumsy circles around their mothers in late April or May, shortly after birth. Cows and younger animals stay in herds in the valleys; adult bulls wander off to be loners and grow to 2,000 pounds.

Bison are deceptively docile. For that reason, and because they are so accessible, it is Yellowstone's most dangerous animal. When agitated, a bison can charge at speeds of up to 30 mph. If you're driving US 191 north of West Yellowstone or US 89 between Gardiner and Yankee Jim Canyon on the Yellowstone River, look for bison crossing the road in the winter and spring—especially at night, when they are barely visible in the blackness. Their eyes do not reflect headlights like deer and elk.

Best viewing: Bison can be seen almost anywhere, but the Lamar and Hayden Valleys are almost a certainty.

BISON: STILL LOOKING FOR ROOM TO ROAM

Though the revered symbol of the American frontier was designated the country's first "national mammal" in 2016, the bison's existence isn't universally valued, especially in Montana. As a result, it is the only wildlife species in the country largely constrained by the boundaries of national parks and refuges.

At issue is that during harsh winters, many bison wander out of Yellowstone to the north and west in Montana in search of forage. Historically, they have been "hazed" back into the park or rounded up for removal to protect cattle from a disease called brucellosis, which has been eradicated everywhere but in Greater Yellowstone. Brucellosis causes cattle to abort their calves. Though rare, and there has never been a documented case of wild bison transmitting brucellosis to cattle (elk are the guilty party when it does occur), the ranching community has been resistant to allowing bison to roam outside the park.

Many conservation groups and state agencies are committed to restoring free-roaming, disease-free bison to wildlife refuges and tribal lands where there are no cattle, and now they are allowed in the entire Gardiner Basin north of the park. "Surplus" Yellowstone bison also have been relocated to two Indian reservations in northeast Montana, with plans to increase the number going to tribes. But the slaughter nevertheless continued in early 2018 as the park culled 1,000 to bring the population to about 4,200.

If you drive US 89 south of Livingston, just before you reach Gardiner you'll notice four ominous-looking, fenced-off areas on the east side of the highway. These are the federal quarantine pens where wandering bison are kept for up to five years. Animals testing positive for brucellosis are slaughtered and the meat distributed to Indian tribes; the remainder are pastured with an eye on one day turning disease-free animals loose on appropriate landscapes. In 2018, another step forward was taken when Yellowstone's superintendent signed a proclamation instituting a quarantine program designed to "augment or establish new conservation or cultural herds of Plains bison, enhance cultural and nutritional opportunities for American Indians, and reduce shipments of Yellowstone bison to slaughter facilities."

BUFFALO OR BISON? TECHNICALLY THE SPECIES IS THE AMERICAN BISON, THOUGH THEY'RE COMMONLY CALLED BUFFALO NEAL HERBERT / NPS

COYOTE Often confused for the larger and longer-tailed wolf, this resilient and adaptable rascal has survived eradication programs and flourishes today—though the return of the wolf cut their numbers in half. Coyotes, or "song dogs," are about one-third the size of wolves, have pointier ears, and yip instead of howl. Interestingly, after wolves were extirpated, coyotes lived in packs; upon wolf restoration the coyote returned to living in pairs. They eat small animals and will patiently wait at a carcass until grizzlies and wolves have had their fill. During spring, look for four to eight pups tagging along behind females after emerging from their dens.

THE CAGEY AND ADAPTABLE COYOTE IS THRIVING AGAIN IN YELLOWSTONE AND GRAND TETON DESPITE EARLY ERADICATION EFFORTS JACOB W. FRANK / NPS

Best viewing: Coyotes are ubiquitous, but the road between Blacktail Plateau and the Lamar Valley regularly produces. You may also see them trotting along other roads, cruising grasslands for rodents, or looking for an unwitting young pronghorn to herd.

EAGLE The bald eagle—America's national emblem and symbol of freedom—is one of America's greatest animal comeback stories. Yellowstone has more than two dozen nesting pairs, compared to 10 in 1986. Bald eagles don't get the trademark white feathers on their heads until they're five to seven years old, so many you'll see are juvenile balds not to be confused with golden eagles. The bald is an opportunistic scavenger and always is the early bird, so to speak, on a carcass.

AN OPPORTUNISTIC BALD EAGLE FEASTS ON LAKE TROUT JIM PEACO / NPS

Amazingly, a half century after bald eagles seemed destined for extinction because of hunting and the pesticide DDT, they've actually become a problem in Yellowstone through no fault of their own. The highly adaptable bird is concentrated around Yellowstone Lake, where historically it used its talons to pluck spawning cutthroat trout from tributaries. But it has turned to fellow avian species due to the trout's dramatically declined numbers. The result: concerning population drops in trumpeter swans, loons, ducks, and other winged species in the park. Given the bald eagle's history and status, human intervention is unthinkable—but it just might come to that.

Best viewing: Almost half of Yellowstone's 14 bald eagle nests are in the Yellowstone Lake area. Look for them in branches along rivers, especially in dead trees, also called "snags."

ELK No animal has had more impact on Yellowstone than the wapiti, and among residents of the Northern Rockies—especially hunters—perhaps no animal is more revered. The stately ungulate, coveted for the massive antler racks sported by big males, once was essentially extinct in the region before efforts by sportsmen's groups restored them. In fact, they did their job too well: Elk overpopulated the park, causing extensive damage to vegetation.

With the restoration of wolves and other factors, including drought, warmer temperatures, and a rise in grizzly bear predation, the population of Yellowstone's famous Northern Range herd dropped from around 20,000 to as low as 4,000 and now back up to 7,500. Biologists think that's a sustainable number; hunters argue it's too few. Either way, scientists say a battered landscape is healing, enabling the return of many other species, such as deer, bighorn sheep, pronghorn, songbirds, and beaver, which became

AN ELK HERD TAKES IN THE SCENE AT MAMMOTH HOT SPRINGS

Some mammals have antlers and some have horns. The difference? Antlers are bones that grow on elk, deer, and moose, and they are shed every fall. Only males have them, and they are used for combat with other males to show dominance during the mating season, or rut. Antlers begin as velvet in the spring, harden, and branch out; a massive antler "rack" is a sign of a healthy animal. Horns are on bison, mountain goats, bighorn sheep, and pronghorn. These have a bony core inside a sheath similar to human fingernails, are permanent, and are on both males and females—with size, shape, and contour being distinguishing factors between genders.

rare without new growth of lush grasses, shrubs, willow, and cottonwood. Wildlife biologists will tell you Yellowstone's herds are "lean and mean," a reference to their overall health.

Elk are among the last mammals to drop their young in the spring, generally late May or well into June. Calves are born unscented and hide in the grasses from grizzlies, wolves, and other predators until strong enough to run. During the fall rut, you'll be treated to the primal sounds of males bugling and challenging other suitors. Another way a bull shows dominance: by wallowing in shallow pits of their own urine and feces. The theory goes that it tells other bulls he is metabolizing fat, food, and muscle, a sign of health and strength. Such instinctive posturing between bulls often takes place between the buildings in Mammoth. Be sure to give them a wide berth. Only one thing is on their minds and they'll charge anything—other elk, humans, pickup trucks—between them and their harem. Fortunately, park rangers are dialed in and constantly rearranging orange cones in an ongoing game of autumn lawn chess with the randy bulls.

Best viewing: The drive from Gardiner through Mammoth, the Blacktail Plateau, and Little America to the Lamar Valley usually produces. They're almost always foraging or lazing on the green grasses at Mammoth. In the winter, the big bulls hang together, often close to the road between Mammoth and Cooke City.

MOOSE Powerful and unpredictable, this long-legged mammal commands respect and space. The moose—in Greater Yellowstone, it's technically the Shiras moose—might ignore you as it browses a few feet away on a trail or chase you for no apparent reason. Because they require old-growth forest canopy, these animals were perhaps hurt most by the 1988 fires. The loss of trees meant less prime habitat. In addition, a debilitating parasite able to survive milder winters has weakened moose and made them vulnerable to predators and weather conditions. The dwindling numbers—about 800 remain in Greater Yellowstone, 200 in the park—are a concern.

Unlike fellow ungulates elk and deer, moose are solitary animals until the rut.

MOOSE ON THE LOOSE NEAR THE SOUTH ENTRANCE BETWEEN YNP AND GTNP JIM PEACO / NPS

The big bulls grow to 1,000 pounds and sport impressive antler racks. Like elk, their young are born in late May and early June.

Best viewing: Look for moose around water, especially marshy areas where willows and aquatic plant life abound. They are often seen along Soda Butte Creek and in Silver Gate, where they seem fascinated by the swing set next to the general store. Just inside the South Entrance and Elk Creek are two other prime spots.

MOUNTAIN GOAT This sure-footed and snow-white favorite of visitors in Glacier National Park was introduced in the mountains along Yellowstone's northern boundary for hunting in the 1940s and '50s and arrived in the park in the 1990s. They're charismatic but not entirely welcome: Biologists worry they are negatively impacting bighorn sheep habitat (Grand Teton National Park officials announced in December 2018 a program to remove all goats from the park, either through lethal means or relocation). But it is highly entertaining to watch them deftly navigate sheer cliffs.

Mountain goats are extraordinary in their ability to cling to the most precipitous terrain. How? A suction cup–like inner sole insulated by hard hooves. A wool coat under "guard hairs" allows them to remain on exposed slopes amid the harshest wind and cold.

Best viewing: Mountain goats are common on the vertical flanks of Barronette Peak and also The Thunderer across from the Pebble Creek parking area in northeast Yellowstone. On occasion they appear in the Gallatin Range in the northeast corner. You'll need binoculars or a spotting scope. Naturally, they're easier to spot in the summer, when their white coats stand out against the granite.

LOOK FOR MOUNTAIN GOATS ON BARRONETTE PEAK OR THE THUNDERER BLUFFS ACROSS FROM PEBBLE CREEK
DIANE RENKIN / NPS

MOUNTAIN LION Once hunted virtually to extinction in the park, these elusive and secretive cats, also called cougars, are rarely seen—though that doesn't mean you're not seen by them. Like the wolf, the mountain lion was part of a predator-eradication program at the turn of the previous century. Anywhere from 15 to 40 live in Yellowstone now, primarily in Black Canyon between Gardiner and the Lamar Valley. Consider yourself lucky if you see one from a distance because mountain lions avoid humans whenever possible. For the record, no cougar attack has ever been reported in Yellowstone or Grand Teton.

Mountain lion kittens are born any time from June to September. Their favorite prey is elk calves, but they'll also pursue mule deer and an occasional pronghorn or bighorn.

Best viewing: Many park veterans have yet to see their first cougar. But wherever mule deer roam, mountain lions are sure to follow. Discreetly. If you're determined, find a roadside spot in Yellowstone's Northern Range. Plop down a lawn chair, pull out binoculars or a spotting scope, search for movement in the cliffs, and . . . hope for a minor miracle.

MULE DEER Midwesterners and easterners are often surprised to discover that more elk than deer are seen in Yellowstone. Mule deer, also called black-tails because of the dark tips on their tails (thus Blacktail Plateau) are fairly abundant—nearly 2,000. But because they tend to spend summers in the forests and high meadows up to 10,000 feet, these nomadic creatures are not as readily spotted. White-tailed deer have taken over many of the river valleys in Greater Yellowstone, but "muleys" remain king of the mountains. Mule deer are distinguishable from white-tails by their larger and lighter-colored ears, black tip on the tails, and a gazelle-like gait called "stotting" in which they land on all four hooves at the same time.

Like bull elk, male mule deer often use their large antler racks to joust during the fall rut. Unlike elk, the males don't maintain harems, instead taking their pick of does herding up—known as yarding—during the winter.

Best viewing: The road from the Lamar Valley to Cooke City is always a strong candidate, but look above river valleys in rocky, forested, or sage terrain.

PRONGHORN Commonly—and mistakenly—known as the antelope, thanks to Lewis and Clark, this graceful and speedy nomad of the sage prairie is a survivor of the last Ice Age and, at 20 million to 40 million years old, the region's sole true native. Reaching speeds of 60 to 65 mph, they're the second-fastest land mammal on the planet, behind the cheetah. And know this: The pronghorn would smoke a cheetah after 40 yards—an ability evolving from outrunning saber-toothed cats long ago. About 5,000 reside in Greater Yellowstone, though only about 500 are in the park. Their populations have been bolstered by the wolf, which reduced the population of a primary predator, the coyote.

Many pronghorn embark on lengthy migrations each spring and winter. In Greater Yellowstone, seven historic migrations have been reduced to one, from Grand Teton National Park to Wyoming's Red Desert. A century ago, about 40 million roamed the Great Plains, but they were hunted to near extinction. Human development continues to fragment their habitat. The pronghorn is a stubborn creature of habit and in some cases will lay down and starve before jumping a new fence, gate, or other obstacle despite extraordinary athleticism.

Best viewing: The open meadows at the North Entrance at Gardiner are almost a sure thing. Chances also are solid along the road from Mammoth to the Lamar Valley, with highest concentrations in the Lamar and Little America.

PRONGHORN ARE COMMONLY SEEN ON THE OPEN RANGE AT YELLOWSTONE'S NORTH ENTRANCE

RED FOX Like their larger cousin, the coyote, the red fox is adaptable and resilient, its stable population in Yellowstone enhanced by the presence of another relative, the wolf. Predation of coyotes by wolves has reduced a prime threat to the fox.

Foxes are thought to inhabit almost all of the park in two subpopulations: one of typical reddish color in the lower elevations and a cream-colored version residing above 7,000 feet. Because they like to hunt at night and in the forest, they aren't as commonly seen as coyotes and even wolves.

Best viewing: Hayden Valley, Pelican Valley, and Canyon are likely prospects, though they can show up just about anywhere. Look for the creamier versions around Cooke City and Silver Gate.

A RED FOX HALTS TRAFFIC AS IT LOOKS FOR FOOD MORSELS ON THE ROAD NEAR MADISON JUNCTION

SANDHILL CRANE The guttural prehistoric call of this majestic bird is one of the park's most memorable wildlife sounds, in the same league as the elk bugle and wolf howl for its echoing across hillsides and meadows. A favorite of famed conservationist Aldo Leopold, the sandhill is frequently seen in pairs and nests in the summer—most notably at Floating Island Lake east of Mammoth. Yellowstone sandhills also tend to be more reddish-brown in color because of iron oxide in the soil spread on their feathers while preening.

The park's sandhills arrive every March and April from New Mexico and Mexico, returning in huge flocks before dispersing into pairs to nest. They prefer damp meadows but can be found on the edge of aspen and conifer forests. Sandhills stand about 4 feet tall and can be heard for miles.

Best viewing: Floating Island Lake once was automatic, but sandhills seem to have temporarily abandoned the small clump of grass—the floating island—to which they once returned every spring. Fountain Flats is another strong possibility along with the Bechler Region, with all its standing water.

WOLF Nowhere in the world is the wolf so readily visible in the wild than Yellowstone, though frequency has tailed off since 2012 for many reasons. The gray wolf was restored in 1995 after a seven-decade absence. Park naturalist James Halfpenny, a noted author on wolves, called it "the greatest ecological experiment of our time." Fourteen were brought to Yellowstone from Alberta in 1995, and another 17 from British Columbia in 1996; still another 35 were released in Idaho over those two years. From those first 66, now about 1,900 in more than 280 packs roam the Northern Rockies, including about 100 in 11 packs in Yellowstone. A profound impact has been evident ever since (see sidebar on wolves in Chapter 4).

Wolves have a defined family structure, starting with alpha males and females. A female will typically bear five pups in a den in the spring after mating in February. About 90 percent of their diet is elk. They hunt systemically, often fail, and it is a myth that they are wanton killers (a rare exception being the occasional domestic sheep flock). Each wolf kill is consumed by a range of critters, from bears and eagles to ravens and invertebrates, and not an ounce is wasted. Carcasses occasionally bring grizzly bears from their dens in the winter. Wolves tend to live up to five years in the park, and the leading cause of mortality is other wolves in fights over territory.

Best viewing: To see a wolf, your best strategy is to look for the "Wolf Man," Rick McIntyre, and his cadre of "wolfers"—either near dawn or dusk, typically in the Lamar Valley or around Slough Creek, home of the Junction Butte pack in 2018. McIntyre, who studies the wolves almost every day and loves sharing information with visitors, uses telemetry to locate collared wolves and to record their habits for the Yellowstone Wolf

U.S. FISH & WILDLIFE SERVICE OFFICIALS CARRY A WOLF TO THE ROSE CREEK ACCLIMATION PEN IN 1995, THE YEAR THE SPECIES WAS RESTORED TO YELLOWSTONE AFTER AN ABSENCE OF 70 YEARS JIM PEACO / NPS

PREENING AND PLAYING IS WHAT RIVER OTTERS DO BEST, OFTEN TO AN AUDIENCE JIM PEACO / NPS

Project. Many of the "wolfers" have vanity license plates identifying their passion for the creature, along with semisophisticated telemetry protruding from their vehicles.

OTHERS If you're fortunate, you might catch a glimpse of the extremely rare wolverine, lynx, pine marten, great gray owl, or peregrine falcon. More prevalent are the badger, beaver, river otter, trumpeter swan, and osprey.

A wildlife treat is to watch a playful family of otters cavort in a stream, especially when they're using snow as a slide. Otters live in the Lamar River and Soda Butte Creek, so seeing them is merely a matter of good timing along the road. Likewise, a few badgers den near roads. Osprey nests are scattered throughout the park, including one you can view from high above in the Lamar River canyon. Roughly 30 trumpeter swans—the largest water birds in North America—live in the park in the summer, and nearly twice that many convene in the winter. Look for them along the Madison and Firehole Rivers as well as the Yellowstone River near Canyon. In the winter, they congregate on the ice-free Henry's Fork of the Snake River in Island Park. Another ideal place, outside the park, is the Red Rock Lakes National Wildlife Refuge in the remote Centennial Valley southwest of West Yellowstone.

WHAT'S WHERE IN GREATER YELLOWSTONE

Practical Information for Your Visit

BEAR SPRAY Regardless of where you plan to be and what time of year you'll be there, bear spray is mandatory. Expect to pay around $40 to $50 for a canister, and purchase it once you're here because airlines won't allow you to fly with it. You can also rent bear spray at many outdoor stores near the parks' entrances and at Canyon Village in YNP.

More bears roam Greater Yellowstone than at any time in more than a century, so your chances of an encounter—though still less likely statistically than getting struck by lightning—are rising. And because of greater access to food sources, thanks largely to wolves, it isn't unusual to see a grizzly stumbling around in the snow midwinter, when they traditionally hibernate. Park employees always carry bear spray, even in January.

Check the label and make sure your canister has at least 7.9 ounces of spray, contains 1 to 2 percent capsaicin, and covers at least 25 feet. Carry it in your hand, on your belt or, better yet, in a chest holster; trust us, it'll be useless in a backpack, pocket, or anywhere else not within instant reach. Know how to use it: Wait until a charging bear is within 25 feet, aim the spray between its head and

GRIZZLY BEARS HAVE MADE A COMEBACK AFTER NEARLY GOING EXTINCT IN THE GREATER YELLOWSTONE ECOSYSTEM NEAL HERBERT / NPS

the ground, and spray in bursts of several seconds.

Disabuse yourself of any notion you're better off with a firearm, though it is now legal to carry them assembled in the parks. Studies routinely show bear spray is effective in 95 percent of encounters. With a firearm, even if you have time to shoot, the likely outcome is wounding the bear, further infuriating it. Only use bear spray on a charging bruin. Helpful hint: Bear spray is not a repellent, so don't spray it on yourself—you'll discover quickly, and miserably, why it deters bears!

When your trip is finished, don't discard your canister in the trash. Find the nearest recycling center at a park hotel, store, ranger station, or visitor center. The airport in Bozeman, Montana, also has a recycling station.

CELL COVERAGE If you need to be plugged in to the outside world, you'll find limited reach. Cell coverage is a divisive issue, with some folks wanting the ability to make dinner reservations as they traverse a park, while others are adamant about retaining the qualities of remoteness. Even so, there are times, such as rescues, when a phone is handy—even crucial.

As of the summer of 2018, cell coverage reached about half of YNP and most of the Jackson Hole valley. Emphasis has been on limiting coverage to developed areas, though reach continues to expand with improved technology.

Within YNP, cell coverage is most reliable around the North, West, and South Entrances, where the towers at Mammoth, Old Faithful, Grant Village, Canyon, Tower-Roosevelt, and Mount Washburn combine with others outside the park to provide optimum signal strength. Yellowstone veterans know that a gaping hole exists from the Lamar Valley to Cooke City, so you might see cars parked late at night at Slough Creek searching for a signal to call home.

In 2018, outgoing Yellowstone Superintendent Dan Wenk signed off on a controversial plan to enhance cell service 38-fold while striving to avoid expanding the footprint. The goal was to increase speed in developed areas; opponents lament that taking and sharing selfies and texting has taken precedent over communing with nature.

Grand Teton also underwent a significant upgrade beginning in 2017 that made service in once-sketchy areas such as Jenny Lake and Signal Mountain more dependable.

The most reliable carriers in both parks tend to be Verizon, AT&T, and CenturyLink.

CLIMATE/WEATHER The old axiom about weather changing every five minutes never rang truer than in Greater Yellowstone, where 4,000- to 10,000-foot-plus elevations mean it can snow in July, and undulating terrain is the perfect recipe for lightning and thunder. Warm and sunny summer mornings can turn to rain, sleet, or even snow by afternoon. Average summer highs are in the upper 70s, with lows in the mid-40s. Winter highs are in the 30s, lows below 10. Subzero weather is routine. Warm jackets and rain gear are important if you're planning to leave your car, lodging, or campsite for any significant time. Remember: You can always remove layers, but you can't add what you don't have. If you're caught in lightning, look for low areas away from water, isolated trees, and high ridges. If that isn't possible, lie flat on the ground, preferably in a low-lying ravine, and wait it out.

Varied topography also means dramatically different weather from Jackson Hole to Yellowstone. The sun can be shining in one area while a downpour is occurring in another. Gardiner at the North Entrance sits in the arid rain shadow of Electric Peak, while the lush forests and standing water of Yellowstone's southwest corner make it a mosquito mecca. Along with cool-weather

THE ABSAROKA MOUNTAINS, NAMED FOR THE APSAALOOKE (OR CROW) INDIANS, FORM AN IMPOSING EASTERN BOUNDARY OF YELLOWSTONE NATIONAL PARK

gear, be sure to bring sunscreen and a hat. Don't let the relatively cool temperatures fool you: It doesn't take long to burn under the intense sun in dry air at high elevation. At 4,500 feet, a sunny, 35-degree day feels warm. And in such dry country, plenty of water is a must. In winter, bring hand and foot warmers for the inside of your gloves/mittens and boots, and sunglasses for eye protection.

EMERGENCIES Dial 911 for any emergency—but be aware that much of Yellowstone and Grand Teton National Parks does not have cell coverage. To report criminal activity or ill-advised human behavior, particularly related to wildlife, call the Yellowstone tip line at 307-344-2132.

FEES
Note: A single seven-day permit for cars purchased at an entrance station once covered both Yellowstone and Grand Teton National Parks, but now is only good for the park at which it was purchased.

Single-entry passes

$35: Standard private, noncommercial automobiles (per park, good for seven days)

$30: Individual motorcycle (per park, seven days)

$20: Single entry by foot, bike, ski, etc. (per park, seven days)

Annual passes

$70: Standard Pass (per park)

$20: Senior Pass (US citizens age 62 and older)

$80: America the Beautiful Pass (valid one year for all national parks and federal recreation lands)

Lifetime passes

$80: Senior Pass (US citizens age 62 and older)

Free: Access Pass for US citizens and permanent residents who are legally blind or disabled; documentation required

Free: Active military and dependents (obtain at federal recreation site)

FIREARMS Firearms are allowed in all national parks, but discharge is prohibited in Yellowstone and guns are not allowed in most facilities. Similar rules apply in Grand Teton, which has an autumn "elk reduction program" for hunters in a portion of the park.

FOOD STORAGE/FEEDING WILDLIFE
The old axiom "a fed bear is a dead bear" is true not only for the fearsome symbol of Greater Yellowstone's wildness, but for all other wildlife as well. Directly feeding wildlife is an obvious no-no; careless food storage by campers, picnickers, hikers, and others is equally problematic.

For all its good intentions, feeding wildlife has two major consequences. Animals accustomed to summer handouts struggle in the winter and starve when people aren't around to serve them, such as at picnic areas. Also, wildlife habituated to humans can become an aggressive hazard and must be destroyed to protect future visitors.

As such, food, trash, and even items with an aroma such as toothpaste and perfumes should be stored in airtight containers. Don't leave unattended food, beverage containers, garbage, coolers, stoves, grills, cooking utensils, cosmetics, toiletries, and pet food/bowls—and don't keep any of the above in your tent. All garbage bins in the parks are now bear-proof, so it is safe to dispose of trash in those receptacles.

If you're in the backcountry, pitch your tent a safe distance from your cooking area and know how to hang your food and related gear from trees to keep it inaccessible to animals.

HOSPITALS/MEDICAL ATTENTION
You can expect first-rate health care either for injuries or illness from all of the clinics in and around the two parks.

Yellowstone NP: Mammoth Hot Springs Clinic (weekdays, year-round), 307-344-7965; Old Faithful Clinic (early May to mid-October), 307-545-7325; Lake Hospital (summer), 307-242-7241

Grand Teton NP: Grand Teton Medical Clinic at Jackson Lake Lodge (mid-May to mid-October), 307-543-2514 (9 a.m.–5 p.m.) and 307-733-8002 (after hours)

Billings Montana: St. Vincent Healthcare Hospital/Billings Clinic, 1233 N. 30th St. (406-657-7000)

Bozeman, Montana: Bozeman Health Deaconess Hospital, 915 Highland Ave. (406-414-5000)

Cody, Wyoming: West Park Hospital, 707 Sheridan Ave. (307-527-7501)

Idaho Falls, Idaho: Eastern Idaho Regional Medical Center, 3100 Channing Way (208-529-6111)

Jackson, Wyoming: St. John's Medical Center, 625 E. Broadway St. (307-733-3636)

Livingston, Montana: Livingston HealthCare, 320 Alpenglow Lane (406-222-3541)

Red Lodge, Montana: Beartooth Billings Clinic, 2525 Broadway Ave. N. (406-446-2345)

West Yellowstone, Montana: Yellowstone Family Medical Clinic, 11 S. Electric St. (406-646-0200)

LICENSES/PERMITS
Backcountry: Between Memorial Day and mid-September, backcountry permits are required for overnight stays at all of Yellowstone's 300 remote campsites. Fees are $3 for backpackers and boaters, $5 for people with horses, mules, and/or llamas. Permits must be purchased within 48 hours of use and

are available daily during the summer at any of nine ranger stations or visitor centers. Annual backcountry passes are $25.

Boating: Boating season is Memorial Day through mid-September. Boats and float tubes are only allowed on lakes and require both permits and aquatic invasive species inspections. For motorized craft, permits and inspections are available at Bridge Bay Ranger Station, Grant Village Backcountry Office, and Snake River Ranger Station. Float tube permits/inspections are also available at Bechler Ranger Station, Canyon Backcountry Office, Mammoth Backcountry Office, Old Faithful Backcountry Office, and the Northeast Entrance. Fees are $5/week for nonmotorized craft and $10 for the season; it's $10 and $20 for motorized, allowed only on Yellowstone and Lewis Lakes.

Fishing: Fishing is open in Yellowstone from Memorial Day through the first Sunday in November. Licenses are $18 for three days and $25 for seven days, but a state license isn't required.

Hunting: No hunting is allowed in Yellowstone National Park.

PETS Suffice it to say, pets and wildlife are like oil and water, and so both parks are equally firm in their rules about where your dog can and cannot be. As the literature notes, these rules are in place to protect humans, pets, and wildlife.

Rule of thumb: Pets can generally go where cars go. They must be on a leash that's no more than 6 feet long and stay within 100 feet (Yellowstone) or 30 feet (Grand Teton) of a road. They are not allowed on any trails. Further, pets are not allowed in any park hotels; they can be in cabins or the Jackson Lake Lodge "classic cottages" for an additional cleaning fee. Pets are allowed in campgrounds but must never be left unattended anywhere, and their food must be stored in airtight, scent-proof containers.

SPECIAL PROGRAMS
Park-sponsored programs range from short ranger-led talks each evening to weeklong adventures into the backcountry guided by Yellowstone Forever. Even if you're a regular visitor, the programs are always fresh and worth your time.

Yellowstone Forever (406-848-2400), based in Gardiner and the heart of the Lamar Valley, is the combined efforts of what was formerly the Yellowstone Association (education) and Yellowstone Park Foundation (fundraising). The organization's Yellowstone Forever Institute offers classes that have turned first-time visitors into lifelong supporters. The group partners with the Park Service to help visitors gain an understanding of the park's flora, fauna, and geology. Spending a week in the institute's rustic cabins amid the quiet of the Lamar Valley ensures a connectedness to the land. Opportunities range from in-depth field seminars and learning programs to private day tours and backpacking adventures.

Ranger-led activities take place at Bridge Bay, Canyon, Fishing Bridge, Gardiner, Grant Village, Lake, Madison, Mammoth, Norris, Old Faithful, West Thumb, and West Yellowstone. **Ranger Adventure Hikes** are at Canyon, Fishing Bridge, Mammoth, Old Faithful, and Tower Junction. In addition, on Friday and Saturday nights during the summer, **Stars Over Yellowstone** partners with the Museum of the Rockies for educational night-sky presentations at the Madison Campground amphitheater. Reservations are required for many activities. Look in the *Yellowstone Today* newspaper provided free at entrance stations for updates on activities. **Junior Ranger Programs** for children ages 5–12 and their families are scheduled during summer and winter. Activities include geyser monitoring, wildlife observation, hiking, skiing, snowshoeing, and ranger-led exploring.

STAYING HEALTHY We don't want your time in Yellowstone to be spoiled by illness, injury, or other maladies. Here are some potential pitfalls as well as tips on how to avoid them.

Altitude sickness: If you're coming from near sea level, it's possible the thin 1-mile- to 2-mile-high air could bring on altitude sickness. Symptoms include shortness of breath, headaches, disorientation, nausea, and nosebleeds. The best antidote is to stop vigorous activity, rest a bit, or move to a lower elevation until symptoms disappear.

Giardia: Even in Yellowstone's pristine waters, a nasty protozoa spread through human and animal waste can make your life miserable. If you need to drink from a lake or stream, purify the water by boiling it, using special tablets, or with a purifier. Giardia symptoms can take weeks to appear, but when they do the intestinal pain is excruciating.

Hantavirus: Although extremely rare, hantavirus is a potentially fatal illness spread through the fresh droppings of rodents, mostly deer mice and voles. It's highly unlikely you'll contract hantavirus even if you do come in contact with or inhale rodent waste, but it's a good idea to steer clear of excrement. If you're in a rustic cabin, check for evidence; if you see droppings, let housekeeping know.

Hypothermia: Even on the warmest days of summer, the right combination of cold temperatures, wind, and wet can quickly drop your body temperature. Hypothermia isn't limited to flipping a kayak or canoe in frigid Lake Yellowstone; a soaking from a sudden storm also can result in dire consequences. Hypothermia begins with uncontrollable shivering, followed by disorientation, and eventually unconsciousness and perhaps even death if untreated. Prevention starts with dressing for all occasions. Avoid wearing cotton and denim because they don't wick dampness. Dress in layers. Wool and polypropylene are terrific for insulation, retaining heat, and drying

quickly. Carry a waterproof raincoat, windbreaker, or shell. In a worst-case scenario, where a hiking partner shows signs of hypothermia, remove wet clothes and wrap yourself around them, preferably skin to skin, to transfer your body heat.

Sunburn: Altitudes are well over 5,000 feet and the air is fairly dry, so it doesn't take much to get a severe burn, even on hazy days. When venturing into the backcountry, cover up skin, use sunscreen of at least 30 SPF, and wear a hat. Sunglasses are a good idea, too, especially in the winter when glare from snow can damage corneas.

Ticks: When it comes to critters, one of the smallest can have some of the most debilitating impacts. The greatest risk today is Lyme disease, first found in eastern states but now in the West. Cover as much skin as possible when walking through brushy areas. After a day of exploring off the beaten path, spend extra time in the shower checking yourself carefully, especially hair and scalp. If you find an embedded tick, use clean, pointy tweezers to remove by twisting like a corkscrew. Be sure to get the insect's head and mouthparts. Neosporin or tea tree oil applied to the bite should reduce swelling and loosen remaining parts.

West Nile Virus: Most of the mosquitoes in the region don't carry West Nile, but some cases are reported each summer, and instances are likely to rise in the Northern Rockies. If you plan to hike in wetter areas where mosquitoes congregate, use insect repellent. The park suggests products containing DEET, but if you prefer to avoid chemicals, try citronella, cedar, or other natural deterrents. You'll want something just to keep the bugs away anyway.

Wildlife: We've saved perhaps the most important for last. Taking precautions and following park guidelines is not only for your own safety but also for the health and well-being of the critters that make this country so extraordinary.

Though many visitors would guess grizzly bears to be the most dangerous creature, most wildlife injuries involve bison. Incidents occur every year because people get too close to these deceptively athletic creatures for photo ops. Before they know what hit them—literally—agitation turns to fury. Give elk space, too, especially during September when they're in rut and acting irrationally. And be especially wary of moose. They can be cantankerous and are prone to pursuing humans for no apparent reason. Park regulations require visitors to stay at least 100 yards from bears and wolves, and 25 yards from all other wildlife. We recommend wider berth, because, well, wildlife is just that—wild and unpredictable. Note for women: It has long been debated whether menstrual odors attract bears, and the question has yet to be fully resolved. Though no evidence suggests bears are attracted specifically to such odors, there's no question they are attracted to scents. The Park Service recommends proper disposal, avoiding scented items, and using internal tampons instead of external pads.

TAXES Good news: Montana doesn't have a sales tax. Bad news: Most of Yellowstone and all of Grand Teton are in Wyoming, where there's a modest 4 percent tax. In neighboring Idaho, the sales tax is 6 percent. Many Montana communities, including West Yellowstone, Gardiner, Red Lodge, and Big Sky, also carry an average 3 percent resort tax.

VISITOR CENTERS
Canyon (307-242-2550, Memorial Day weekend to mid-October) has natural

FORTUNATELY, THIS BISON ISN'T AGITATED—YET. HUMANS ARE ASKED TO GIVE WILDLIFE AT LEAST 25 YARDS OF DISTANCE

history and geology displays and book sales in the lobby. The Canyon Visitor Education Center has two floors of interactive exhibits about Yellowstone's supervolcano.

Fishing Bridge (307-242-2450, Memorial Day weekend to late September) is recognized for its "parkitecture" exterior that's served as the prototype for several national park buildings. It's home to exhibits showcasing fauna and geology, and there are books for sale.

Grant Village (307-242-2650, Memorial Day weekend to late September) sheds insight on Yellowstone's fire history, most notably the massive 1988 blazes that burned one-third of the park. A film called *Ten Years after the Fire* is a must-see.

Madison Junction (307-344-2876, early June to late September) has information and a bookstore. Included is a junior ranger station with educational activities for children ages 5–12.

Mammoth (307-344-2263, year-round) is newly renovated. The Albright Visitor Center, named after the first superintendent, Horace Albright, serves as park headquarters and houses a variety of new exhibits related to early explorers, Indians, and mountain men. A small theater shows films and videos every half hour during the summer and on request in the winter.

Norris Geyser Basin Museum (307-344-2812, Memorial Day weekend to late September) showcases exhibits about thermal features and a bookstore.

Norris Museum of the National Park Ranger (307-344-7353, Memorial Day weekend to late September) details the evolution of official park rangers through videos and exhibits in a 1908 soldier station. You'll even get a chance to hobnob with actual former rangers who volunteer.

Old Faithful (307-545-2751, late April to early November and mid-December to mid-March) has an expansive newer clock forecasting its namesake geyser's next eruption.

Books, maps, videos, and souvenirs are available for purchase.

Ongoing Events and Festivals

ONGOING EVENTS *Montana Shakespeare in the Park:* From May to September, a traveling group of thespians offers free nightly plays throughout Montana and into Idaho and Wyoming, including communities in the Greater Yellowstone area. Check their website for the schedule.

Cody, Wyoming: **Cody Nite Rodeo** (307-587-5155), 8 p.m. nightly, June 1 to August 31, Cody Stampede Rodeo Grounds.

Driggs, Idaho: **Symphony on Sunday**, July to September, City Center Plaza. **Teton Valley Rodeo** (208-354-8005), Fridays from June to August, Teton County Fairgrounds.

Jackson, Wyoming: **Jackson Hole Rodeo** (307-733-7927), 8 p.m. Wednesday and Saturday, Memorial Day weekend through Labor Day weekend. Jackson Hole Rodeo Grounds.

Teton Village, Wyoming: **Grand Teton Music Festival** (307-733-1128), June to August, has for more than a half century brought nightly classical music concerts featuring internationally renowned symphony musicians in Walk Festival Hall in Teton Village.

Victor, Idaho: **Music on Main** (208-399-2884) takes place every Thursday evening beginning in late June and continuing into early August. The nonprofit Teton Valley Foundation puts on the free series, which supports the Teton Valley Animal Shelter. The ecoconscious group rents steel cups or allows you to bring your own for refreshment refills.

West Yellowstone, Montana: **Wild West Yellowstone Rodeo** (406-560-6913), Wednesday through Sunday, June to August, West Yellowstone rodeo arena (6 miles west of town on US 20).

FESTIVALS
February

Jackson, Wyoming: **WinterFest** (307-690-4824), sponsored by Jackson Hole Food & Wine, is an offshoot of the group's summer festival. It is three days of sipping and nibbling with some of the area's top wine, cocktail, and beer makers.

March

Cooke City, Montana: The annual **Spring Fling & Hog Roast** (406-838-2495) at Soda Butte Lodge is an antidote for cabin fever and gets the high mountain town enthused for spring. Auction, music, and dancing lead up to the main course: a hog roast. Proceeds go to charity.

West Yellowstone, Montana: The **World Snowmobile Expo** (406-646-7701) is six days of racing in the self-proclaimed snowmobile capital of the world—conducted at Expo Central, the SnoCross track, and the airport.

May

Jackson, Wyoming: **Elkfest** (307-733-3316) features an elk-antler auction and mountain-man rendezvous at the Teton County Fairgrounds. Antlers are collected by Boy Scouts from the nearby National Elk Refuge and are sold to help with the annual feeding of the elk. **Old West Days** (307-733-3316), Memorial Day weekend, boasts lots of Old West activities—including mountain-man rendezvous, chuckwagon dinners, horses, rodeo events, and shootouts—at Teton County Fairgrounds.

June

Cody, Wyoming: **Plains Indian Museum Powwow** (307-587-4771) features singing, dancing, arts and crafts, and Indian food from all over the region at the Robbie Powwow Garden at the Buffalo Bill Center of the West.

Jackson, Wyoming: **Jackson Hole Food & Wine Summer Festival** (307-690-4824) is three days of wine (and beer) tasting and meals from Jackson Hole's top restaurants and chefs from around the country, all to benefit Hole Food Rescue. **Plein Air Fest** (307-733-5771) brings more than 50 painters to the sculpture trail at the National Museum of Wildlife Art, where they set up easels and capture their surroundings in paint.

Red Lodge, Montana: The **Red Lodge Music Festival** (406-256-5210) features nine days of concerts and other events conducted by students and professional musicians. Talent shows and other recreational activities are part of the festivities.

July

Alta, Wyoming: **Targhee Fest** (307-353-2300) is all about music in the mountains and the lifestyle it engenders.

Driggs, Idaho: **Teton Valley Summer Festival** (208-354-2500) is an annual event at the Driggs airport famed for the

FOR 80 YEARS AND RUNNING, THE CODY NITE RODEO HAS PROVIDED WESTERN-STYLE FAMILY ENTERTAINMENT

launch of hot-air balloons, but also features a crafts fair, parade, fireworks, and other activities.

Jackson, Wyoming: **Art Fair Jackson Hole** (307-733-8792) is a competitive arts and crafts fair for nearly 175 artists that takes place at Miller Park. **Teton County Fair** (307-733-5289) is a weeklong event at Teton County Fairgrounds that includes the usual fair fare—rodeo, 4-H competitions, beauty queens, a demolition derby, wildlife, food, music, and exhibits—with a Western flair. **Grand Teton Music Festival** (307-733-1128) is considered one of the top orchestral-music gatherings in the nation. Started in 1962, the event lasts six weeks and is a retreat of sorts for classical musicians.

Livingston, Montana: **Livingston Roundup Rodeo** (406-222-3199), Fourth of July weekend, Park County Fairgrounds. PRCA-sanctioned event with a $200,000 purse. **PBR Livingston Classic**, late July, Park County Fairgrounds (bull riding included).

Red Lodge, Montana: **Home of Champions Rodeo** (406-446-2422), Fourth of July weekend, Red Lodge Rodeo Grounds.

August
Alta, Wyoming: **Grand Targhee Bluegrass Festival** (307-353-2300) is entering its fourth decade of bluegrass music, arts and crafts, food booths, and children's entertainment.

Gardiner, Montana: At **Brewfest** (406-848-7941), microbrews, wine, and entertainment are the highlight of this annual fundraiser for the Gardiner Chamber. It takes place in Arch Park, next to the Gardiner High football field, with Electric Peak as the backdrop.

September
Cody, Wyoming: **Rendezvous Royale** (307-587-5002) is a celebration of the arts that combines the Buffalo Bill Art Show and Sale, Buffalo Bill Center of the West's Patrons Ball fundraiser, Cody High Style fashion and custom-furniture show, and Boot Scoot & Boogie street festival featuring styles of the West.

Jackson, Wyoming: **Jackson Hole Fall Arts Festival** (307-733-3316) presents a wide array of music, cowboy poetry, and cuisine, along with gallery walks, workshops, and artist receptions. The highlight is the Taste of the Tetons food expo. The renowned **Jackson Hole Wildlife Film Festival** (307-200-3286) is a conservation- and science-oriented gathering of more than 700 people dedicated to celebrating the natural world through media. Films, science summits, and education highlight the festivities.

West Yellowstone, Montana: For 60 years, the **Knothead Jamboree** (406-646-1093) has brought up to 1,000 square dancers to the Union Pacific Dining Lodge. The name? Once upon a time, anybody who journeyed more than 100 miles to go square dancing was considered a "knothead."

October
Jackson, Wyoming: **Jackson Hole Wildlife Film Festival** (307-733-7016) features some 900 filmmakers from more than 30 countries who gather at Jackson Lake Lodge, where scientists, naturalists, and other wildlife enthusiasts view and discuss wildlife films. The event culminates with a ceremony in which some 23 awards are at stake. In alternating years, science media are highlighted.

November
Yellowstone Ski Festival (406-646-7097) gathers more than 3,500 Nordic skiers at the Rendezvous Ski Trails to celebrate the beginning of the season with races, shows, sales, etc.

WEST ENTRANCE

West Entrance to Madison Junction / Madison Junction to Norris / Norris to Canyon Village / Madison Junction to Old Faithful / The Bechler Region

Gateway Communities: West Yellowstone, Island Park

✳ Overview

If there's any doubt which entry point gets the most intense traffic in the summer, one glance settles the question. The West Entrance looks like a toll booth on a Chicago freeway, and traffic can be backed up just as far—a half mile to West Yellowstone. The town sits hard on the park's lodgepole-blanketed western boundary, and the contrast is striking both coming and going. What's the main attraction? Two words: Old Faithful.

BISON GRAZE ON RICH SPRING GRASSES BEHIND OLD FAITHFUL INN

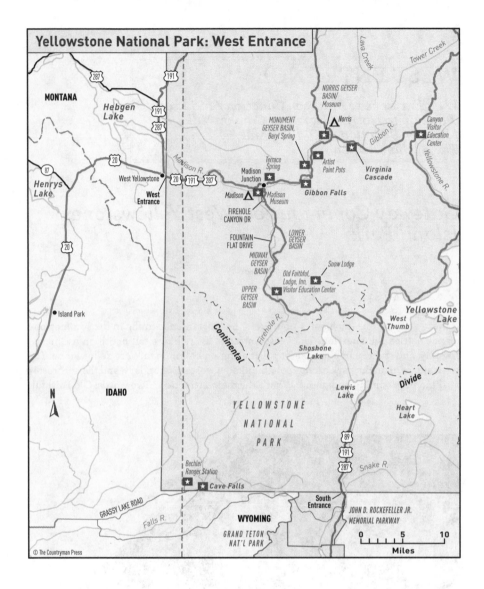

Yellowstone's signature landscape feature is a mere 30 miles from the West Entrance, a stretch that can have a rush-hour feel, with frequent assists from plodding herds of bison and photo ops with elk and an occasional bear. The image is reinforced at Old Faithful itself, where the Park Service built a cloverleaf interchange to accommodate traffic.

This region is the heart of Yellowstone's geyser country, with not only Old Faithful but the world's tallest active geyser, Steamboat, and the spectacularly colorful Grand Prismatic Spring. The Madison, Firehole, and Gibbon Rivers are three of the most revered fly-fishing streams, all settings for photos of anglers with a bison and/or geothermal feature as a backdrop. In addition, this country provides the most discernible examples of the caldera, especially at Madison Junction and Gibbon Falls. Wildlife frequently roam the geyser basins and meadows across the Madison River.

Another reason to like this part of Yellowstone: The 14-mile newly paved road between Madison Junction and Norris, upgraded because of repair work around Gibbon Falls, is easily the smoothest and safest stretch for bicycling. It was a welcome upgrade for cyclists unnerved about the prospect of getting whacked by Winnebago mirrors on shoulderless roads in most of the park.

The west boundary has two roads entering the park that do not have entrance booths. US 191 carves a 20-mile corridor in the northwest corner along the Gallatin River and Grayling Creek. Several trails lead away from the busy highway into the park, all into wild country with wolves and grizzly bears.

Another entrance, in the southwest corner, leads to the underappreciated Bechler Region. The Bechler is also

ARROWLEAF BALSAMROOT BRIGHTENS A MEADOW IN THE BECHLER REGION OF YELLOWSTONE

known as Cascade Corner because of its array of waterfalls. The only way in to this remote area is via a 26-mile drive on pavement, gravel, and dirt from Ashton, Idaho.

✳ Getting Here

There isn't much that can be called large in West Yellowstone—except its airport runway. Yellowstone Airport's 8,400-foot strip of asphalt is one of the longest in Montana, a necessity when you play host to the president of the United States. Yes, Air Force One has landed there, and so can you if you take SkyWest from Salt Lake City to West Yellowstone (WYS) between late June and late September. The airline offers two flights daily during the week and three on weekends. You can also rent a car from Avis, Budget, and Big Sky Car Rentals.

The more common arrival point via air is Bozeman Yellowstone International Airport (BZN) at Gallatin Field. The state's busiest airport, served by United, Delta, Alaska, American, Frontier, Allegiant, and several regional airlines, continues to expand. Though some service is seasonal, the former little college cow town offers direct flights from Chicago, Detroit, New York, Newark, Atlanta, Dallas/Fort Worth, Houston, Phoenix, Las Vegas, San Francisco, and Los Angeles, along with longstanding connections through Salt Lake City, Seattle, Denver, and Minneapolis.

Another option is to fly into Idaho Falls, Idaho. SkyWest, United Express, Allegiant, and SeaPort Airlines serve Idaho Falls Regional Airport (IDA) year-round from Salt Lake City, Denver, Las Vegas, and Phoenix/Mesa. Thanks to both parks, seasonal service is available from Minneapolis, Los Angeles, and Oakland.

✳ Along the Way

FROM BOZEMAN, MONTANA

Those who arrive in Bozeman have two choices for reaching West Yellowstone by car: the serpentine 89-mile drive south on US 191 through the Gallatin River Canyon or the longer (by 25 miles) but 70-mph shot through the sweeping Madison River Valley.

The Gallatin option is narrow and beautiful, slicing into a 20-mile stretch of the park (no charge) on US 191. If the picturesque river looks familiar, you might recognize it from the movie *A River Runs Through It*. Much of the classic was filmed in the lower canyon near a striking vertical rock outcropping called Storm Castle. The Gallatin might be the premier road-accessible, whitewater-rafting stream in Montana when the water is high in the spring and early summer. At House Rock, just below a bridge over the river, pull into a parking area to watch rafters and kayakers navigate the so-called Mad Mile. Farther upstream is Big Sky, home of one of the nation's most picturesque winter and summer destination resorts, with the full complement of restaurants, lodging, and outdoor recreation opportunities, plus the only stoplight between Four Corners and West Yellowstone.

All that said, US 191 is also one of Montana's most dangerous stretches, as evidenced by the more than 100 white crosses along the road signifying a fatal accident. Many locals prefer to go the extra 25 miles via US 287 through Ennis to West Yellowstone. This route has its perks, too: fly-fishing on the world-famous Madison River, the Earthquake Lake Visitor Center commemorating a massive 1959 temblor that killed 28, and a worthwhile detour at Ennis to the history-rich frontier mining communities of Virginia City/Nevada City, where there are enough attractions to seize an entire day.

FROM IDAHO FALLS/POCATELLO, IDAHO

At Idaho Falls, take the West Yellowstone exit off I-15 onto US 20 and head northeast through the seed-potato fields of the Upper Snake River Plain through Rigby, Rexburg, St. Anthony, and Ashton. Rigby, of all places, fancies itself the birthplace of television, and you'll want to save time for the Farnsworth TV & Pioneer Museum. US 20 continues north through a few more miles of farmland before crossing the Henry's Fork of the Snake River and rising into forested foothills into the Yellowstone caldera toward Island Park and West Yellowstone.

If time permits, we highly recommend—actually, we insist—that you turn east at Ashton on ID 47 and drive the especially photogenic Mesa Falls Scenic Byway. Stop and smell the pines and experience the grandeur of Upper and Lower Mesa Falls on the Henry's Fork on this 29-mile paved detour. The river drops dramatically from the caldera onto the Snake River Plain at Upper Mesa Falls. It's believed to be the last falls undisturbed by humankind in the Columbia River system. ID 47 returns to US 20 just north of the Osborne Bridge across the Henry's Fork, at the south end of Island Park, famed for the "Longest Main Street in America." If your legs need a stretch, stop at Harriman State Park, named for the family that punched a Union Pacific railroad spur from Ashton to West Yellowstone. The so-called Railroad Ranch borders the Henry's Fork, considered a dry-fly-fishing shrine.

LOWER MESA FALLS ON THE HENRY'S FORK OF THE SNAKE RIVER IS A HIGHLIGHT ON THE SCENIC ROUTE BETWEEN ASHTON AND ISLAND PARK, IDAHO

✳ Gateway Communities

WEST YELLOWSTONE, MONTANA

No gateway community has more of a summer theme-park vibe than West Yellowstone, a town that sprang from a pine forest simply to serve tourists who jam the wide streets and sidewalks. In the late 1800s, visitors to the West Entrance came to this broad, forested bowl via wagon from Virginia City, Montana, about 70 miles to the northwest. After the turn of the century, Union Pacific President E. H. Harriman saw a business opportunity and punched a rail line through from Pocatello, Idaho, to the town's current site. The Oregon Short Line was finished in 1907. A year later, the town of West Yellowstone was founded.

The settlement originally was named Riverside, identical to a soldier station inside the park, even though the Madison River is 2 miles away. However, having two Riversides was confusing, so in 1910 the town was renamed Yellowstone. That only created

BEFORE YOU WERE HERE

Described by some historians as the fiercest Plains Indian tribe, the Blackfeet are more known for dominance in the Glacier National Park region. But the nomadic warriors frequently made their way as far south as the area that became Yellowstone National Park.

Blackfeet warriors often skirmished with Crow or Shoshone Indians before returning to the country in northern Montana and southern Alberta they described as "The Backbone of the World." The Blackfeet also were notorious for killing white trappers and settlers, taking a shoot-first-ask-questions-later approach. Despite their enmity toward whites, it was the Blackfeet who showed a Jesuit priest named Xavier Kuppens the wonders of the Yellowstone region, most notably the Firehole Basin and Grand Canyon of the Yellowstone.

Once the Plains Indians were subdued, the Blackfeet were relegated to a reservation east of Glacier. Some were still allowed to roam freely in the park as part of the Great Northern Railroad's "See America First" publicity campaign. The idea was to provide wilderness authenticity, including Indians, to the visitor experience for East Coast elites. The campaign ended during the Great Depression in the 1930s.

The best places in the region to learn more about the Blackfeet are at the Albright Visitor Center and Buffalo Bill Center for the West in Cody.

TWO BANNOCK INDIAN GIRLS POSE IN THE LATE 1800s. THE BANNOCK BUILT A TRAIL ACROSS THE PARK TO ACCESS BISON HUNTING GROUNDS. NPS

more confusion between the town and park, so in 1920 "West" was added. Early on, heavy snows and some of the lowest temperatures in the nation sent residents scurrying for warmer climes in the winter.

The isolation afforded Rat Pack characters from early Las Vegas days, savory and otherwise, to hide out. The only evidence of that era today is in a single motel: Best Western Desert Inn. The community has just under 1,200 residents, with a strong Latter-Day Saints contingent reflected in five churches. Also prominent is a year-round Hispanic population, along with seasonal eastern European workers.

BISON, REAL AND OTHERWISE, ARE A PART OF WEST YELLOWSTONE'S FABRIC

Once the state began plowing US 191 north to Bozeman in the winter, the town grew into a year-round playground. Rail passenger service ended in 1970, but the introduction of snowmobiles around the same time created new prosperity. Unfettered access to the park lasted more than three decades, until tourist and even resident complaints about noise, pollution, and stress to animals compelled the Park Service to ban the machines. Today, after years of uncertainty and rancor between the town, park, and conservation groups, a limited number of quieter, cleaner machines, along with motorized snowcoaches—custom touring vans equipped with skis and tracks—are allowed in Yellowstone.

In the summer, West is crowded with tourists who come to explore the park and fly-fish in the Madison and Henry's Fork Rivers. Lodging is abundant and expanding, with many small mom-and-pop operations alongside chain hotels. West Yellowstone has a central reservations system for lodging (406-646-7077), providing easy access to well over 500 rooms.

Between its two frenetic seasons, West Yellowstone takes a deep breath in spring and fall, called "shoulder seasons." Only a handful of businesses and restaurants remain open, and the town appears to have rolled up its streets. But if you're looking for a little less hustle and bustle, plan your trip for these small windows.

ISLAND PARK, IDAHO

Island Park has long boasted the "Longest Main Street in America," a 33-mile north–south ribbon of US 20 that cuts a narrow swath through lodgepole pine roughly paralleling the Henry's Fork. The town, no more than 500 feet wide in places, was incorporated in the 1940s for ease of licensing businesses scattered throughout the area. From the name Island Park, you might expect to see a series of islands in the river, but the designation actually refers to meadows, or "islands," of open land amid the forest. Early travelers through the country would "park" in these meadows overnight before moving on to the next open space, or "island."

Much of the focus was on resource extraction—mining, timber, ranching—until a gradual shift toward tourism and trophy homes beginning in the 1970s. The forests south of town once were clear-cut to Yellowstone's western edge, a harsh line fading but still visible on satellite photos from space. The practice was discontinued to protect grizzly bear habitat, and the forests are thickening again, with signs along US 20 revealing when they were replanted.

Today, Island Park has an interesting mix of residents and guests. Harriman State Park and the highly developed Box Canyon section of the Henry's Fork lure Nordic skiers and fly anglers in their Orvis togs. Toward the north at Mack's Inn, the woods are a labyrinth of snowmobile and ATV trails. The town is still a series of land islands, but now those are full of motels, gas stations, sporting goods stores, and cabins for rent. Advocates have been pushing to create an Island Park Caldera National Monument that would recognize the scenic and recreational value of the area, but locals are split on the idea. Some also are pushing for wildlife overpasses and underpasses on US 20 so critters can cross safely—drivers should be vigilant.

✳ Hitting the Road

WEST ENTRANCE TO MADISON JUNCTION (14 MILES)

Much of this section of road is in thick forest. About 2 miles after the entrance, the hallowed Madison River appears like a wide, shimmering jewel on the left. You'll also see remnants of the 1988 fires, mostly in the bleached, ghostly spires of old pines now barely poking above thick stands of 30-year-old trees (see sidebar on the 1988 fires). One of the park's two bison herds frequents the roadway during annual migrations to and from lower elevations, often snarling traffic. This has also been the most heavily used entrance by snowmobilers since the 1960s.

About 6 miles into the park, the clearly marked 1-mile Riverside Drive paralleling the main road allows for a more casual and closer look at the broad and shallow Madison's sparkling riffles. At 7 miles in is the Seven Mile Bridge over the Madison. Just before it, look at the sage embankment on the other side of the river. You'll notice a heavily trafficked game trail used by bison, wolves, elk, and other wildlife after fording the river. Bison are especially fond of this spot for safely coaxing their calves across, positioning them upstream so they can brace against their mothers' flanks.

Upstream from the bridge on the south side of the road is a broad meadow where bison and elk are almost always grazing in the shadow of 8,235-foot Mount Haynes, and where moose occasionally linger. And wherever elk are, wolves can't be far behind. Bears like this country, too. By the way, Mount Haynes and 7,500-foot National Park Mountain provide the first glimpse of the Yellowstone caldera rim. Before reaching the T at Madison Junction, you'll arrive at Madison Campground. The junction is at the confluence of the famed Gibbon and Firehole Rivers, forming the Madison.

MADISON JUNCTION TO NORRIS (14 MILES)

Once one of the more rugged sections of road, this stretch was tamed considerably when it was repaved, rebridged, and rerouted. A larger parking area was fashioned out of rock above 84-foot Gibbon Falls at the edge of the caldera. Once notorious for traffic jams, Gibbon Falls now offers plenty of room for sight-seeing without slowing those in a hurry to get to Norris and beyond. Only the road between Madison Junction and Old Faithful has more thermal features. In fact, many people prefer Norris Geyser Basin for the less-crowded boardwalks and trails.

Norris is also the hottest, oldest, and most rapidly changing thermal basin in the park and home to the mighty but fickle Steamboat. The world's tallest geyser can slumber for 50 years, then awaken without warning. In recent years, it has erupted several times, including 2018, much to the awe of a handful of surprised witnesses.

The first few miles of this drive follow the meandering Gibbon River, a magnet for trout anglers—humans, sandhill cranes, and herons alike. In barely a mile is Terrace Spring, a thermal area with hot Terrace Spring and cooler Bath Spring. There are two picnic areas along the route, one at Tuff Cliff and the other at Gibbon Falls. Once arriving at the spacious new parking lot above the falls, you're on the rim of the caldera.

The next noteworthy stop is the spectacularly blue-green Beryl Spring, near the edge of the road, which vents (literally) at passing vehicles. At almost 200 degrees

AN IMPROVED PARKING AREA HAS ENHANCED VIEWING AT GIBBON FALLS

Fahrenheit, the spring is one of Yellowstone's warmest and likes to spew its boiling waters to heights of 4 feet. Nearby fumaroles add to the feistiness of this hot spot.

Up next is the trailhead for Monument Geyser Basin: a mile-long climb leading to several fizzling-out geysers. Beyond the trailhead and past sloshy Gibbon Meadow—a great place to scan for elk, bison, and more exotic critters—is the turnoff for the colorful Artist Paint Pots. Newcomers and veterans alike find themselves mesmerized by, and giggling at, the gurgling cream-colored pots reached via a short trail up a hill.

Finally, reserve substantive time for Norris Geyser Basin. Have your camera ready for more than 50 thermal features viewed from a labyrinth of trails adding up to more than 2 miles. Grab a brochure at the Norris Geyser Basin Museum and take one or both of the loop trails—Porcelain Basin and Back Basin—through a sensory feast of aromas, colors, soundscapes, and otherworldly landscapes. Among the highlights: Black

STEAMBOAT GEYSER IS THE WORLD'S LARGEST NATURAL FOUNTAIN BUT IT CAN BE FICKLE, GOING YEARS WITHOUT ERUPTING JACOB W. FRANK / NPS

Growler Steam Vent is a classic fumarole, Ledge Geyser shoots water more than 200 feet sideways, Whirligig Geyser swirls and twirls its waters, and Emerald Spring showcases a rainbow of colors.

And then there's Steamboat. It doesn't show its fiery wares often, but when it does it's the most spectacular geyser in the world in terms of sheer height (more than 350 feet). The wildly unpredictable geyser, with two vents spaced 15 feet apart, went from 1911 to 1961 without a single eruption, then suddenly blew its top 29 times in 1964 alone. In 2013, Steamboat sent vapors nearly 300 feet for nine minutes, ending an eight-year hiatus. It erupted again in 2014, went silent for nearly four years, then excited spectators several times in 2018. In its full glory, water can shoot to the length of a football field or longer for up to 40 minutes, requiring a cooling-off period of a couple of days. For the record: Until 1985, Excelsior Geyser in Midway Geyser Basin claimed the mantle as world's tallest, but it went dormant that year and is now listed as a mere hot spring.

It's difficult to believe today, but Grand Loop Road once cut through the heart of Norris Geyser Basin. The Park Service rerouted it a half century ago, to the benefit of guests and geysers. This is a surreal place to come in the winter via snowcoach, when heated water mixes with frigid air to create a wonderland often accented by the steamy breath of frosty bison.

NORRIS TO CANYON (12 MILES)

This largely forested stretch is the middle section of the figure-eight Grand Loop, most of it on the north edge of the caldera. A route sometimes called the Norris Cutoff is relatively nondescript by park standards. It boasts a handful of modest hikes, provides close-up examination of scorched remnants of the famous 1988 fires, and even has an exhibit describing a 1984 windstorm once reported as a tornado.

The drive from west to east is a steady climb, and it's conceivable to start amid bare ground and wind up 12 miles later in a field of snow at Canyon Village, the gateway to some of the park's most spectacular views.

Less than 2 miles into the drive from Norris is the turnoff for Virginia Cascade, a 60-foot plunge on the Gibbon River that, like Gibbon Falls, drops dramatically from the caldera rim. The difference: a twisting, descending, 1.7-mile loop drive on pavement to view the falls, with precious little parking for those who want to gape at the waters pouring into the canyon. A picnic area at the end of the loop is one way to stretch your legs and to see the cascade. Back on the main road, look for the parking area for exhibits about fire and the freakish wind shear in 1984 that blew down hundreds of lodgepoles. Nobody was hurt, but a few folks on the Virginia Cascade Road were stranded for several hours.

On the final 8.5 miles, you'll rise onto Solfatara Plateau past five trailheads (see "Hiking") that lead to Ice Lake, Little Gibbon Falls, and Grebe Lake before reaching Canyon Village. This is a busy hub where the sprawl is partially masked by a thick pine forest, though recent innovative renovations have reduced the footprint. The sparkling Canyon Visitor Education Center offers the usual assortment of information along with exhibits about the area's stunning topography and geology.

MADISON JUNCTION TO OLD FAITHFUL (16 MILES)

Geysers, geysers, geysers. That's the synopsis of this mystical section of well-traveled road that follows the Firehole River to Lower Geyser Basin and Fountain Flat Drive. The route begins at the confluence of the Firehole and Gibbon Rivers.

Within a few miles, you'll have access to Lower, Midway, and Upper Geyser Basins—the latter being home to Old Faithful—and a fourth thermal area called Fountain Paint Pots. Though Old Faithful is known worldwide, equally impressive and infinitely more colorful are Grand Prismatic Spring and Excelsior Geyser, both at Midway Geyser Basin. It's easy to be mesmerized for hours gazing at nature's handiwork.

Before embarking on this route, wander through the free Madison Museum. This National Historic Register building (1929) contains a handful of touchable items and

THE GIBBON RIVER FLOWS TOWARD THE EDGE OF THE YELLOWSTONE CALDERA   JIM PEACO / NPS

THE 1988 FIRES: REBIRTH OF THE FIRST NATIONAL PARK

Almost completely unnoticed, a small wildfire began on June 14, 1988, in a place called Storm Creek near the historic Silver Tip Ranch north of the park boundary. By the end of June, three more lightning-caused fires were burning, also largely unnoticed as the Park Service allowed them to do what nature intended, planning to intervene only if structures were threatened.

Nobody gave much thought to the blazes until July 1, when smoke from the so-called Fan Fire near Gardiner, Montana, curled upward in full view. It was just a precursor. Before the month was out, howling winds, high temperatures, and the worst drought in Yellowstone's recorded history conspired to create what would be known as the "Summer of Fire." An eerie glow would last for two months, and before the summer took its last smoky breath, nearly 800,000 acres—about a third of the park—were consumed by 51 conflagrations, 42 caused by lightning and 9 by humans. The "devastation" was sensationally transmitted into America's living rooms each night by network television.

From the moment that first fire was ignited until rain and snow blanketed the park on September 11, the "tragedy" in Yellowstone was the focus of a stunned, angry, and grieving nation. Government officials argued over policies that had ranged from the old Smokey Bear suppress-every-fire philosophy to the so-called "Let Burn" doctrine of 1972, which guided

ONE-THIRD OF YELLOWSTONE NATIONAL PARK BURNED IN 1988
NPS

also serves as an information station and Yellowstone Forever bookstore. If you're not in a hurry, take the 2.2-mile Firehole Canyon Drive beginning just south of Madison Junction. The route winds through conifers and past a cascading stream with excellent fishing holes. A mile into the scenic detour is 40-foot Firehole Falls. Another mile leads to the Firehole swimming hole, a delightful 75 degrees but often crowded on warm days.

Back on the main drag 3 miles later, an old freight route now called Fountain Flat Drive leads west across a picturesque plain toward Lower Geyser Basin. At 11 square miles, it is Yellowstone's largest geyser area. In another 1.5 miles is a parking or staging area for hikers and bicyclists who want to continue to Midway Geyser Basin. The prettiest of the 17 springs in Lower Geyser Basin might be the brilliant blue Ojo Caliente

decisions in '88. Residents of gateway communities such as Cooke City and West Yellowstone helplessly watched flames draw near, their livelihoods and homes threatened. Vice President George H. W. Bush was forced to cut short a fishing excursion. Tourists in the park and folks back home watched nightly as much of America's first national park went up in flames, never to look the same in our lifetimes.

They saw tens of millions of scorched trees. They saw charred remains of elk. They saw smoldering remnants of cabins. And they saw more than 25,000 firefighters living in grimy tent cities as they battled the blazes, at a hefty cost to taxpayers, mostly in an effort to save lives and historic structures. By August, some two dozen fires were burning a mosaic pattern across the park. Ash fell halfway across Wyoming, and smoke plumes could be seen in surrounding states. On August 20, 1988, dubbed Black Saturday, hurricane-force winds forced officials to close the park completely for the only time in its history (until fiscal sequestration in 2013). Eighteen days later another 100,000 acres burned, turning 20 cabins near Old Faithful to cinders.

How could this happen, Americans wondered, and more to the point, how could the Park Service let this happen? When snow mercifully halted the carnage, reporters packed their notebooks, TV trucks lowered their satellite dishes, and government officials turned to other matters, leaving the rest of the Summer of Fire story untold.

What Americans wouldn't see on TV or in the headlines—except on nature programs and in reports buried in newspaper travel sections—was the miracle of regeneration, a turnaround so rapid and remarkable that even biologists and naturalists were awestruck. As Park Service officials began assessing the fallout, they didn't have to wait long for hopeful signs. Fewer than 400 large mammals perished, about two-thirds of them elk. Only a handful of bison, bear, moose, and deer died. Smoke inhalation was the primary culprit. Wildflowers such as fireweed and Indian paintbrush, along with grasses and forbs, rose quickly from the ashes. They provided forage for deer, elk, and bison in places where they once couldn't roam because of a tangled understory of dead and dying timber.

Only a tiny fraction of the park burned hot enough to sterilize the soil. Millions of "serotinous" lodgepole cones that depend on fire to open and root have created stands more than 30 feet tall. Weaker wildlife ultimately perished at the paws of predators in the harsh winter of 1988–89, leaving the fit to survive, a direct link to today's flourishing populations.

More than three decades later, the rebirth continues to be astonishing. Though officials feared Yellowstone would cease to be one of America's favorite destinations, a record 4 million visit annually, and the number continues to climb. The burned areas are more a source of fascination than despair. Wildlife gravitate to the new growth in open spaces, making them more visible to amateur photographers. Gateway communities thrive as never before. The upshot: The ecosystem works and self-regulates. Even cataclysmic fires are part of the process.

(Spanish for "hot spring"). Believe it or not, a stately park-style hotel—the Fountain—stood here during the stagecoach era from 1891 until 1917, when it was rendered obsolete after the automobile made it possible to zip through to Old Faithful.

Next up on Grand Loop Road is the Fountain Paint Pot Trail, where you can see all four of the park's geothermal types. This is a great place to observe mud pots, but there are six geysers, a handful of fumaroles, and some hot pools, including 200-degree Celestine Pool.

On Firehole Lake Drive, the most attention-seeking geyser is across the main road from Fountain Paint Pot Trail: the entertaining and relatively predictable Great Fountain Geyser. Its 30-minute eruptions, which spit steamy water anywhere from 100 to 220 feet, occur roughly every 12 hours. You can watch from your car. Check the board at the site or Old Faithful Visitor Education Center for the next estimated eruption time.

Dubbed "Hell's Half-Acre" by famed writer Rudyard Kipling, Midway Geyser Basin has two showcase thermal features. One is the extinct Excelsior Geyser, which once sent water and rock 300-plus feet into the air and now, as a hot spring, dispatches 4,050 gallons of scalding water per minute into the Firehole River. Excelsior was the largest geyser in the world before likely muting itself through the sheer force of its own violent eruptions. The other is Grand Prismatic Spring, where a blue, green, and turquoise center is dramatically offset by rusty reds, browns, and oranges on the perimeter. At 370 feet in diameter, Grand Prismatic is the largest hot spring in the park. Though a boardwalk hugs an edge of the spring, to fully appreciate it, hike the new Grand Prismatic Spring Overlook Trail on the flanks of the burned slope to the south. Also camera-worthy here is the brilliant Turquoise Pool.

About 2 miles south of Midway Geyser Basin is Upper Geyser Basin, where the prime attraction needs no introduction. Before venturing into the madness at Old Faithful, you might stretch your legs on two quick walking tours: Biscuit Basin and Black Sand Basin. Biscuit Basin, named for the small biscuit-shaped formations that once surrounded Sapphire Pool, is a 0.75-mile walk on a boardwalk amid numerous pools and geysers. In the same neighborhood, Black Sand Basin has an equally impressive collection of thermal attractions. Another eye-catcher: Morning Glory Pool, which still shines even though coins and other garbage tossed by tourists have altered the color over time.

Your arrival at Old Faithful Village is announced by the sight of the decidedly out-of-place cloverleaf interchange leading to the historic Old Faithful Inn. You will also be led to other services, including two gas stations, lodging, restaurants, cafeterias, gift shops, employee dormitories, and bleachers in a crescent shape around the centerpiece geyser. The cathedral-esque, Gold-level LEED-certified, $27 million Old Faithful Visitor Education Center is not to be missed. The center's primary purpose is to provide a thorough and compelling education about geothermal activity.

Once you've seen the eruption, walk the trail behind Old Faithful from Geyser Hill toward Midway Geyser Basin. There are dozens of pools and geysers, and you'll escape some, though not all, of the crowds.

YELLOW-BELLIED MARMOTS DART IN AND OUT OF THEIR ROCK CAVERNS ALONG TRAILS IN BOTH PARKS

THE BECHLER REGION

Far from the masses, the Bechler Region, also known as Cascade Corner, is a well-kept secret that provides a memorable experience if you're a hiker, horseback rider, angler, waterfall aficionado, or simply enjoy a refreshing swim on a warm summer day. Yellowstone's wettest region showcases more waterfalls than the rest

MORNING GLORY POOL BRIGHTENS UP ITS CALCIFIED SURROUNDINGS JIM PEACO / NPS

of the park combined, a few spots suitable for hot-potting if you know where to look (they are not marked), and fantastic fishing.

The Bechler lies hard against the park's southwest corner. To get there, head due east out of Ashton, Idaho, on ID 47. About 4 miles out of town, the road bends to the northeast in wide-open country, and you'll see a sign at the intersection of Marysville Road for Yellowstone National Park. Veer east and continue as the road turns to gravel and becomes Cave Falls Road. Just before the park boundary the road forks, with options to turn left for Bechler Ranger Station or to continue straight to Cave Falls on Falls River. If you have to pick one, choose the falls. The upper falls are the showstopper, though the lower chute is worthy of a photo op, too.

It takes some effort to fully immerse yourself in the region, which is why folks at the historic little ranger station are wont to waive the entrance fee if you simply want to poke around on trails leading toward the Pitchstone Plateau and Old

EXPLORERS WHO MAKE THE DRIVE TO THE BECHLER ENTRANCE ARE REWARDED WITH SOLITUDE

CAVE FALLS IS ONE OF THE MOST IMPRESSIVE OF MANY PLUNGES IN YELLOWSTONE'S CASCADE CORNER

Faithful. After all, you can't get anywhere from here unless you're up for serious hiking or packing. During the short summer, the prolific amounts of water and swarms of mosquitoes make it inhospitable for many.

The ranger station, over 100 years old, has a stash of backcountry information. The list of waterfalls accessible from here is impressive: Bechler, Ouzel, Dunanda, Iris, Union, and Colonnade, just to name a few of dozens. It's a haven for wildlife drawn to marshy areas, especially sandhill cranes, moose, and both types of bears. "Problem" bears are sometimes relocated here due to the remoteness. Because many trails require fording streams and mosquitoes can be relentless, we recommend waiting until late summer or fall to explore the Bechler.

✳ To Do

ATTRACTIONS
West Yellowstone: The most popular attractions in town are the highly visible and neighboring **Grizzly & Wolf Discovery Center** (406-646-7001) and **Yellowstone Giant Screen Theatre** (406-646-4100), formerly IMAX. The Discovery Center is the easy yet safe way to get up close and personal with two of Yellowstone's more famous denizens, as well as with birds of prey. As of 2018, the center was home to seven grizzlies, including Sow 101, a survivor in the wild for 20 years before human carelessness allowed her and her cubs access to pet food and garbage. Three small wolf packs add to the educational experience. The Yellowstone Giant Screen Theatre is a six-story theater that offers a bird's-eye view of YNP on a 60-by-80 screen—the largest in a 12-state area. Among regularly playing films is *Yellowstone,* with dramatic footage of landscapes, waterways, and wildlife. Rotating in are films from wild places far away. In the stately Union Pacific Building, the **Yellowstone Historic Center** (406-646-1100, May

THE DAY THE EARTH SHOOK

Quake Lake (406-682-7620, May to September), about 25 miles northwest of West Yellowstone, is a worthy detour for an eerie perspective on recent geological history. On August 17, 1959, two faults just outside Yellowstone moved simultaneously and caused an earthquake that registered 7.5 on the Richter scale. A massive landslide roared down Sheep Mountain into the Madison River in eight seconds, killing 23 unsuspecting campers. Five more campers were washed away as floodwaters raged over the dam at Hebgen Lake upstream. Some 370 aftershocks were counted, and 298 geysers erupted, some for the first time in recorded history.

The landslide became a natural dam on the Madison and created a 38,000-acre lake 6 miles long. The spires of inundated trees still poke through the water like haunting sentinels, and the site of the landslide remains obvious. Just how powerful was the quake? Water-softener magnate Emmitt Culligan had a home on Hebgen Lake constructed during the Cold War to endure a nuclear attack. Unbeknownst to Culligan and his architect, the home was built on a fault line. When the earth quit trembling, one side of his fortresses was 15 feet higher than the other. A Forest Service visitor center overlooks the slide site, with a boardwalk, exhibits, and video room helping visitors marvel at Mother Nature's awesome power.

to September) provides an in-depth look at the cultural history of the park and events that shaped it—especially transportation and the railroad spur that once dead-ended outside the back door.

Island Park: About 3 miles south of America's Longest Main Street is **Harriman State Park** (208-558-7368), a.k.a. the Railroad Ranch. The ranch was constructed in 1902 by the Guggenheim family and Averell Harriman, owner of the Union Pacific Railroad. Harriman, who also founded Idaho's Sun Valley Resort, built a spur line from Pocatello,

IRIS FALLS IS ONE OF THE MORE IMPRESSIVE DROPS ON THE BECHLER RIVER DIANE RENKIN / NPS

ANGLERS CAST A FLY TO TROUT ON THE FAMED FIREHOLE RIVER   JIM PEACO / NPS

Idaho, to West Yellowstone. The ranch, gifted to the state of Idaho in 1961, has 27 buildings, 30 trails weaving in and out of pine and sage, and access to world-class dry-fly
fishing on the Henry's Fork. Today the land is a state park, though a failed bill in the
Idaho legislature in 2018 threatened to return the land to the Harriman family, which
is split on the continuing drama.

RECREATION IN YNP

FISHING   Never heard of the **Bechler River**? Many people haven't, largely because few
venture to this remote corner of the park. The Bechler is accessible only from Ashton, Idaho—unless you hike 30 miles from Old Faithful. Although the cutthroat and
rainbow trout encounter relatively few anglers, they are surprisingly wary; grizzlies
are common in the area, so make sure you have bear spray. You'll have much more
company on the **Firehole River**, which epitomizes the pure dry-fly Yellowstone fishing
experience, especially in June and July. On cloudy days, pale morning duns and caddis
flutter above the river and lure trout to the surface. The fish aren't large, but they're
feisty. Hatches tend to occur late morning, but you'll want to arrive early to stake out
prime holes and to wait for the water to boil.

Farther downstream, the **Madison River** and trout fishing are inextricably linked,
like Bogey and Bacall. Famed local angler Charles Brooks once described the Madison as the world's largest chalk stream, a reference to its nutrient-laden calcium
bicarbonate. Birthed at the junction of the Firehole and Gibbon Rivers, the "Maddy"
meanders westerly and leaves the park near West Yellowstone before turning north.
Though fishing is solid in YNP, the river is best known for a 40-mile stretch between
Quake Lake and Ennis that produces large rainbows and browns. The **Gibbon River**
is another angler favorite. From its source at Grebe Lake to the confluence with the
Firehole, anglers move up and down the easily walked meadows for rainbows, browns,
or the rarer Arctic grayling.

SWIMMING Of the park's three designated swimming areas, two are reached via the West Entrance. The **Firehole River Swimming Area**, off Firehole Drive south of Madison Junction, is favored for its "just right" temperature due to a combination of hot and cool water mixing. The swimming hole is between modest rapids; body surfing the waves will get you to calm water and provide an adrenaline rush to boot. Swimming is prohibited when water is too high or swift. **Madison Campground Warm Springs** is just that—warm. A 100-degree spring trickles into the Madison River, where 50-plus temperatures are better suited for trout. Convergence near the bank makes for a comfortable 80 to 90 degrees, dandy for a refreshing dip on a warm summer day. In the winter you'll have the place to yourself.

RECREATION OUTSIDE YNP

FISHING Twisting through a thickly forested canyon between the more renowned Madison and Yellowstone Rivers, the **Gallatin River** is sometimes overlooked, even by residents. The fishing isn't as publicized, but it merits attention on several counts. One, it's the first river in Montana to be declared "navigable," meaning the public is allowed access below the high-water mark even where a stream flows through private property. Two, this literally is the river that ran through "It." Many memorable scenes from the 1992 film *A River Runs Through It* were filmed in the canyon. Best of all, fishing for rainbows and browns is outstanding, especially during the harshest of summer months. While the sun bakes the broad Madison and Yellowstone, the Gallatin's emerald-green waters stay cool and shaded by canyon walls, commonly producing trout 20 inches or larger.

To the south, Idaho's nutrient-rich **Henry's Fork of the Snake River** is birthed from a crystal-clear spring southwest of Yellowstone. To get a glimpse of the mammoth trout

"HOT-POTTING" IS ALLOWED IN THE THERMALLY HEATED FIREHOLE SWIMMING AREA NEAR MADISON JUNCTION NPS

HIKING

Madison Junction Area: The brisk, easy, 1-mile Harlequin Lake jaunt, about 1.5 miles west of Madison Campground, meanders through charred pines to a small lake where mosquitoes like to congregate. Purple Mountain, which begins 0.25 mile north of Madison Junction, is a moderate trail through burned conifers, with better views than Harlequin—and fewer mosquitoes. The route climbs 1,500 feet and offers a good look at where the Firehole and Gibbon Rivers join to become the Madison. Two Ribbons is a short, pretty, wheelchair-accessible boardwalk through regenerated forest along the Madison River 5 miles east of the West Entrance. You're likely to encounter bison and possibly elk.

Old Faithful Area: The breezy Fairy Falls/Twin Buttes hike ends at 197-foot Fairy Falls, one of the highest in the park. The creek curls and drops through a lush forest where elk, bison, coyotes, and eagles are known to roam or soar. With several options for access, it's suitable for a leisurely 5-mile stroll or exertive 7-mile jaunt. The trailhead is reached via the Steel Bridge parking area 1 mile south of Midway Geyser Basin or at the Fountain Flats parking area. Fountain Paint Pot, 8 miles north of Old Faithful, offers close-up views of geysers, hot springs, fumaroles, and mud pots on a short loop trail. Few trails offer a better perspective of geothermal activity than Geyser Hill Loop, which winds by Beehive, Castle, Daisy, and Firehole geysers. A few geysers, such as Anemone, erupt every few minutes. Named for its hive-like shape, Beehive shoots higher than Old Faithful. Castle looks like the name implies and erupts about every 12 hours, shooting spray up to 75 feet. The Morning Glory Pool was once one of the park's most brilliant, though years of tourists tossing coins and junk from the road have tempered its hues and spurred algae growth.

Popular with bicyclists, the Lone Star Geyser trail is a flat, paved 5-miler through pines to a powerful geyser. Lone Star goes off about every three hours and never disappoints. The trailhead is 3.5 miles southeast of Old Faithful at Kepler Cascades parking area. Slip away for solitude among pines, meadows, and rock on a moderate 6.8-mile jewel called Mallard Lake trail, reached from the cabin at Old Faithful. For a terrific perspective on Old Faithful, try the 2.4-mile Mystic Falls hike. Many folks turn back after reaching the 70-foot falls, but we suggest veering right where the trail forks for a climb up a series of quad-testing switch-

that lurk in the Henry's Fork, drive east of Island Park to Big Springs and peer over the bridge railing at the fat rainbows gorging themselves. Downstream from Island Park Reservoir, the Henry's Fork has two prime angling areas: Box Canyon and Railroad Ranch. The 3-mile Box Canyon stretch between Island Park and Last Chance is rapid water where nymph anglers go deep in pocket water for trophy fish. Farther downriver, at Railroad Ranch, is the world-renowned dry-fly portion, where rising fish tease and shrug at less-than-perfect presentations on the mirror-like surface. Fishing remains excellent on the Snake River Plain below Ashton.

For a less crowded but nonetheless rewarding outing, try fishing for cutthroats, rainbows, and brookies in **Falls River** in the southwest corner of the park as its sparkling waters tumble toward the Snake. You can fish the section flowing through seed-potato fields east of Ashton or follow Marysville Road until you nearly arrive in Wyoming. Travel down the rugged Forest Service road to exceptional fishing uninterrupted by anything but an occasional moose or grizzly.

SKIING (ALPINE) *Big Sky:* **Big Sky Resort** (406-995-5000), the vision of former NBC newsman and Montana native Chet Huntley, has become the state's poshest ski destination. After absorbing neighboring Moonlight Basin in 2013, it is now the country's

backs ending at an overlook. The Upper Geyser Basin fans out below, with Old Faithful in the background. Finally, another excellent way to get an overview without too much exertion is the Observation Point Loop, a 1.1-mile trail that rises 200 feet above Upper Geyser Basin. Keep an eye out for bison and signs of forest regeneration from the 1988 fire.

BEEHIVE GEYSER SHOWERS SPECTATORS WITH AWE   JIM PEACO / NPS

second-largest ski resort behind Park City in Utah. Towering Lone Mountain receives 400 inches of snow each year. The 85 named runs, including a whopping 6-miler, ensure shorter lift lines. Vertical drop is 4,350 feet, and skiable terrain grew to 5,800 acres with the addition of Moonlight Basin. The resort also has a family-oriented snow-tubing park and is in the midst of a $150 million, 10-year upgrade called "BigSky2025," dedicated to even loftier enhancements.

SKIING (NORDIC) *West Yellowstone:* So much emphasis has been on snowmobiles, it's easy to forget about some of the best Nordic snow around, especially at **Rendezvous Ski Trails** (406-646-7701). Some 20-plus miles of groomed trails traverse gently rolling terrain through wildlife-rich national forest land that hosted the US Olympic Biathlon Trials in 1988. Passes are required from November 15 to March 31. Thanks to a cooperative effort between the Forest Service, West Yellowstone Chamber of Commerce, and Ski Education Foundation, a season-long pass is a mere $40 ($75 for families) and a one-day pass is $8.

Big Sky: About two-thirds up the hill toward the downhill resorts is **Lone Mountain Ranch** (406-995-4644). Roughly 46 miles of groomed trails on a variety of terrain are navigable even by novices. In 2018, trail passes were $20 for adults, $180 for 10-day passes, and $230 for a season.

SNOWMOBILES: AFTER FOUR DECADES, A SOLUTION

Snowmobiles arrived on the Yellowstone scene relatively late, in 1963. Once the Park Service made the decision to allow them inside its boundaries, it wasn't long before sleds became a major part of West's economic fabric. Certainly this was also true in Gardiner, Cooke City, Cody, and Jackson, but nowhere more than in West Yellowstone and Island Park. By the 1990s, as many as 2,000 were entering the park on peak weekends, queuing up 30 or 40 deep at the West Entrance. Often the whine of snowmobiles cruising the streets of West Yellowstone was more prevalent than auto traffic.

By the late 1990s, an increasing number of people were coming for winter solitude and quiet. Snowshoers, Nordic skiers, snowcoach riders, wildlife watchers, and a growing number of residents were increasingly disenchanted with the noise and air pollution. Park Service employees collecting fees wore gas masks to protect them from carbon monoxide. Biologists also feared snowmobiles were stressing resident wildlife, especially bison, when winters were harsh enough. In 2000, mindful that some 75,000 snowmobilers were entering over 100-day periods, the Park Service announced its intention to phase out the activity in the park. Panicked, West Yellowstone, with about 60 percent of the park's snowmobile traffic, filed suit.

For nearly 15 years, the dispute raged, the pendulum swinging between each side, depending on court decisions and environmental-impact statements (EIS). Finally, in 2012, the Park Service released a supplemental EIS—its seventh in 12 years—arriving at a permanent solution. In the final ruling, a limited number of snowmobiles and snowcoaches are allowed to enter. Most people must be with certified guides aboard four-stroke sleds equipped with so-called Best Available Technology (BAT); a few private groups are also allowed. All parties seem content with the new rules, and West Yellowstone and Island Park have been able to get on with promoting their winter businesses without persistent uncertainty. Interestingly, studies show people who come for weeklong snowmobiling excursions spend one day in the park and the rest of their time riding the labyrinth of trails and high-marking in Montana and Idaho.

BISON AND SNOWMOBILES ROUTINELY SHARE THE ROADS IN THE WINTER JACOB W. FRANK / NPS

THE RENDEZVOUS SKI TRAILS IN WEST YELLOWSTONE ONCE HOSTED THE OLYMPIC BIATHLON TRIALS

SLED DOGS *Big Sky:* **Spirit of the North Adventures** (406-995-3424) runs half-day trips daily out of Big Sky Resort at Lone Mountain and in the Gallatin National Forest out of West Yellowstone. Spirit of the North lets you operate your own dog-sled team of Alaskan huskies or lets you sit back, relax, and leave the mushing to them. The operation was started by Jessie Royer, a teenager at the time, who has since competed in more than a dozen Iditarods in Alaska, finishing as high as fourth. Royer's parents, Jim and Connie Sperry, own the business now.

SNOWCOACHES *West Yellowstone:* Six companies are authorized to offer treks into the park's interior, most notably to Old Faithful but also to Norris Geyser Basin and the Grand Canyon of the Yellowstone. Wildlife enthusiasts and others in the community have been pushing for snowcoaches as a cleaner, quieter, warmer, and more efficient way for groups of people to see Yellowstone's majesty in the winter.

SNOWMOBILING *West Yellowstone:* Outside the park are hundreds of miles of trails, with rugged mountain terrain ever more accessible as technology improves. West Yellowstone, self-described "Snowmobile Capital of the World," has at least 13 rental facilities—including six permitted to lead park tours—and loads of information at the Chamber of Commerce (406-646-7701).

Island Park: Numerous trails dip and bob through the forests between the "islands" and push up against Yellowstone's western boundary in the Caribou-Targhee National Forest. Another popular sled playground is the Centennial Mountains to the west. The Idaho side is easily accessible; be sure to obey signs prohibiting entry into the wilderness study area on the Montana side.

✳ Lodging

LODGING IN YNP

Old Faithful Area: ♿ ❚❚ **Old Faithful Inn** ($$$$, 307-344-7901, May to October), the grande dame of Yellowstone and National Historic Landmark, is more than a century old. It remains the most visited human-made attraction in Yellowstone, thanks mostly to a geyser of some renown out the back door, making lodging difficult to secure. The original 1904 log structure, fondly called the Old House, towers seven stories and showcases peeled log staircases and balusters, plus walkways designed by architect Robert C. Reamer to reflect nature's perfect imperfections. At the top, 92 feet from the floor, is a crow's nest where musicians once played. The centerpiece is a massive floor-to-ceiling stone fireplace. The old structure has survived earthquakes, including the monster 1959 temblor that collapsed the dining-room chimney, and barely escaped the '88 fires. Interpretive tours can be arranged.

The lodge's 327 rooms have been renovated to mesh history with contemporary comforts, yet original fixtures such as clawfoot tubs remain. Room choices range from basic without bath to rooms with views and suites. Despite heavy foot traffic between Memorial Day and Labor Day, it's still possible to find a cozy corner to relax with a good book in an original log rocker.

For the more budget-conscious who want proximity to Old Faithful Inn, geysers, and fishing the Firehole River, **Old Faithful Lodge Cabins** ($$, 307-344-7901, May through September) are next door. The 130 semiprimitive cabins are split between the Frontier, with private baths, and Historic, with communal showers and toilets. A store, gift shop, and dining hall are in the main building. And we'll let you in on a secret: The best views of the geyser are from their cafeteria.

✿ ♿ ❚❚ **Old Faithful Snow Lodge and Cabins** ($$/$$$, 307-344-7901, May to October/December to March) is Yellowstone's newest accommodation, constructed in 1999 to blend seamlessly with its surroundings. What sets the Snow Lodge apart is it's open during the winter. Adventurers are destined for a treat, with intimate confines plus solitude amid steamy geysers and congregating wildlife, especially bison. Getting there is part of the fun. Snowcoaches and snowmobiles bring most folks from West Yellowstone, about 30 miles away, though some intrepid trekkers will arrive on skis. The lodge comprises 100 attractive rooms with full baths. The Western cabins are akin to a comfortable motel room; Frontier cabins are duplexes and more vanilla but comfortable. An upscale dining room, lounge, and store also are on-site. When all costs are added, you're looking at about a grand for a weekend winter getaway—a bargain considering where you are and where the crowds aren't.

BEST LODGING OUTSIDE YNP

West Yellowstone: Because West Yellowstone has so many lodging options, we've divided our selections into three categories based on rates: Budget, Middle of the Road, and Higher End.

In the *Budget* category, a favorite is **Al's Westward Ho Motel** ($, 406-646-7331, May to October), with its front-row view into Yellowstone National Park across the street. Recently remodeled rooms are clean and simple with basic amenities. The **Lazy G Motel** ($/$$, 406-646-7586) is out on the quieter end of town, and other than April and early November, the clean and welcoming 15-room mom-and-pop is always open. The **Evergreen Motel** ($$, 406-646-7655, April to October) began as an auto court in 1931 and retains the same aura. It's comfortable, affordable, and the hanging petunia baskets reveal TLC. Built in 1912, **Madison Hotel** ($/$$, 406-646-7745,

May to October) offers a range from cheap (14 hostel or economy rooms with bathroom down the hall) to standard and deluxe rooms with private baths. President Warren G. Harding and actors Wallace Beery and Gloria Swanson are said to have bunked there. For intimate touches, **Yellowstone Inn** ($$, 406-646-7633, May to October) ranks high for best value with character. Log cabins and rooms with warm wood accents, some with full kitchens and wood-burning fireplaces, have a cabin-in-the-woods feel but in-town convenience.

For *Middle of the Road* lodging, the Best Western chain has three unique properties in West Yellowstone. The 🐾 ♿ **Crosswinds Inn** ($$$, 406-646-9557, May to October) is a two-story on the north edge of town with 70 rooms, indoor pool, spa, and continental breakfast. The 🐾 ♿ **Desert Inn** ($$, 406-646-7376)—so named because of the town's Las Vegas influence six decades ago—is a comfortable three-story with 74 rooms, indoor pool, and hot breakfast just two blocks from the park entrance. The 🐾 ♿ **Weston Inn** ($/$$$, 406-646-7373, May to October) is also a three-story structure, with 66 nonsmoking rooms, heated outdoor pool, and hot tub across from the city park. In the heart of downtown is 🐾 ♿ **Brandin' Iron Inn** ($$, 406-646-9411)—80 basic rooms with a fridge, plus two indoor hot tubs to soothe after a day in the saddle. 🐾 ♿ **ClubHouse Inn** ($$, 406-646-4892, May to October), near the Grizzly & Wolf Discovery Center, is one of the plusher hotels for the price. An indoor heated pool, whirlpool, and exercise room add value, plus there's no charge or restrictions on pets (one guest brought a goat).

🐾 ♿ **Holiday Inn West Yellowstone** ($$/$$$, 406-646-7365) is a desirable full-service lodging choice, especially in the winter, thanks to an indoor pool, exercise room, hot tub and dry sauna, sled rentals, and organized snowcoach tours. More like a village, 🐾 **Hibernation Station** ($$/$$$, 406-646-4200, closed November) is a tightly grouped collection of 50 cabins with homey log interiors, a few with kitchenettes and fireplaces. 🐾 ♿ **Stage Coach Inn** ($/$$$, 406-646-7381) is a large, modernized facility with 88 Western-themed rooms and heated underground parking for the snowmobile set. The lobby's old stone fireplace, sweeping staircase, and mounted animal heads are a reminder of the wildness nearby.

To escape the intensity of a West Yellowstone summer, ♿ **Super 8 by Wyndham** ($$$, 406-646-9584, May to October) is a 44-room getaway 8 miles west of town in the evening shadow of Lion's Head Peak. You might suffer from sticker shock for a Super 8, but that's West Yellowstone in the summer. You do get a continental breakfast, sauna, and guest laundry at no extra charge. 🐾 ♿ **Yellowstone Lodge** ($$/$$$, 406-646-0020) is an attractive three-story offering 80 spacious rooms, a continental breakfast (waffle maker, too), indoor pool, and hot tub. If you want to be far from the chaos, about 35 miles north of town is 🐾 **Cinnamon Lodge** ($/$$$$, 406-995-4253), a cluster of 14 cabins in a wide variety of shapes, sizes, and rates in an energetic little adventure beehive on the Gallatin River.

If you desire a step up into *Higher End* lodging, check into one of Park Gate Lodging group's three distinct properties. 🐾 ♿ **Gray Wolf Inn & Suites** ($$/$$$, 406-646-0000) has 103 rooms on three floors, an indoor pool, hot tub, dry sauna, limited continental breakfast, and heated underground parking garage—a definite perk in winter. The ♿ **Yellowstone Park Hotel** ($$/$$$, 877-600-4308, April to October) emulates boutique-style lodging with 63 larger rooms boasting creature comforts such as fine bedding, fluffy bathrobes, and slippers. Last in the collection, 🐾 **Explorer Cabins at Yellowstone** ($$/$$$$, 877-600-4308, April to October) is glamping in modern cabins with oversized bathrooms and showers, stocked kitchenettes and complimentary s'more ingredients meant to promote communal fireside chats.

Also on the high side is ClubHouse Inn's sister property, 🐾 ♿ **Kelly Inn West Yellowstone** ($$$/$$$$, 406-646-4544). Log furnishings in 78 ample rooms—a handful of Jacuzzi suites among them—large indoor pool, sauna, hot tub, and hot breakfast in the morning set it apart. Note: Summer rates roughly double winter rates, but they don't charge for pets. Though it doesn't look like much from the outside, the eco-oriented 🐾 ♿ 🍴 **Three Bear Lodge** ($$$/$$$$, 406-646-7353) showcases reclaimed building material from a fire in 2008 that destroyed the historic (1932) digs. Much of the salvaged wood has been crafted into furnishings and other distinctive decor such as towel racks. Newer on the scene is the offbeat (no lobby) and Asian-themed **Tao's Inn** ($$/$$$$, 406-646-6838, May to October), with 16 rooms—single kings and double queens—for those looking for quiet with a touch of class. Rates vary dramatically from season to season. Another newcomer to the lodging party is the boutique-ish and adults-only **1872 Inn** ($$$$, 406-646-1025). Attention to the finer details is exemplified in capacious Montana lodge-style rooms, a breakfast buffet emphasizing healthy, and his and hers everything.

Island Park, Idaho: Just off US 20 is 🐾 🍴 **Angler's Lodge** ($$/$$$, 208-558-9555), an attractive 15-room motel with log accents. All rooms (and restaurant) overlook the meandering Henry's Fork of the Snake River—which stays ice-free in the winter and is a haven for trumpeter swans and other waterfowl. On the edge of national forest land near Island Park Reservoir and Henry's Lake is 🍴 **The Pines at Island Park/Phillips Lodge** ($$$, 208-558-0192), an appealing selection of one-, two-, and three-bedroom handcrafted log cabins, each with satellite TV and private hot tubs. The lodge dates to the late 1800s and is a draw for repeat clientele. Geared to anglers, 🐾 🍴 **TroutHunter Lodge** ($$/$$$,

208-558-9900, May to October) is a functional motel with 11 rooms—each with a fly-tying desk—on the banks of the Henry's Fork. Special rates for the budget-minded angler or guided fishing trips can be arranged, and a vast array of gear is available in their full-service store. In front of a towering pine grove is 🍴 **Ponds Lodge** ($/$$$$, 208-558-7221), a fast riser in the Island Park lodging competition. A restaurant, saloon, and store serve four-bedroom cabins with fireplaces and five economical bunkhouse units.

BEST ALTERNATIVE LODGING OUTSIDE YNP

West Yellowstone: 🐾 ♿ 🍴 **Bar N Ranch** ($$$$, 406-646-0300, May to October, three-night minimum), 6 miles west of town, is cowboy luxe—right down to plush bathrobes. Seven lodge rooms and eight multiroomed cabins are equally enticing choices, and a gourmet country-style breakfast an added perk. The restaurant, renowned for an extensive wine cellar, is open to the public for dinner during the summer. The ranch offers gazing at the Gallatin and Targhee Ranges plus blue-ribbon trout fishing on the South Fork of the Madison River flowing through the property. Located on a Bannock Indian migration route, **Parade Rest Guest Ranch** ($$/$$$, 406-646-7217, May to September) is 10 miles north of West Yellowstone. Fifteen cabins ranging from the original 1912 Homestead to more modern options, and a dining hall, recreation room, outdoor hot tub, and equestrian facilities complete the parade. Many guest ranches blend the Old West with creature comforts, but not ✪ **Elkhorn Ranch** ($$$$, 406-995-4291, June to September) in the upper Gallatin River Valley. At the request of many repeat guests—some families have vacationed there since the 1950s—the Elkhorn has remained largely unchanged, retaining its genuine rustic persona. The 1930s lodge and cabins are plenty comfortable and the meals outstanding, but those are a mere backdrop to the sensational setting.

If you seek even greater peace and tranquility, albeit a bit off the beaten path, check into one of three restored homesteads at ✪ **J Bar L Ranch** ($$$/$$$$, 406-596-0600, May to October) in the Centennial Valley near Red Rock Lakes National Wildlife Refuge. Rockefeller heir Peggy Dulany bought the vast and remote cattle ranch, and for economic diversification restored the Sears & Roebuck Smith Place, Anderson House, and Brundage Cabins to host travelers and groups. The ranch's draw is a drawback for some: It's a s-l-o-w 25-mile drive on washboarded gravel and sand.

Island Park: 🏕 ♿ ⅋ **Island Park Cabins at Eagle Ridge Ranch** ($/$$$, 208-558-0900, May to October), 19 miles west of central Island Park, is a collection of three varying cabins. Tent campers are welcome and allowed access to restrooms and showers. The ranch touts access to Sheridan Lake, a privately owned fishery on which only eight rods a day are allowed.

CAMPING *West Yellowstone:* There's a plethora of camping opportunities in or near town, starting with the immaculate 🏕 **Yellowstone Grizzly RV Park & Cabins** ($/$$, 406-646-4466, May to October), which resembles a small village right down to the paved roads. The Grizzly has tent camping, three styles of cabins, and a multitude of RV sites, including premium 70-foot pull-throughs backing up to the Gallatin National Forest. 🏕 **Yellowstone Cabins & RV Park** ($/$$, 406-646-9350, May to September), another community-type setup in town, has seven tightly squeezed RV sites (limited to 32 feet and shorter) and seven 1946 duplex camp cabins with wood paneling, log furniture, and private bathrooms. Gas grills, picnic tables, and a hot tub are on the grounds. About 7 miles outside of town in the Gallatin National Forest is **Yellowstone Park/Mountainside KOA**

($/$$, 406-646-7662), highlighted by 175 RV pads, tent sites with a table and fire pit, deluxe cabins on Denny Creek, and a stocked fishing pond.

Hebgen Lake Area: 🏕 **Kirkwood Resort & Marina Cabins** ($/$$, 406-646-7200) on Hebgen Lake has a few tent-camping spots, 20-plus RV slots, and 11 cabins of various sizes. You'll also find a convenience store, gas, and public dock where you can launch a rented pontoon or fishing boat. In the winter escape for ice fishing and Nordic skiing on nearby trails. From US 191, **Madison Arm Resort** ($/$$, 406-646-9328, May to October) is 5.5 miles. The busy compact property on Hebgen Lake has 52 full hook-ups with a couple of pull-throughs for RVs up to 36 feet, 30 tent sites on the lake, and five relatively modern cottages. The resort's marina rents boats and bikes. **Yellowstone Holiday RV Campground & Marina** ($/$$, 406-646-4242, Memorial Day to Labor Day), on Hebgen Lake's north shore, caters to families and reunions with 16 camp cabins (some with private bath), 36 large RV sites with full hook-ups, and a central cooking facility for large groups.

✳ Where to Eat

DINING IN YNP

Old Faithful: Meals in the **Old Faithful Inn Dining Room** ($/$$$, 307-545-4999 or 307-344-7311, B/L/D, May to October), known for its parkitecture design, might be more memorable for the grand ambiance than the food, but it's a definite "must do" at least once. Breakfast and lunch, highlighted by all-you-can-eat hot buffets, are first-come, first-served but dinner is by reservation only. Yellowstone National Park Lodges, the concessionaire for food and lodging under the Xanterra banner, has made a concerted effort to raise the bar with more sustainable and regionally sourced ingredients.

Recent additions include enticing dinner entrées such as gourmet macaroni and cheese with elk bratwurst, grilled quail under Flathead cherry glaze, and spaghetti squash with roasted veggie ragout. If you just want a light bite and/or beverage and refuge from the fray, consider drinks and appetizers at the **Bear Pit Lounge**. **Old Faithful Lodge Cafeteria & Bake Shop** ($/$$, B/L/D, May to September) has less formal lunches and dinners, and seating near the windows may offer a peek at the geyser. The cafeteria is open only for lunch and dinner; the bake shop offers breakfast all day and serves sandwiches and wraps. **Bear Paw Deli** ($, B/L/D, May to October) seats 70 but works well for grab-and-go breakfasts, sandwiches, salads, and scoops of ice cream through the evening.

Next door to the inn at Old Faithful Snow Lodge, **Obsidian Dining Room** ($$/$$$, 307-344-7311, B/L/D/Br, May to October and December to March) delivers a creative menu and slower pace. The Obsidian's objective is to "provide the highest quality food with the softest footprint," so they partner with sustainable purveyors. Montana Wagyu beef burgers, roasted pheasant, bison short ribs, and wild Alaska sockeye salmon are a few standout selections. The intimate environs are definitively Western with wildlife accents and service a notch above. Reservations can only be made in the winter. **The Firehole Lounge** offers a warm welcome with a large fireplace, comfy chairs, and a broad selection of cocktails and microbrews. The **Geyser Grill** ($, B/L/D, April to November and December to March) will get you out the door and on to adventure with a quick-fix sandwich, soup, salad, burger, or ubiquitous huckleberry ice cream.

BEST DINING OUTSIDE YNP

West Yellowstone: If you're seeking extraordinary dining with remarkable ambiance, this isn't your place. The whole idea of "being here" is to experience "out there," and restaurants in West Yellowstone are in lockstep with that theme. That said, plenty of excellent meals await in West.

To get the day started or for a takeaway lunch, you can count on **Ernie's Bakery & Deli** ($/$$, 406-646-9467, B/L year-round) for exceptional eats—homemade bread for sammies—and friendly service. If you're interested in updated road conditions, SNOTEL (SNOwpack TELemetry) reports, or current earthquake activity, visit their informative website. A mainstay currying favor is **Running Bear Pancake House** ($/$$, 406-646-7703, B/L), named for a stuffed black bear watching over patrons from just below the ceiling. Breakfast is always served—yes, get the pancakes—and portions are generous. For a diversion from the norm and if you're not in a hurry, squeeze into cozy **Euro Café** ($$, 406-646-1170, B/L) for made-to-order eggs Florentine or Benedict, signature crêpes, and biscuits smothered in gravy.

Three Bear Restaurant ($/$$, 406-646-7353, B/D, May to October and December to March) can be counted on for above-average breakfasts still under $10 (except steak and eggs) served promptly. Steak and seafood dinners are equally inviting, but during the winter season meat 'n' taters are the go-to entrée, notably bison sirloin tips. On the quick-stop list is eco-sensitive **Morning Glory Coffee & Tea** ($, 406-646-7061, B/L), with fair-trade coffee beans from around the globe, roasted on-site, to be sipped in-house or shipped to your home.

For a midday break, you can squelch those gushing hunger pangs at **The Gusher Pizza and Sandwich Shoppe** ($/$$, 406-646-9050, L/D, May to October and December to March) with pizzas, subs, salads, and decent pie; take-out or free delivery is offered, too.

Canyon Street Grill ($/$$, 406-646-7548, B (summers)/L/D), a 1950s-style café complete with a black-and-white checkered floor and red-and-chrome booths and table sets, will get your motor revved up with typical soda-fountain grub. And they use locally produced Wilcoxson's ice cream for tasty floats, malts, and shakes. During the summer, you'll find fast and reasonably priced taco trucks, one on Canyon Street near Big Sky Anglers (formerly Bud Lilly's Fly Shop) and the other on US 20 heading toward Targhee Pass.

After a day of wildlife touring, ✪ **Wild West Pizzeria & Saloon** ($$, 406-646-4400, L/D) gets our WOW award for consistently Wonderful Out of this World pizzas made from scratch using Wheat Montana flour and a secret red sauce, salads beyond the tip of the iceberg, Montana brews, and spot-on service. A centrally located full-service bar has TVs in every direction, pool tables, and Pittsburgh Steelers Hall of Famers jerseys pinned to the ceiling. Another pizza-plus option is **Pete's Rocky Mountain Pizza Company** ($$, 406-646-7820, L/D), where you can satisfy your burger, steak, or vegetarian tastes as well as quench your thirst with beer and wine; take-out and delivery are available. **Café Madriz** ($$$, 406-646-9245, D, May to September), one of a few true ethnic choices, sports small and slightly crowded environs reminiscent of Spain's tapas bars. True to its roots, you may order small plates (papas bravas) or traditional meals (paella) to savor on long picnic-style tables. Newer on the West scene, French-influenced **Serenity Bistro** ($$$, 406-646-7660, D) presents lovely appetizers, soup, salads, entrées, and a wine list in, yes, a serene setting—indoors and out, weather permitting.

Another upscale option, ✪ **Madison Crossing Lounge** ($$, 406-646-7621, D, May through October) has decidedly fine dining sans fine-dining prices along with an extensive wine list. Recommended: flat-iron steak, pan-seared trout, or huckleberry burger. If you are hankering for a simple burger 'n' fries accompanied by a sporty atmosphere, **Bullwinkle's Saloon and Eatery**'s ($$, 406-646-7630, L/D, closed November) crowded and

family-friendly dining room is your place for wild game, steaks, and seafood. You'll get along with owners Dennis and Jackie LaFever if you root for the Green Bay Packers while watching pro football on one of 15 TVs. Locals and tourists in the know favor **Buffalo Bar Restaurant & Casino** ($$, 406-646-1176, B/L/D), where the motto is "Don't drink downstream from the Buffalo." The decor is classic frontier rustic, epitomized by a bucking bison mount; bar bites (hog handles in huckleberry sauce or a soft pretzel with homemade queso) and dinner offerings (bison meatloaf with mashed taters) raise their game. For slightly brighter ambiance and slightly pricier fare, **Slippery Otter Pub** ($$/$$$, 406-646-7050, L/D) charbroils their burgers and hand cuts their fries, and locals rate their steaks "best in town." If you're feeling fancy, head out of town a few miles west on US 20 to **Bar N Ranch**'s ($$$$, 406-580-5756, B/D, May to September) intentionally Wild West dining room. The Bar N works magic on a burly mountain man burger (bison, elk, antelope, or wild boar) or 16-ounce buffalo rib eye complemented by an award-winning wine list. While vegetarians might not be the main audience, they aren't forgotten (Mediterranean quinoa, veggie burger).

Hebgen Lake Area: A little secret: West Yellowstone locals like to journey out for breakfast at **Campfire Lodge Resort** ($, 406-646-7258, B, June through September), a hideaway in a cuter-than-cute campground along the Madison River above Quake Lake. Larger-than-your-plate hotcakes and cinnamon rolls are the big draw. The one-of-a-kind **Happy Hour Bar** ($$$, 406-646-5100 or 406-646-7281, L/D), May to October and December to March) grills up hand-cut steaks, bison and beef burgers, halibut, and shrimp under a ceiling heavily festooned with brassieres, panties, and boxer briefs. A cattywampus deck and dock on the lake add even more character and make a Bloody Mary (secret family recipe) or

Moscow Mule ("copper on the deck") even more refreshing.

Island Park: At **Angler's Lodge Restaurant** ($$/$$$, 208-558-9555, B/L/D) you might catch glimpses of fly anglers or trumpeter swans on the Henry's Fork of the Snake River while dining in their comfortable, log-walled environs. During warmer times, enjoy views from the deck overlooking the river; on colder days, sit near the front-and-center stone fireplace. At the family-friendly **Lodgepole Grill** ($$/$$$, 208-558-0192, L/D), history creaks from the planked floors of rebuilt Phillips Lodge. Dinner entrées range from meat-centric to fish or pasta, plus you'll find a full bar and decent wine list. High on the "if you're in the area" list is dinner and a show at **Mack's Inn Playhouse** ($$$, 208-558-7871, May to September) in the form of spoofs such as *Butch Cassidy and the Sunburnt Kid!* and Western plays. It isn't as intimate since the opening of a 10,000-square-foot facility seating 320, but it still makes for a memorable evening. Reservations are required.

NORTH ENTRANCE

North Entrance to Mammoth / Mammoth to Norris / Mammoth to Tower Junction

Gateway Community: Gardiner

✻ Overview

For the history buff, the North Entrance—the only entrance station open year-round to automobile traffic—is your place. When you leave old-town Gardiner you'll find yourself craning your neck at the massive stone Roosevelt Arch, constructed during the summer of 1903—31 years after the park's creation. President Theodore Roosevelt laid the cornerstone at a landmark near where early well-heeled tourists disembarked from passenger trains and boarded horse-drawn carriages for rides into Yellowstone. Recent construction has enabled drivers to bypass the arch en route to the two kiosks at the North Entrance, but many tourists still choose the old way for photo opportunities and selfies.

About 5 twisting miles up the road from Gardiner is Mammoth Hot Springs, site of the park's current headquarters and formerly Fort Yellowstone. The stately row of former officers quarters—now housing for park employees—is a reminder of the era (1886–1916) when the military was brought in to establish order when squatting, vandalism,

THE MAMMOTH COMMUNITY SERVES AS HEADQUARTERS FOR YELLOWSTONE NATIONAL PARK

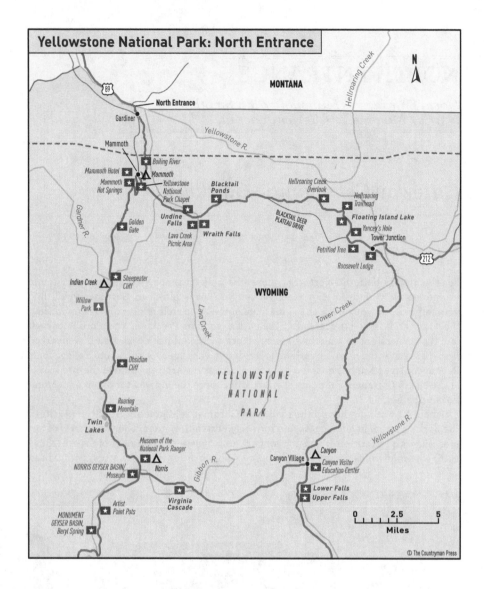

poaching, and general lawlessness were rampant. Also oozing history are the renovated Albright Visitor Center and Mammoth Hot Springs Hotel.

The centerpiece is Mammoth Hot Springs itself. If there's a close runner-up to Old Faithful in terms of natural geothermal wonders that define Yellowstone, it's these steamy, constantly shifting, bleach-white terraces that shape and reshape the terrain every day. Nowhere in the world is there a better example of travertine sculpting at work. New pools and pour-over springs emerge almost overnight.

At Mammoth, options are to head east toward Tower Junction or south to Norris. In the winter, the road to Norris—with ongoing improvements—is open to vehicle traffic only to the upper end of Mammoth Hot Springs. From there, it's a scenic snowmobile and snowcoach ride to Old Faithful or Canyon Village. The road east to Tower crosses the Gardner River on the second-highest bridge in Wyoming. This route remains open year-round and leads to the Lamar Valley, the Northeast Entrance, Silver Gate, and

ROOSEVELT ARCH'S CORNERSTONE WAS LAID BY PRESIDENT THEODORE ROOSEVELT IN 1903

Cooke City. Plowing stops at Cooke City for the winter, so you'll return the way you came.

The 18 miles to Tower Junction cross the Blacktail Deer Plateau, known for prolific bison and dramatic views of the Hellroaring Creek drainage. The 21 miles to Norris include the park's most challenging road-construction achievement at Golden Gate. From there, miles through forest and meadows lead to what many believe to be the most spectacular geyser basin.

✳ Getting Here

The drive to the North Entrance on US 89 south of Livingston, Montana, might be the most riveting of the five entrances. Even though the northern end of the gorgeous Yellowstone River Valley has its fair share of ranchettes and trophy homes, and the river has been unnaturally channeled to combat flooding, these distractions pale against the magnificent Absaroka and Gallatin Mountain backdrops to the east and west. Livingston is about 25 miles east of Bozeman Yellowstone International Airport at Gallatin Field (BZN) on I-90 and 100 miles west of Billings Logan International Airport (BIL). At Exit 333, turn south on US 89 and squeeze through a narrow slot where the Gallatin and Absaroka Mountains pinch together to behold some of the most eye-pleasing landscapes anywhere.

✳ Along the Way

It's easy to see why the 50-mile stretch from Livingston to Gardiner is called Paradise Valley. People have long been drawn to the valley, for evolving reasons. Indigenous peoples came to hunt game in the winter. Wildlife was plentiful because notoriously ferocious winds routinely scoured the valley of snow.

Quirky Livingston might not look like much from the freeway, but its showy mountain backdrop, nostalgic redbrick character, and reinvention as an artist colony after Burlington Northern Santa Fe Railroad shuttered most of its diesel repair facility in the 1980s, lures people from around the world. More professional writers per capita work their magic there than anywhere in the United States. Living in Livingston does require some toughness: The winter winds are so potent that empty railroad cars are known to topple over. The local joke: How can you tell the wind has stopped? Everybody has fallen down.

To get some sense of what Paradise Valley was like before its "discovery," turn left onto East River Road about 4 miles south of Livingston. Follow the road along the base of the Absarokas through little Pine Creek and Pray. Past the junction for Chico Hot Springs, it rejoins US 89 about 20 miles north of Gardiner. The ever-popular Chico has historic and contemporary lodging, a five-star restaurant and always-hopping bar, and of course a hot pool. In Emigrant, across from the Sinclair dinosaur, there are a few more worthy stops: historic Old Saloon for food and live music in the summer, funky Follow Yer' Nose BBQ for smoked carnivore sensationalness, and Wildflour Bakery for yummy wholesome goods.

North of the US 89 bridge across the Yellowstone River is another detour worth taking: the Old Yellowstone Trail. A scenic gravel route starts at an obvious outcropping called Point of Rocks and roughly follows the old Park Branch Line Railroad grade. Look for eagles, bighorn sheep, elk, white-tailed deer, and mule deer, especially in the spring before snowmelt in the high country. Before returning to US 89 on the iron bridge at the Carbella fishing access site, consider remaining on the dirt road. Above the railroad grade in Yankee Jim Canyon are remnants of a toll road built in the late

CENTURY-OLD ADVERTISING IS STILL VISIBLE ON BOULDERS ALONG THE YANKEE JIM CANYON TOLL ROAD

BEFORE YOU WERE HERE

As you drive from Livingston to Gardiner, you will be entranced by the towering mountain range to the east named for the Indian tribe that once inhabited the region. Absaroka, pronounced Ab-SORE-ka in Montana and Ab-sa-RO-ka in Wyoming, means "children of the large-beaked bird" in the Crow language.

The Apsaalooke—their tribal name in Siouan language—once roamed a vast territory that included much of what is now eastern Montana and northern Wyoming. It was the Crow who took trapper/explorer John Colter to see geysers, hot springs, and fumaroles, making him the first Anglo to observe the landscape that would become Yellowstone National Park.

The Crow historically were enemies of the Sioux and Cheyenne, so when the Indian Wars began on the Plains, the tribe aligned with the US government. Several Crow scouts lost their lives at the Battle of Little Bighorn, fighting alongside Gen. George Armstrong Custer. They believed helping the Army would ensure their status on most of their traditional homelands. Cooperating did pay some dividends, however slight, in that the Crow's current 3.3-million-acre reservation in southeast Montana is one of the nation's largest. Nevertheless, it's a fraction of what was initially promised. The Little Bighorn National Battlefield is on the Crow Reservation about an hour's drive east of Billings on I-90. Relatively new at the Park Service site is a monument to tribes who fought on both sides of the Indian Wars.

For more on the Crow culture, if you're headed to Cody, Wyoming, the Plains Indian section of Buffalo Bill Center of the West is a great resource. Also, the visitor center at Little Bighorn has an extensive museum and bookstore. An even richer assortment of books is available across US 212 at the Custer Trading Post.

1800s. Advertisements painted on boulders for businesses such as a mercantile are still visible.

Back on the main road, US 89 cuts through Yankee Jim Canyon before emerging into the Gardiner Basin. You'll probably see bison in the spring and winter. Many leave the park's deep snows in search of forage. Until 2011, they were rounded up and stashed at the Stephens Creek corrals, visible in the distance at the base of the Gallatin Mountains. Others were transferred to one of four quarantine pens on the east side of the highway—obvious by the tall double fencing and red-and-white US government warning signs. Today, these last remnants of wild herds that roamed the Great Plains by tens of millions—a genetic treasure trove—are allowed to wander. Their presence demands extra attention by drivers, especially at night. You'll know you're in bison country when you see 35 mph caution signs and drive over the oversized metal cattle guard.

As you pass Corwin Springs near Devils Slide rock formation, look west across the Yellowstone for a row of cottonwood trees marking a straight line toward the base of the Gallatins. This is Reese Creek and the Yellowstone National Park boundary. Also, you'll see several large, fenced exclosures where the Park Service is attempting to restore vegetation to a treeless plain.

✳ Gateway Communities

GARDINER, MONTANA

Of all the gateway communities to Yellowstone, Gardiner has the most raw and rugged persona, fitting its semiarid surroundings. It was created in 1880 entirely for the purpose of serving park visitors, though mining, ranching, hunting, and fur trapping certainly had an influence. The story goes that two men, J. C. McCartney and H. R. Horr, were angry with park officials for forcing them to leave their ranch and bathhouse at Mammoth when Yellowstone was created. To spite the government, they laid out the town against the park's northern boundary.

Today, Gardiner sits on steep, rocky benches sandwiching the frothy Yellowstone River below, and in the rain shadow of dramatic Electric Peak. The old part of town faces the park and connects to the newer section by a high bridge over the Yellowstone. It is best known as the site of the Roosevelt Arch and was the hub of activity for a half century after the Park Branch Line of the Northern Pacific Railroad arrived. By 1883, Gardiner had 21 saloons serving about 200 full-time residents.

Today, the town has its share of lodging, dining, and shops, including an excellent grocery store, the Gardiner Market. Many park employees reside in or around Gardiner, along with many other mammals. Wildlife such as bison, elk, and deer routinely roam the streets, and the high school football field is the only one in America where bison and elk are occasionally chased away before spring competitions. A raucous time to visit is Memorial Day weekend for the annual Hell's A-Roarin' Horse Drive. Hundreds of equines tear through town from the fairgrounds to the Hell's A-Roarin' Ranch near Jardine.

Human traffic snarls have been partially mitigated by the Gardiner Gateway Project, completed in 2016. It created the Arch Bypass Road for those who want to avoid hordes of picture takers, reconstruction of the Gardiner Train Depot, and enhancement of Arch Park above the high school.

✳ Hitting the Road

NORTH ENTRANCE TO MAMMOTH (5 MILES)

Even though the Gardiner Gateway Project has sped up entrance traffic, lines can be long—though there are worse places to idle. Scan the desert-like sage and grasslands on either side for bison, elk, and pronghorn. You'll notice a gravel road coming in from the west. This is a one-way route that starts behind the hotel at Mammoth Hot Springs and provides a great sense of seclusion along with terrific views of the Gardiner Basin.

After a short drive past the Rescue Creek trailhead, the road and Gardner River squeeze together for a serpentine rise through a canyon. The spelling isn't a typo: the river and town are spelled differently. Named for fur trapper Johnson Gardner, the river gets it right. Look for bighorn sheep clinging to the sheer pumice slopes on your left or sipping from the river on your right. About 3 miles into the drive, you'll pass a sign marking the 45th parallel, the midway point between the North Pole and the equator. Next is the WELCOME TO WYOMING sign.

After a second bridge you'll see parking on both sides of the road for the Boiling River soaking area, one of three places where hot potting is allowed. It's a short walk along the river to the spot where the 115- to 140-degree waters of the Boiling River pour out of the ground and race about 100 yards to the 50- to 60-degree waters of the Gardner River, creating idyllic pools. Once a rowdy place where locals let off steam with drunken binges and vandalism, tightened Park Service restrictions have made it more family friendly. There are no facilities for changing clothes, so come with a posse and a big towel or prepare to walk in a wet bathing suit back to your car—a true test of mettle during the winter. Boiling River is closed during high water in the spring.

From the parking area, the road rises precipitously, unveiling views of steamy water. Rugged alluvial cliffs to the east rise above the lower reaches of the Black Canyon of the Yellowstone River, which is only slightly less spectacular than the Grand Canyon of

RESCUE CREEK TRAIL CROSSES AN ARID PLAIN SOUTH OF GARDINER TOWARD THE YELLOWSTONE RIVER
JACOB W. FRANK / NPS

the Yellowstone upstream. You'll pass the Lava Creek trailhead and two barren knolls that were favored for taking photographs when visitors arrived via carriage. Soon to come into view amid scraggly juniper and limber pine is Mammoth Campground. YNP's lone year-round campground is one of the more comfortable places to pitch a soft-sided tent, especially for those who lose sleep over prowling bears. Farther up the hill on your left is an elementary school and a neighborhood of simple, ranch-style houses for employees.

Mammoth almost always has elk grazing on oases of green lawns. In September, during rut, single-minded bulls with giant antlers square off—occasionally with a vehicle or tourist—as they pursue and protect their harems. Among animal sounds, there's nothing quite like the bugle of a bull elk echoing across the mountains and valleys.

Make your first stop in Mammoth the Albright Visitor Center, an original stone building that serves as an anchor for the park's headquarters. Named for superintendent Horace Albright (1919–29), the center underwent a major upgrade that improved accessibility, addressed earthquake concerns, and enhanced exhibits reflecting YNP's history, wildlife, and culture. This is a great place for information as well as for backcountry permits before heading deeper into the park.

Up the road even farther are the travertine terraces at Mammoth Hot Springs. The ever-evolving springs are split into upper and lower terraces, both with excellent boardwalk access and viewing platforms with interpretive sites. The dominant white rock deposits were left by rain and snow runoff that passed through fissures in the earth's surface and reemerged as carbonic acid. The stunning variety of colors, ranging from brown and yellow to azure and teal, are due to the dramatic array of microorganisms, temperature variances, and acidity associated with the hot water. On the

Directly across the Gardner River Valley from Mammoth is the 7,841-foot peak of Mount Everts, named for 1870 Washburn–Langford–Doane Expedition member Truman Everts. In September of that year, Everts was separated from his party, his horse, and all of his supplies, with the exception of two knives and an opera glass. He managed to start a fire with his opera glass but fell asleep, starting a blaze that destroyed his knives and singed his hair. Everts survived by eating thistle root and spending nights near the heat of thermal features. After 37 days he was rescued by two men searching for him.

COW ELK GRAZE ON THE MAMMOTH GREEN UNDER THE PROTECTIVE WATCH OF AN EDGY BULL JIM PEACO / NPS

upper terrace, dead conifers protruding from pools are stark evidence of just how rapidly change occurs. Calcium carbonate (travertine) also accumulates rapidly, forming lips that dam the water and kill vegetation.

About 2 tons of travertine is dispersed each day, and terraces can grow as much as 8 inches a year. Pools that exist today could be gone in 5 or 10 years and others will have formed. If time is an issue, head straight to New Blue Spring on the upper terrace. Other pools of note are Canary Spring, Angel Terrace, and Palate Spring. Between the terraces and the commercial area, you'll notice an erect hunk of 2,500-year-old dormant travertine called Liberty Cap. It was named in 1871 by the Hayden exploration party for its resemblance to French military caps.

MAMMOTH TO NORRIS (21 MILES)

Much of what Yellowstone symbolizes is covered in this scenic north-to-south journey. From mountains, thermal features, and wildlife to the dramatic road construction at Golden Gate, you'll encounter numerous "gee-whiz" moments. The first mile reaches the upper terraces and then a gate that's closed in the winter except to snowmobile and snowcoach travel. Beyond the gate begins a gradual climb through pine and aspen past ghostly shaped hoodoos that provide a sneak peek at similar configurations scattered throughout the backcountry. A short, one-way side trip on what was a stagecoach road provides a close-up look at these odd stone columns.

A 0.5-mile drive past The Hoodoos is Golden Gate, a.k.a. Silver Gate and Kingman Pass, once described by Rudyard Kipling as "The face of virgin Nature." Construction was completed in 1885 after requiring 1,275 pounds of dynamite to blast through solid rock. The canyon wall is so vertical that a 228-foot wood trestle was required. Today, a concrete bridge wraps around the wall on the way to Swan Lake Flat. When you reach the pass, you'll have dramatic views of Glen Creek tumbling over 47-foot Rustic Falls into a chasm. The plateau is also known as Gardner's Hole because the river cuts a V-shaped course off the flanks of the Gallatin Range to its speedy meeting with the Yellowstone at Gardiner.

THE ROAD TO GOLDEN GATE IS OPEN TO NONMOTORIZED TRANSPORTATION FOR A FEW WEEKS IN THE EARLY SPRING

Bison and the occasional grizzly bear move across Swan Lake Flat. The open stretch provides panoramic views of mountains in all directions and also serves as the starting

THE TRAVERTINE TERRACES AT MAMMOTH HOT SPRINGS ARE EVER CHANGING

SHEEPEATER CLIFF IS A SERIES OF COLUMNAR BASALT CLIFFS FORMED BY LAVA FLOWS 500,000 YEARS AGO

point for four worthwhile hikes—including a trek to the top of Bunsen Peak to the east. As you continue south through forest, you'll pass the turnoff for the striking columnar basalt of Sheepeater Cliff along the Gardner River. Stop at the picnic area and appreciate the 500-year-old lava columns. Indian Creek Campground is next before arriving at aptly named Willow Park. The thick willows are classic moose habitat, so be on the lookout.

Moving southward, with 10,236-foot Mount Holmes and 9,894-foot Dome Mountain looming to the west, you'll arrive at Obsidian Cliff, an archaeologist's treasure. Because of its sharpness, obsidian was a favored volcanic rock for tools. Pieces from so-called Glass Mountain have been found as far away as Ohio, Kansas, and Michigan. Obsidian Cliff, considered one of America's first industrial areas, became a National Historic Landmark in 1996, and removing any pieces is strictly forbidden.

Going 4 miles past Obsidian Cliff, roll down your car window and listen for Roaring Mountain. The barren, steamy, 400-foot mountainside actually hisses. Roaring Mountain sends the remnants of 200-degree water into the air as steam. Not as effusive as it once was, it's still a classic example of a fumarole. Beyond Roaring Mountain on the west side of the road is Twin Lakes, separated by a modest divide that sends waters from each into different basins.

Before arriving in Norris, stop at the Museum of the National Park Ranger on the road to the campground. The museum is housed in a rebuilt 1908 cabin that was one of the first soldier stations; only three of its type remain. Displays mark the evolution of park rangers and include a 25-minute movie, *An American Legacy.* The museum is mostly staffed by retired Park Service employees who are a wealth of institutional knowledge. With help from Yellowstone Forever, YNP is raising funds to enhance exhibits and films.

MAMMOTH TO TOWER JUNCTION (18 MILES)

This stretch offers an eye-pleasing mix of conifer, sage, and high plain, with a dramatic crossing of Gardner River on Wyoming's second-highest bridge and even more striking views across the Black Canyon of the Yellowstone River into the Hellroaring Creek drainage. Nearly all of Yellowstone's wildlife species are here. Before departing Mammoth, consider a short walk up Old Gardiner Road behind the hotel for a snapshot of the entire grounds.

As you depart Mammoth to the east, you'll pass the row of old officers' quarters that house park personnel. Look for elk grazing on the lawns and perhaps a wedding taking place at the stone Yellowstone National Park Chapel, where Mass is still conducted on weekends. At 200 feet high, the Gardner River bridge is one of the most breathtaking in the region. Built in 1939, it is surpassed in height in Wyoming only by the span over Sunlight Creek in Sunlight Basin northwest of Cody. From the bridge, the road narrows and begins a notable rise above Lava Creek toward Undine Falls, actually a series of falls totaling about 100 feet high and named for mythological water spirits. It's a good idea to drive vigilantly—bison regularly use this stretch as a migratory route between Gardiner Basin and higher elevations. About 0.5 mile above the falls is Lava Creek Picnic Area, always busy because of its bucolic setting and sparkling waters that beckon trout anglers. This is also the southern terminus of Lava Creek Trail, which begins slightly north of Mammoth and includes part of an old Bannock Indian hunting trail.

In contrast to Undine Falls, Wraith Falls is modest in volume even though its height (90 feet) is about the same. It's a 0.5-mile walk from the parking area through a meadow of wildflowers and Uinta ground squirrels. At 1 mile past Wraith Falls is the beginning of the Blacktail Plateau, once the western territorial edge of the popular Blacktail wolf pack. The Blacktails were birthed in 2009 by perhaps the most famous and most photographed wolf since restoration—302M, a.k.a. Casanova. The rogue wolf achieved rockstar status and was the subject of the film *Rise of Black Wolf* by Emmy Award–winning

NORRIS GEYSER BASIN SERVES UP SURREAL SURROUNDINGS IN THE WINTER JIM PEACO / NPS

videographer Bob Landis. The arrival of the assertive Mollie's pack from the Pelican Valley in 2012 signaled the end of the much-watched Blacktail and Agate packs. As of 2018, the preeminent packs in the area are the Junction Buttes and Wapitis. Around the shores of boggy Blacktail Ponds look for bison, coyotes, goldeneye ducks, sandhill cranes, and the occasional black bear.

THE BULL ELK "SIX" WAS FAMED FOR HIS FIERCE DEFENSE OF HIS HAREM DURING MATING SEASON

Coming up on the south side of the road is Blacktail Deer Creek Trail, which begins as a short walk to the cabin once inhabited by Mary Meagher, a park biologist and author who could distinguish and identify individual bison. You'll begin to notice hundreds of large boulders sprinkled across the plateau's wide-open spaces. These are glacial "erratics," left over from the last great ice retreat. Look closely and you'll note many erratics have a single conifer tree growing from the base. The boulders create their own microclimates, providing just enough shade, water, and protection from the elements for growth otherwise not possible.

About 2 miles past the ponds and trailhead is a brief walk on an interpretive trail with insight into all the fiery turmoil underfoot. In another mile is the Blacktail Plateau Drive, a 7-mile, one-way gravel diversion that rises and falls through dramatic country. More than a century ago, when Yellowstone was toured by the elite, many service roads similar to this existed so staff could bring supplies to hotels and stores without being

BULL SNAKES ENTANGLED DURING MATING SEASON ARE OBLIVIOUS TO ONLOOKERS

GLACIAL ERRATIC BOULDERS ARE STREWN THROUGHOUT THE NORTHERN RANGE, EACH SEEMINGLY WITH ITS OWN PET TREE DUE TO THE MICROCLIMATES THEIR PRESENCE CREATES

seen. Remnants of such roads are still visible. The highlight of this detour is The Cut—a canyon that once served as an Indian trail.

If you choose to bypass Blacktail Plateau Drive, you'll pass Phantom Lake on the south side of the road. It is so named because it routinely vanishes during summer months. Soon after, you'll notice a captivating panoramic vista opening up on the left. Shortly you'll have an opportunity to break out binoculars and spotting scopes at the Hellroaring Creek Overlook. In the spring and fall, the distant hillside split by tumbling, cottonwood-lined Hellroaring Creek often is blanketed by elk and bison, with the occasional wolf pack or grizzly bear wandering through.

At 2 miles past the overlook is Floating Island Lake, featuring a tiny clump of reedy materials where sandhill cranes once nested every year. This has become a marvelous viewing area for other wildlife as well, including grizzly bears and ducks. As you continue on with more striking views, the road will make a sharp right turn and you'll be looking into the deadfall-cluttered Elk Creek Valley. Unlike other areas that were burned in the famous 1988 fires, this one has not regenerated well, in part because the Wolf Lake blaze burned so hot it sterilized the soil. Vegetation has been slow to return, but that's a boon for wildlife watchers. Black bears, moose, wolves, fox, bison, and other megafauna are common, routinely causing traffic jams.

As the road horseshoes across Elk Creek and bends back to the east, you'll

A GRIZZLY BEAR TAKES A TURN ON A BISON CARCASS

Though technically it's true that Yellowstone became the world's first national park in 1872, it wasn't the first land set aside by the US government for such protections. Coincidentally, the first was all about hot springs: In 1832, President Andrew Jackson designated the federal Hot Springs Reservation on 5,550 acres in Arkansas. Then, in 1864, President Abraham Lincoln created the Yosemite Grant in California. But management of both Hot Springs and Yosemite was turned over to their states. Yosemite didn't officially become a national park until 1890, and Hot Springs didn't join the ranks until 1921. Yellowstone wound up as the first national park simply because Wyoming (1890 statehood), Montana (1889), and Idaho (1890) were still territories.

reach the turnoff for the Petrified Tree. It's a 0.5-mile drive to see the lone remaining entombed redwood remnant in an area that once had several. Most were removed or destroyed by vandals or artifact hunters, and the lone holdout now endures behind iron bars. Anyone willing to hike off the beaten path can find more impressive examples on Specimen Ridge, where ancient forests are stacked on top of one another—including giant redwoods.

Looking north before arriving at Tower Junction, a broad plain with a handful of grazing bison will come into view. Though Yellowstone is as healthy ecologically as it has been since its creation in 1872, this is a place to ponder human intervention and impacts. Called Yancey's Hole, the area where Roosevelt Lodge's cookout facility is now located once had a hotel and saloon amid a soggy landscape where beavers were hard at work creating valuable wetlands. When wolves were eliminated and elk populations subsequently rose, trees, shrubs, and grasses were overpowered. Without trees, beaver disappeared—and so did the wetlands, leaving the relatively arid area you see today. Humans aren't completely hands-off now, either; Roosevelt Lodge staff often haze black bears away before tourists arrive in horse-drawn wagons for their steak-and-beans cookouts in Yancey's Hole.

At Tower, a ranger station is on the right, followed by a Sinclair service station and entrance to Roosevelt Lodge—a rustic setting cherished by locals and seasonal workers who want to get away from the madding crowds of summer.

✳ To Do

ATTRACTIONS

Gardiner: The **Yellowstone Heritage and Research Center** (307-344-2662), a state-of-the-art facility housing a wide variety of artifacts, photographs, journals, and other memorabilia of historical value. Though mostly for research and storage, the public is welcome to view displays and free public tours are on Tuesdays and Thursdays at 10 a.m. from Memorial Day through Labor Day. Space is limited so make an appointment to conduct research in the archives and museum collections 8 a.m. to 5 p.m. Monday to Friday.

BISON BABIES BEGIN TO SHOW IN LATE APRIL AND EARLY MAY NEAL HERBERT / NPS

RECREATION IN YNP

FISHING The **Yellowstone River**, the longest undammed river in the United States, is one of America's most prolific trout streams. It alternatively meanders, cascades, and tumbles violently through the park, creating prime habitat for threatened Yellowstone cutthroat populations as well as for rainbow, brown, and brook trout. Though technically only the cutthroats are native, other species have reproduced naturally for so long they are de facto wild—and fight like it. Cutthroats averaging about 16 inches tend to inhabit the river above the Upper Falls of the Grand Canyon. Below the falls, rainbows, brookies, and browns dominate. Wading or bank fishing is mandatory in park streams, where float craft aren't allowed. As is the case with most rivers, the most resourceful will prevail. Scramble into the canyon or hike into the backcountry above Yellowstone Lake; your rewards will be tranquility and less wary trout. Once the river leaves the park at Gardiner it broadens and meanders, but fishing remains world-class well past Livingston to the mouth of the Clarks Fork of the Yellowstone River at Laurel, Montana.

If you're a parent or grandparent looking to introduce your child to fishing, take the family to the **Gardner River**, a delightful little stream trickling to its confluence with the Yellowstone at Gardiner. Just upstream from the North Entrance, before the river tumbles over Osprey Falls, it is fed by Panther, Obsidian, and Indian Creeks in a meadow shadowed by Bunsen Peak. All four streams may be fished with worms by children 12 and under.

SWIMMING Generally, waters are either too hot or too cold for a swim, and soaks are discouraged because of the instability of ground where thermal features and streams converge. It's illegal to swim, bathe, or soak in any of Yellowstone's thermal springs or pools. Damage to the environment can occur, and the thermal areas can be a health hazard because of scalding temperatures, waterborne fungi and bacteria, and acidity. That leaves streams warmed by thermally heated waters. Although swimming is permitted in the lakes of Yellowstone, it's not advised due to the frigid water temperatures.

Boiling River Hot Springs is the best and busiest spot in Yellowstone for soaking. The Boiling River emerges from the ground off North Entrance Road between Gardiner and Mammoth. Water temperature varies depending on river depth, so the soothing spot might change each time you're there. The Park Service has restrictions to eliminate some of the rowdiness, trash, and car burglaries that once plagued the area. It's against regulations to move rocks or dig to create pools, and swimsuits are required. The only private changing facilities are the parking lot outhouses.

RECREATION OUTSIDE YNP

HIKING North of Yellowstone is some of the wildest country in the region, with hiking trails to match. At the end of the 12-mile Tom Miner Basin Road, which leaves US 89 at the northern entrance to Yankee Jim Canyon, is a trailhead for the **Gallatin Petrified Forest**. Much like Specimen Ridge in Yellowstone, this 26,000-acre area has 30-million-year-old trees once buried by lava flows. The trail starts at Tom Miner Campground in the Gallatin National Forest but eventually crosses into the park. Take another trip through more recent history on **Yankee Jim Canyon Road** about 5 miles north of Gardiner. You can reach it by turning off US 89 at Tom Miner Basin and hugging the Yellowstone River southward on the old railroad grade until you reach the well-marked interpretive site. Instead of walking on the flat railroad bed through the canyon, take the still-discernible old road up the side of the hill and back down to where it meets the

HIKING

Mammoth Area: Get a good overview of the Mammoth area on the 5-mile **Beaver Ponds Loop** hike through pine and aspen forest, past beaver ponds, and into wildflower-rich meadows that belie the stark beauty of the hot springs area. Look for elk, pronghorn, beaver, deer, and moose. Keep your eyes and ears open for black and grizzly bears on the trail, which starts between Liberty Cap and the stone house at Mammoth Terraces. **Blacktail Deer Creek** is a memorable and moderate 12.5-mile trail along a creek by the same name that tumbles more than 1,000 feet to the Yellowstone, where a steel suspension bridge leads to the **Yellowstone River** trail. Continue along the river on the dusty path to Gardiner at the North Entrance. Bring a fly rod; you're sure to have some of the Yellowstone's best fishing waters to yourself.

TAKING IN SOLITUDE AT ALTITUDE ON ELECTRIC PEAK NEAL HERBERT / NPS

Perhaps the easiest hike with the greatest mountaintop rewards in Yellowstone is **Bunsen Peak**, which can be as few as 2 miles or as many as 10. Views include Mammoth Village and the Gallatin, Madison, and Absaroka mountain ranges as well as the Yellowstone River valley. The 3.5-mile **Lava Creek** trail follows the Gardner River and then turns east by the towering bridge toward Undine Falls. **Osprey Falls** is a rugged trail in a starkly beautiful area not often seen by visitors despite its proximity to the Mammoth-Norris Road. You might share the first 3 miles of the Old Bunsen Peak Road with mountain bikers until you reach the actual Osprey Falls trail. At the rim of Sheepeater Canyon, the trail drops about 700 feet in less than a mile to 150-foot Osprey Falls on the Gardner River. You're in a deep canyon here, looking up at 500 vertical feet of walls. The spray from the falls will offer a refreshing respite from what's likely to be a warm hike in the summer, and the fishing can be great. Be especially bear aware on this trail. The first trailhead North Entrance visitors see is for the 8-mile **Rescue Creek** hike, an initially deceiving trek that includes a dramatic 1,400-foot climb out of the Gardner River Canyon. Another lesser-known jaunt with great rewards is **Sepulcher Mountain**, which has a strenuous 3,400-foot ascent to 9,652 feet west of Gardiner. Check with rangers for bear activity. The easiest hike in this part of Yellowstone is **Wraith Falls**, an excellent place for families or anyone wanting a quick break from driving. Minutes after leaving the parking area, after a quick 1-mile stroll past sage and Douglas fir, you'll be at the falls on Lupine Creek.

Norris Area: Though not as popular as the Fountain Paint Pots viewing area, Artist Paint Pots is an easy, 1-mile round-trip walk on a boardwalk and trail through burned pines that brings visitors up close and personal with two mud pots. Anyone seeking a little solitude will savor the 8-mile round-trip Cygnet Lake hike through marsh and burned lodgepole to a tiny lake; bring mosquito repellent and keep diligent watch for signs of bears. Grizzly Lake isn't a grizzly hangout, but few hikes in Yellowstone paint a more vivid portrait of fire history than this 4-mile round-tripper through spires of charred pine. Burns are visible in every direction once you drop about 300 feet to the rim of the lake—some from the historic 1988 blazes and another from 1976. Like Grizzly Lake, the 0.5-mile Ice Lake trail features the ghostly remains of lodgepole burned in 1988; unlike Grizzly, this easy hike ends in a lush green forest and is a great jumping-off point for other hikes and handicap-accessible backcountry campsites. If you want geyser viewing without the crowds, try the modestly rugged Monument Geyser Basin hike from Artist Paint Pots up a steep, mile-long trail to gnarled cones, including the Thermos Bottle Geyser. An interesting hike that combines thermal features, lodgepole forest, springs, a creek, and even some park power lines is the relatively easy Solfatara Creek, which has a gentle 400-foot gain. The Wolf Lake Cut-Off is a 6-mile round-trip hike that starts along the Gibbon River before veering toward Wolf Lake through burned lodgepole past Little Gibbon Falls.

WILDFLOWERS REWARD HIKERS ON BUNSEN PEAK TRAIL JIM PEACO / NPS

railroad bed. The 120-year-old stone wall to support the road is still there, along with painted signs on boulders advertising other-era businesses in Gardiner. When the railroad was constructed early in the twentieth century, the old road became obsolete.

RIVER RUNNING For a mountain-birthed stream that flows for 678 undammed miles to the Missouri, the **Yellowstone River** has surprisingly little whitewater outside the park. In fact, there are only two stretches, and both are short: the Gardiner town run and Yankee Jim Canyon. Both are Class III at best, but their proximity to Yellowstone's North Entrance and easy access from US 89 make it possible to spend a half day in the park and another half on the river. The town run requires hauling boats about 100 yards down a modestly steep trail from town to where the Gardner River thunders into the Yellowstone. Most trips range from 8 miles in a half day to 17 miles in a full day. You can choose from a variety of companies near Gardiner that offer these floats; some have rigged up impressive pulley systems to reach the river below their shops.

SLED DOGS *Emigrant:* **Absaroka Dogsled Treks** (406-223-6440) operates out of Chico Hot Springs north of Gardiner and runs primarily Siberian huskies on trails in the Gallatin and Absaroka Ranges from Thanksgiving until the end of March, snow permitting. Full-day treks, half-day adventures, and two-hour rides are available, as well as clinics.

✳ Lodging

LODGING IN YNP

Mammoth: Yellowstone's oldest lodging, **Mammoth Hot Springs Hotel** ($$, 307-344-7311, May to September and December to March), was renovated in 2018, in part to meet earthquake standards. The original National Hotel was built in 1883, the current structure in place since 1913, and final major reconstruction completed in 1937. Back then, the hotel was a cornerstone of park activity. Today, history adorns the halls in the form of photographs and creaking floorboards. As part of Mammoth Hot Springs Hotel's recent makeover, a wing was added and rooms now have private baths. Cabins consist of four Hot Tub cabins with private hot tubs and showers, Frontier cabins with showers, and Rustic cabins with just a sink. A quiet lounge and bar adjacent to the lobby soothes with local brews, craft cocktails, snacks, a grand piano, and a giant US map inlayed with 15 types of wood.

There's a gift shop and Bear Den Ski Shop for rentals and tours.

ALTERNATIVE LODGING IN YNP

CAMPING *Mammoth Hot Springs:* The most popular, **Mammoth** ($20, 307-344-7381), is open year-round with 85 sites amid sagebrush, juniper, and limber pine in the driest corner of the park. The campground, considered luxe because of flush toilets and pay showers, fills quickly. Expect to have company from the Mammoth area's ubiquitous elk herd. An occasional pronghorn or black bear might wander around the fringes.

Norris: Even larger than Mammoth is **Norris** ($20, 307-344-7381, May to September), another prized location with 100 mostly tent sites, flush toilets, two marked 50-foot pull-through RV sites, and five more for 30-footers set amid pines. In the woods above Golden Gate and past Swan Flats is the more primitive **Indian Creek** ($15, 307-344-7381, June to September), with 10 sites for 35-foot pull-through RVs and 35 more for 30-footers.

BEST LODGING OUTSIDE YNP

Gardiner: **Absaroka Lodge** ($/$$, 406-848-7414) is basic, but oh the views: All rooms have attached balconies that seem suspended above the hurtling Yellowstone River. The Absaroka once made the cover of *National Geographic* magazine, though the stars of the photo were two bison. Among chain motels, the modern, log-sided ⓑ ⫤ **Comfort Inn** ($/$$$, 406-848-7536, April to October) on the north end stands out. With 77 rooms, it isn't too large, the hot breakfast is better than most, and two indoor hot tubs plus the Antler Pub & Grill (late April to late October) are a bonus. For a quainter experience, ◎ ⚘ ⓑ **Riverside Cottages** ($$/$$$, 406-848-7719) are a snug collection of cute yellow cabins, a fourplex, and split-level suites with private balconies above the river. The outdoor hot tub on a platform deck affords "the best views in Gardiner." In the drive-to-your-door department, ⚘ **Jim Bridger Court** ($$/$$$, 406-848-7371, May to October) is a tight semicircle of

small mountain-style log cabins suited to the budget-conscious. ⫤ **Cowboy's Lodge and Grille** ($$$, 406-848-9178) offers a multitude of lodging picks, including five beautifully appointed multiroom suites in a complex behind the restaurant. Only one has any semblance of a view, toward the river, but handsome interiors compensate. For lodging with personality and unique touches, ◎ ⓑ **Park Hotel Yellowstone** ($$/$$$$, 406-223-7007) is a delightful addition to bunking options. Each room is Yellowstone through and through, from a shower with a tile inlay of the Roosevelt Arch to original photos

BLACK BEARS ARE FREQUENTLY SEEN AT THE YELLOWSTONE RIVER PICNIC AREA, A.K.A. "BEARMUDA TRIANGLE"
NEAL HERBERT / NPS

"AS A MATTER OF FACT, I DO OWN THE ROAD" NPS

café, starting with a studio and finishing with a two-room suite that includes a fireplace and deck.

Jardine: **Crevice Mountain Lodge** ($$$, 406-223-0148, June to September and December to April), a guest ranch and hunting lodge 5 miles east of Gardiner, is an outpost that puts guests as close to the Yellowstone backcountry experience as possible without sacrificing comforts. At 8,300 feet on Crevice Mountain and on the migratory route for the famed Northern Range elk herd, hunters, wildlife watchers, and photographers will find nirvana in three traditional Western log cabins (each sleeps up to six) and trails that lead directly into the park.

Emigrant/Pray: The eco-conscious ✪ **B Bar Ranch** ($$$/$$$$, 406-848-7729) in upper Tom Miner Basin is the quintessential Montana experience, right down to an abundance of wildlife that includes

of grizzlies; it might just be our favorite overnight stop in Gardiner. Another noteworthy addition: ¶ **Wonderland Café & Lodge** ($$, 406-224-2001) is determined to make a year-round go of it with six spacious suites above a Euro-style

POSTCARD PERFECT: THE WEST BUNKHOUSE AT B BAR RANCH ACCOMMODATES UP TO 10 PEOPLE

moose, grizzly bears, beavers, and coyotes. The B Bar is nearly at the end of the road, on the last private land before Yellowstone Park's northern boundary. Rent the west bunkhouse for your family or group of up to eight, stay in the west wing of the main lodge, or book Reed Cabin on the dirt road into the ranch.

Back in Paradise Valley, Carol and Pete Reed go the extra river mile to pamper and accommodate guests at **Paradise Gateway B&B and Guest Cabins** ($$/$$$, 406-333-4063). Four rooms in the main log home are bright and cheery; the three cabins on their riverfront acreage are private and uniquely Montana. For that ultimate in Paradise (Valley), ☉ **Rivers Bend Lodge** ($$$$, 206-228-5448) was designed by the Reeds' son Jeff, who grew up wishing for his own riverside retreat. Every detail has been carefully considered, most notably a casting rock embedded into the ground just a few feet above the blue-ribbon trout waters.

On the National Register of Historic Places, ☉ 🐾 ♿ ⑪ **Chico Hot Springs Resort and Day Spa** ($$/$$$$, 406-333-4933) is as popular with locals as with out-of-towners for thermally heated outdoor pools, a five-star dining room, and an energetic saloon adjacent to the pool that comes with window beverage service. The main lodge and Warren's Wing (for actor Warren Oates) ooze history, and rooms vary in style and comfort. Older rooms are creaky, Lower Lodge and Fisherman's Lodge more upscale. New on the scene: Cowboy Camp Conestoga wagons and The Caboose on the hill overlooking the resort. A few more miles up the road toward Livingston is 🐾 ♿ ⑪ **Yellowstone Valley Lodge** ($$$$, 406-333-4787, April to October), once a respite for travelers heading to YNP. Today it's a set of warmly decorated cabin-style units on the banks of the Yellowstone River; a larger bunkhouse and cabin make for a good group getaway. Competing with both is the new and distinctive 🐾 ♿ ⑪ **Sage Lodge** ($$$/$$$$, 855-400-0505), also on the banks of the

Yellowstone midvalley. Suites in the lodge have the finest of accoutrements, and "cabins" with double-sided gas fireplaces and private bathrooms are anything but primitive. Also on the grounds are a full spa, two restaurants, and a bar, all with panoramic views.

ALTERNATIVE LODGING OUTSIDE YNP

The spectacular ♿ **Mountain Sky Guest Ranch** ($$$$, 406-333-4911, May to October) is a former working ranch tucked into a picturesque Gallatin Range canyon 4.5 miles from US 89. Thirty 1920s guest cabins with one, two, and three bedrooms are sprinkled among pine and fir trees. Seven-day-minimum (in the summer) rates include meals and the use of the tennis courts, heated pool, sauna, horseback riding, the trout pond (with instruction), yoga, fitness room, extensive hiking program, and access to the 18-hole Rising Sun Golf Course. Three-night minimums are offered in May and early June. 🐾 ⑪ **Pine Creek Lodge & Café** ($/$$, 406-222-3628) showcases six recycled shipping containers for whimsical lodgings that sleep from two to eight. Eclectic and colorful furnishings blend with modern niceties such as a fridge, coffeemaker, and tiny attached patio, but toilets and showers are in a shared bathhouse. Pine Creek is a happening place in the summer, with live music on an outdoor stage across from the "containers."

CAMPING *Gardiner:* For an up-close and personal experience with the Yellowstone River, **Yellowstone RV Park and Campground** ($, 406-848-7496) is a snug 48 sites on a dusty bluff about a mile from the North Entrance. River access is limited because of the steep embankment. Feel the call of the wild at 🐾 **Rocky Mountain RV Park & Cabins** ($, 406-848-7251, April to October) on a hill well above Gardiner on the east side of the river facing Electric Peak. Amenities include mini-golf, grass tent sites, grills, and a communal campfire.

If Forest Service campgrounds and solitude are more your speed, we suggest **Tom Miner Basin Campground**, a 12-mile drive on gravel to the end of Tom Miner Road. This off-the-radar spot has 16 sites abutting Yellowstone's northern boundary. Trailheads lead to petrified forests on the way up to Devil's Backbone on the Gallatin National Forest. With a hefty population of grizzlies, you'll want to be especially attentive about proper food storage.

Emigrant: Parallel to US 89 is ✿ **Yellowstone's Edge RV Park** ($, 406-333-4036, May to October), with a tidy side-by-side row of full hook-up sites right on the west bank of the river. The check-in office has a small store and cabin suite ($$$) above that sleeps up to six. With about a mile of river frontage, **Mallard's Rest**, a primitive 13-site campground with fishing access, is a cool spot to camp or just hang out and watch the rafters, kayakers, and anglers float past. It also has a much-used boat launch for put-in or take-out on the Yellowstone.

Pine Creek: Diane and Terry Devine run a smooth, family-oriented operation at ✪ ✿ **Livingston/Paradise Valley KOA** ($, 406-222-0992, May to September) in the pines and right on the banks of the 'Stone. An indoor swimming pool will cool off the kids, and there's a small boat for river enthusiasts. A covered pavilion provides a perfect platform for group picnics, DIY sing-alongs, or church services on Sunday morning. Cook your own meals or walk a country mile to the famous Pine Creek Café. For an even more alternative camping adventure, **Luccock Park Camp** ($, 406-223-8131, May to October) is a Methodist church camp open to all. A combination of log and 1950s-style, wood-plank cabins can accommodate from 2 to 33, with elbow room to spare. For a modest $55 per person per day (2018) you get a bed,

community shower, and three meals prepared on-site. You may be sharing the grounds with a youth camp, a family reunion, or a retreat, but it just adds to the personality.

✱ Where to Eat

DINING IN YNP

Mammoth Hot Springs: Food choices are limited at this entrance, but we've enjoyed meals at the **Mammoth Hotel Dining Room** ($$/$$$, 307-344-7311, B/L/D, April to October and December to March), the first and only four-star certified-green restaurant in a national park and one of only 25 in the entire country. A unique mix of casual and formal ambiance blends with the 1930s history emanating from the walls of a large, open dining room. Breakfast includes a "Healthy Yellowstone" component, but the all-you-can-eat buffet is still the signature. Lunch is a step up from the mundane, with no fewer than 10 items sourced within 500 miles, including the Wyoming Legacy beef burger and elk sliders. Same goes for dinner entrées such as Montana meatloaf certified by the Western Sustainability Exchange and fettuccine with Yellowstone Grassfed Beef meatballs. Reservations are accepted for dinner only during the winter, but if you're forced to wait, there's a small bar (with TV) on the main floor to the right of the entrance that serves drinks and apps. Along those lines, the bar inside the Map Room draws a good draft, shakes a mean cocktail, and pours a good glass of vino.

For a quicker and more standard meal, **Mammoth Terrace Grill** ($/$$, 307-344-7311, B/L/D, April to October), next to the dining room and across from the general store, offers a serviceable assortment of burgers, chicken, fries, breakfast sandwiches, and more, with an increasing emphasis on healthy choices.

Yellowstone General Stores ($/$$, 406-586-7593) doesn't have a restaurant, but you can grab sandwiches, snacks, and beverages ranging from sodas and juices to beer and wine.

BEST DINING OUTSIDE YNP

Gardiner: A frontier town often chided for homogenous cuisine, Gardiner doesn't have four-star restaurants, but the food and value are solid and improving. Starting with breakfast spots, **Yellowstone Grill** ($/$$, 406-848-9433, B/L) gets kudos for a creative menu that includes homemade delights such as Thai wraps and burritos. Also a bakery with breads made on-site, it has become especially popular for its omelets, burritos, and tacos. A promising newcomer is ✪ **Wonderland Café & Lodge** ($/$$, 406-224-2001, B/L/D), with its farm-to-table and handcrafted meals plus homemade scones and muffins. A bonus: They're vowing to remain open year-round.

As for lunch, among the more famous burger joints in the ecosystem is **Wild West Corral** ($, 406-848-7627, L/D, May to September), once home to "Helen's Hateful Hamburger." Helen, along with her crusty attitude, is gone. But the drive-in remains a summer mainstay for ice cream, shakes, and burgers. If your tastes lean to the healthier green side, **Tumbleweed Bookstore and Café** ($, 406-848-2225, B/L/D) has great soups, a few sandwiches, espresso drinks, and fair-trade coffee to savor while perusing new and used books on the Yellowstone region. On the other side of the river, don't let the bland exterior and roughneck persona dissuade you from a light bite and drink at ✪ **Two Bit Saloon & Restaurant** ($/$$, 406-848-7743, L/D). Burgers, tacos, and hand-cut fries are a few mentionables made in front of folks perched on bar stools. High-top dining tables flank pool tables in the adjacent add-on. Friendly service, value pitchers, and bargain prices make it a return stop for us.

For dinner, fans of BBQ and brisket will appreciate **Cowboy's Lodge and Grille** ($/$$, 406-848-9175, B/L/D). Wildlife mounts on the wall are all Montana, but the food reflects the tastes of its Georgia owners. The best pizza and microbrews in town are served at ✪ **K-Bar Pizza** ($/$$, 406-848-9995, L/D), a well-worn bar that looks as if it has been frequented hard and put to bed wet but is always busy. Even with billiards, casino machines, and a jukebox, it's still suitable for kids. **The Yellowstone Mine Restaurant** ($$/$$$, 406-848-7336, B/D), a longstanding Gardiner staple, attracts folks despite a local reputation for overpriced steaks, seafood, and pasta. The old-timey, gold-mine decor and large-screen TVs are a plus. Always on the move, **The Raven** ($$, 406-848-9171, D) has found a home on Park Street across from the park. The steakhouse has the key regionally oriented elements, including bison steak, elk lasagna, and huckleberry soufflé or strawberry-rhubarb sorbet for dessert. If you hit the right night, usually Thursday or Saturday, you'll be treated to live music.

Corwin Springs: About 6 miles outside Gardiner is the on-again, off-again, on-again ✪ **Lighthouse Restaurant** ($/$$, 406-848-2138, D Wednesday to Monday, May to September), easily recognized by its namesake replica out front. Owner/chef Victor Kaufman and his wife, Tanya, serve fresh, healthy cuisine that brings various corners of the globe to this remote outpost. It's still Montana, so you can also chow down on a bison burger accompanied by a generous side of hand-cut fries. Prices are reasonable for the quality, so you can afford to save room for dessert. Whether the Lighthouse remains in Corwin Springs is another question: As of fall 2018, the Kaufmans were searching for digs in Gardiner.

Emigrant: What's not to love about the **Dining Room at Chico** ($$$, 406-333-4933, B on Sunday/D), famed for exceptional gourmet dining? The setting is Western, with a small lounge in back serving drinks and appetizers. The extraordinary mainstays are beef Wellington for two, Gorgonzola filet mignon, rack of lamb, or pork chops from a local purveyor. Flanking the outdoor pool is **Chico Saloon** ($$, L/D), with a separate menu highlighted by rockin' ribs and perfect pizza, and a dress code that ranges from swimsuit to glitz-studded country garb. Several small TVs surrounded by baseball caps are usually tuned to sports channels, as is the big screen above the shuffleboard table. Throw in a few video poker machines and a small stage with a dancing area and you've got a Montana-style good time. Weekend music creates an even more entertaining atmosphere; patrons under 21 are allowed until 8 p.m. Big changes have been ongoing at **Old Emigrant Saloon** ($/$$, 406-333-4482, B/L/D), where they have been "serving outlaws and cowgirls since 1902." The

rustic saloon still operates under the watchful eye of a half-dozen bighorn sheep mounts, but an outdoor music stage and upgraded menu boost the appeal. Highlight: Paradise Valley Testicle Festival in late May. **Yellowstone Valley Grill**, in the lodge at Yellowstone Valley Ranch ($$$, 406-333-4787/406-333-4162, D), is back in business, making a go at a serene riverside location. Mingle with lodge guests or local folks out for the evening in an intimate dining room while enjoying the best local farmers and ranchers have to offer.

Pine Creek: The best times at **Pine Creek Lodge & Café** ($$, 406-222-3628, Br [weekends]/D, Wednesday to Sunday) are summer nights when live music is played on a small platform in a grassy yard beneath the Absarokas. A narrow stream with a footbridge trickles by your lawn chair. Mind you, the best food is served inside, in the dining room or on the screened porch, and reservations are a must.

NORTHEAST ENTRANCE

Northeast Entrance to Tower Junction /
Tower Junction to Canyon

Gateway Communities: Red Lodge, Cooke City, and Silver Gate

✳ Overview

Want to escape the crowds? Spend your time around Yellowstone's least-busy gated entry. Though certainly the Northeast Entrance has its share of visitors, numbers are limited largely by available services in the tiny gateway communities. In addition, there are fewer natural attractions beyond the rugged beauty of the towering Absaroka Mountains and the wildlife, which typically scatters to the high country in the warmest months. So while many visitors are clustered around Old Faithful, Yellowstone Lake, and Mammoth Hot Springs, the Northern Range and the Lamar Valley remain relatively sedate.

Truth be told, the best time to visit the so-called American Serengeti generally is anytime but the summer. Traditionally, elk and bison congregate in the Lamar in the winter. Spring is spectacular because animals are still typically in the valley, accompanied by newborns. Autumn is no slouch either, especially September, when bull elk are in rut, bears are fattening up for the winter, and wolves are more intent on looking for any weak prey.

Most scenes in Yellowstone nature films are shot in the Lamar Valley. This is because of the prolific wildlife and also because the road from Mammoth to Cooke City is the only one open to automobile traffic year-round. For much of the year, however, you can access this area only from the North Entrance. The Northeast Entrance isn't staffed in the winter because there's no need—Cooke City is the end of the road. The Beartooth Highway (US 212) from Red Lodge has only a brief window, from June to October. WY 296, which veers southeast to Cody east of Cooke City, is closed by deep snows on Colter Pass until May. A proposal to plow the 8 miles between Cooke City and the Pilot Creek snowmobile staging area has gained traction in recent years but has yet to come to fruition.

For summer visitors, the Beartooth Highway is unparalleled. The Beartooths are Montana's highest and brawniest mountains. Instead of the craggy peaks associated with the larger Absarokas, this ancient range is broad-shouldered. You'll feel as if you're on top of the world, with precipitous half-dome drops resembling Yosemite's El Capitan. When you're touching the clouds on the plateau, look for mountain goats, marmots, and maybe even a wayward grizzly bear.

WY 296, dubbed the Chief Joseph Scenic Route, is one of Greater Yellowstone's better-kept secrets. Most visitors who reach Cody continue westward up the scenic North Fork of the Shoshone River Valley to the East Entrance. Those who instead head

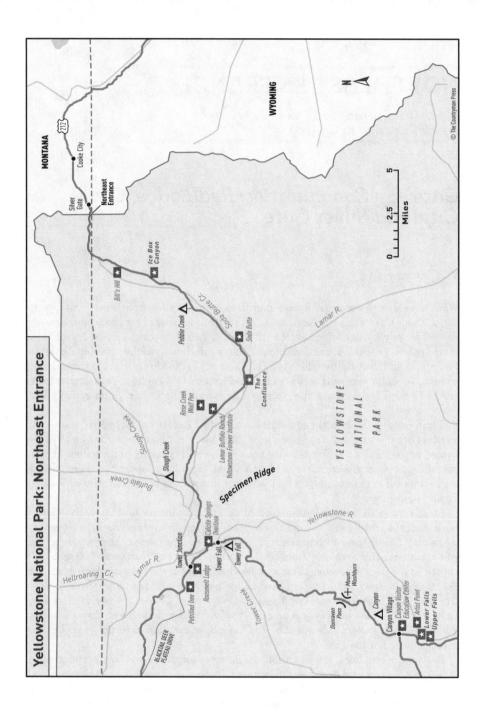

Yellowstone National Park: Northeast Entrance

MONTANA
WYOMING
© The Countryman Press

N

212
Cooke City
Silver Gate
Northeast Entrance

Ice Box Canyon
Bill's Hill
Pebble Creek
Soda Butte Cr.
Soda Butte
Lamar R.

The Confluence
Rose Creek Wolf Pen
Lamar Buffalo Ranch/ Yellowstone Forever Institute

Slough Creek
Slough Creek
Buffalo Creek

YELLOWSTONE NATIONAL PARK

Specimen Ridge

Yellowstone R.

Calcite Springs Overlook
Tower Junction
Tower Fall
Tower Fall
Hellroaring Cr.
Lamar R.
Roosevelt Lodge
Petrified Tree
BLACKTAIL DEER PLATEAU DRIVE
Tower Creek

Dunraven Pass
Mount Washburn
Canyon
Canyon Village
Canyon Visitor Education Center
Artist Point
Lower Falls
Upper Falls

0   2.5   5
Miles

northwest are in for a treat. The 46-mile highway navigates the spectacular Sunlight Basin and follows the route used by the Nez Perce Indians as they eluded the US Army for most of the summer of 1877. The Clarks Fork of the Yellowstone River cuts a daunting 1,200-foot canyon before it leaves the so-called Absaroka-Beartooth Front. The area is characterized by vast tracts of sage, pine, and jagged 3.2-billion-year-old rock

IN THE SPRING THE LAMAR RIVER FILLS WITH RUNOFF FROM THE DISTANT ABSAROKA MOUNTAINS

of many hues. The views west from Dead Indian Pass—also called Chief Joseph Pass—are beyond striking. Once over the summit coming from Cody, stop at Sunlight Creek and look over the railing of Wyoming's tallest bridge. The drive is no less gripping up to Cooke City, past guest and working ranches, climaxing with extraordinary views of pointy Pilot and Index Peaks.

✳ Getting Here

Aesthetically, you can't go wrong with either of the two approaches to the Northeast Entrance. From the north, you'll arrive (in the summer) via the dramatic Beartooth Highway (US 212), which rises to nearly 11,000 feet above sea level in a state where the highest point is 12,799 feet. Equally riveting is the route from Cody over 8,080-foot Dead Indian Pass through Sunlight Basin. Either way, if you're coming by air we suggest Billings Logan International Airport (BIL), which is served by seven major airlines, including Delta and United. Cody's Yellowstone Regional Airport (COD) is reached by Delta and United regional carriers from Salt Lake City and Denver, but flights are fewer, aircraft are smaller, and service can be fickle because planes can't land when rare cloud cover drops to 600 feet or lower.

From Billings, head west on I-90 to Laurel (Exit 434), then drive south past the refinery on US 212/330. In 12 miles, at Rockvale, you'll reach a fork in the road: US 212 veers right to Red Lodge and US 310 continues straight toward Lovell, Wyoming. The more eye pleasing of the two routes is US 310 through Fromberg, Bridger, and, after veering right onto MT 72, the tiny blip of Belfry. At Belfry, take County Road 308 over the hill through Bearcreek to Red Lodge or continue south to Cody.

From Cody, it's 12 miles north on WY 120 to the junction of WY 296 and the beginning of the spectacular Chief Joseph Scenic Byway.

BEFORE YOU WERE HERE

In 1877, the Nez Perce tribe of eastern Oregon, northern Idaho, and western Montana began their famous summer march to freedom under Chief Joseph, their revered and often-quoted leader. That ill-fated journey, ending with Joseph's poignant "I Shall Fight No More Forever" speech on a frigid October morning in far northern Montana, included a brief foray into 5-year-old Yellowstone National Park.

Their flight began in eastern Oregon, when war broke out between the US Army and a band of Nez Perce who refused to sign a treaty relegating them to a reservation. The march, with the Army in hot pursuit, would last 126 days and cover 1,177 miles on what is now known as the Nee-Me-Poo Historic Trail.

On August 23, 1877, about 800 Nez Perce with 2,000 horses entered Yellowstone from Targhee Pass near the current town of West Yellowstone. It was two weeks to the day after they suffered major casualties at the Battle of Big Hole near present-day Wisdom, Montana. During their 13 days in the park they encountered about 25 tourists. On their second day, they took 11 hostages—nine tourists and two prospectors—before eventually either releasing them or seeing them escape. Separate Nez Perce scouting parties killed one tourist at Otter Creek in the Canyon area and another on a ranch near Gardiner, Montana. The tribe continued to elude the Army through the heart of the park, eventually moving up the Lamar River, crossing the Absaroka Mountains, and descending through the mouth of the Clarks Fork of the Yellowstone River. Their trail through Yellowstone remains sacred to the Nez Perce today.

For more information on the Nez Perce and their story, the visitor center at the Big Hole National Battlefield west of Wisdom has books, videos, and presentations. No place along their trail of tears is more haunting than the Big Hole Battlefield.

CHIEF JOSEPH AND HIS NEZ PERCE PEOPLE WERE PURSUED BY THE ARMY THROUGH YELLOWSTONE TERRITORY IN 1877 NPS

THE NEZ PERCE OCCASIONALLY CAME TO THE YELLOWSTONE REGION FROM THEIR PRIMARY TERRITORY IN EASTERN OREGON AND NORTHERN IDAHO NPS

✻ Along the Way

If Billings is your landing spot, you'll instantly be tantalized by snowcapped mountains to the distant southwest. As you head south from Laurel and the mountains draw closer, you might have the tendency to be in a hurry. We suggest you take your time.

On a hot summer day—and Billings generally is the hottest of Montana's major cities—pull into Rockvale's old-school Quick Stop Drive In for a huckleberry milkshake. You'll have to order at the window, but there's a redwood-covered slot and picnic table for each vehicle. At Rockvale, decide whether to take US 212 or 310. Though neither fork to Red Lodge will make any book about scenic drives, the right is slightly faster while the left, along the Clarks Fork, is slightly more interesting.

If you take US 310, at the junction for Edgar head east into the tiny burg hugging the railroad tracks and nurse a cold Coors beer at the nondescript red-brick Edgar Bar, known for its hand-cut steaks, Montana-sized prawns, and heady clientele. No less than Joe Coors himself has been a frequent visitor because local farmers provide barley for his brews. It's also definitely worth continuing 23 miles east on gravel to Plenty Coups State Park, where the two-story home of the spiritual Crow chief still stands next to a sacred spring.

Between sleepy Fromberg and only slightly less sleepy Bridger is a rest stop on the east side of the highway where you can read about the ancient residents of the area, ranging from humans to dinosaurs. From there, you'll continue to play peek-a-boo with the Clarks Fork to Belfry—yes, home of the Bats—and the westward turn for 14 miles to Red Lodge. The bonuses on that route are the Bearcreek Steakhouse & Saloon—famed for pig races—and site of the Smith Mine disaster, worst in Montana history; take a few moments and walk the Bearcreek cemetery on the hill just before town for a somber snapshot of the area's historic ethnic diversity.

If you do choose the straighter shot to Red Lodge on US 212, this one amid sprawling pastures along Rock Creek, little Roberts has a general store with a menagerie of junk and the one-of-a-kind Roberts Café. A rest area just before Roberts offers space to stretch your legs or to picnic under cover next to the creek.

Coming from Cody, you're in for much more of a visual and geological feast. The only blip of civilization is at Crandall, where Chief Joseph RV Park (May to October) offers fuel, basic groceries, liquor for sale, cabins, and a bar.

✻ Gateway Communities

RED LODGE, MONTANA

This busy little burg of 2,000 at the foot of the brawny Beartooth Mountains is the largest on the least-traveled corridor to Yellowstone. Originally a coal-mining town, Red Lodge has been best known for years as the starting point for the breathtaking drive on the "Highway to the Sky" into the Beartooths. The influx of tourists helped offset the shutting down of the coal industry. Red Lodge has moved away from its grimy roots and capitalized on all its outdoor possibilities, the arts, and the Beartooth Highway. Skiing, mountain biking, golfing, fishing, and chilling out at the town's namesake brewery are favored activities, and Red Lodge offers numerous events. Like Cody, Red Lodge is a din of Harley-Davidson motorcycles in the summer. On July 4, Red Lodge can get almost as wild and woolly as in its days of yore.

Be sure to save at least an afternoon and probably a day or two to explore the rich history, colorful saloons, trendy boutiques, and stellar candy store in this Telluride-esque town. Once a raucous community with more than 20 saloons and ethnic neighborhoods such as Little Italy, a decidedly tamer but still vibrant Red Lodge was named for a breakaway band of Crow Indians that raised a red tepee. The town is squeezed between grassy benches along Rock Creek and against the broad eastern shoulder of the Beartooths. For all but the four-plus months of the year that Beartooth Pass is open, Red Lodge is essentially the end of the road. It then becomes a winter destination for skiing and snowmobiling, and in the shoulder seasons offers numerous unique events designed to bolster a year-round economy.

COOKE CITY, MONTANA

You can only get to Cooke City by going through Wyoming, and for about half the year it's only from the west. In the winter, the highway dead-ends in a pile of snow on the upper east end of the former mining town. Plowing from Mammoth through Yellowstone ends here in a narrow community of mostly motels, restaurants, a couple of gas stations, and a few homes for the hundred-plus hearty, year-round residents.

In the late 1800s, Cooke City—named for a Northern Pacific president who never visited and refused to build a railroad there, much to the town's chagrin—was a bustling gold-mining town with two smelters, two sawmills, and two hotels. Today, the main drag is abuzz with snowmobiles in the winter, most headed to terrain high above town to the northeast. Cooke City typically gets tons of snow, often lingering until late June. In the summer, it's more of a traditional gateway tourist community. Evidence of

A MOOSE CONSIDERS CHECKING IN TO THE RANGE RIDER IN SILVER GATE, ONE OF THE LARGEST FREESTANDING LOG STRUCTURES IN THE COUNTRY

the 1988 fires is starkly visible on the north side of what was then morbidly referred to as "Cooked City," when the town's demise seemed assured until the wind shifted at the last moment and the fires skirted the northern edge. Soda Butte Creek cuts a channel on the south side of town, and its thickly wooded corridor is a busy migration route for grizzly bears.

SILVER GATE, MONTANA

Silver Gate received its name for the silver haze that seems to hang over the 10,000-foot peaks to the immediate southwest. Despite the similarities in their settings, in many ways it is the antithesis of Cooke City a mere 3 miles away. Peace and proximity are the draws of this tiny hamlet within brisk walking distance of the Northeast Entrance. The Absaroka Mountains surrounding the town are some of the most dramatic in the region. Keep your camera handy: It isn't unusual to see moose, bison, or even one of those grizzly bears foraging along Soda Butte Creek. Like Cooke City, the town was barely spared from the 1988 fires.

✳ Hitting the Road

NORTHEAST ENTRANCE TO TOWER JUNCTION (29 MILES)

For those of us who frequent Yellowstone, no road offers more unbridled anticipation than the route going to and from the Northeast Entrance. You are about to enter an area rich in wildlife, especially in the spring and fall and, usually, the winter. The wildness of this area is evident quickly.

From the entrance, you'll begin a gradual descent along Soda Butte Creek through forests of pine, spruce, and fir. Soda Butte is unique in that it's the only major headwaters other than the Yellowstone River itself that starts outside the park and flows into it. The forest density makes wildlife viewing a challenge at first, though rest assured there are plenty of grizzlies. Look for moose nibbling on willows along the creek and the occasional mule deer. Slightly more than 4 miles inside the park boundary, you'll notice a dramatic sheer face rising to the north. This is Barronette Peak, named for a gold prospector and early guide named Jack Baronette, who built the first bridge across the Yellowstone River within the park; the misspelling of his name lives on. You'll need strong binoculars or a spotting scope, but if you scan the outcroppings closely, chances are you'll spot mountain goats clinging precariously to the cliffs. Also in this area is a conspicuous sage knoll just north of the road called "Bill's Hill"—the place where, with Barronette Peak as a backdrop, then-president Bill Clinton was dropped in via helicopter in 1996, putting closure on a controversial gold mine proposal by famously declaring that "Yellowstone is more precious than gold." The mine site, about 3 miles outside the northeast corner of Yellowstone above Cooke City, would have included a waste-tailings pond the size of 72 football fields in a seismically sensitive area at the source of streams flowing into Yellowstone and the Absaroka-Beartooth Wilderness. About 3 miles farther west from Bill's Hill is Ice Box Canyon, which quite literally never sees sunlight. Ice outcroppings linger well into the summer.

After roughly 10 miles, you'll pass Pebble Creek Campground and enter marshy Round Prairie, the first hint of what lies ahead. Though an occasional bull bison will wander into Silver Gate, especially a fellow affectionately named Jackson, this is the first place you're likely to spot significant numbers of the shaggy beasts. Wolves and moose are occasionally seen, too. A short drive later you arrive in the eastern end of the Lamar Valley, where the wildlife viewing begins in earnest. The first landmark is the conical Soda Butte, an extinct hot spring next to the road recognizable by the unmistakable whiff of sulphur as you drive past. As bison forage on the grasses in the valley, scan the aspen and pine tree lines for wolves and grizzlies. You might also notice some fenced-in areas on sage hillsides on the north side of the road, with thick groves of aspen inside. These are elk exclosures, erected more than a half century ago, before wolves were restored, to determine what would happen if the prolific herds weren't able to browse relentlessly on grasses and tree shoots.

At 15 miles inside the park you'll reach a place known simply by park regulars as The Confluence. Braided channels of Soda Butte Creek and the Lamar River meet here for a beefed-up short run to the Yellowstone. Welcome to the hub of the park's wildlife-watching universe. In recent years, wolf packs have denned in the woods just to the north and regularly crossed the road in search of food in the broad valley. Bighorn sheep are frequently seen on the rocky outcroppings, often within a few feet of the road. Otters playfully slide in and out of the creek and river. Eagles fish for cutthroat trout and hunt for ducks. Bison and elk graze the grasses, moose wander into the willow lowlands, and the mighty griz appears regularly.

About 3 miles later, the Lamar Ranger Station/Buffalo Ranch comes into view. It is here that the bison, which once thundered across the prairies by the tens of millions, made its last stand around the turn of the previous century. They were fed hay propagated in the valley and also grazed on planted nonnative timothy grasses on the

ICE BOX CANYON NEVER SEES SUNLIGHT, WHICH MAKES FOR ICICLES WELL INTO THE SUMMER JIM PEACO / NPS

SODA BUTTE CONE SHINES WITH THE FIRST RAYS OF DAYLIGHT ON A SPRING MORNING   JACOB W. FRANK / NPS

benches. For a half century they lived this way, until in 1968 the park opted for a more natural management system.

For another brush of history, hike the well-worn trail along Rose Creek behind the Buffalo Ranch for about a mile until you reach a dilapidated chain-link enclosure with several large, weather-beaten doghouses inside. This is what's left of one of the acclimation pens where the Rose Creek wolves restored to Yellowstone in 1995 were kept for about two months until their release. Also at the Buffalo Ranch is Yellowstone Forever, where educational classes are frequently conducted by the nonprofit's engaging staff. One of the great advantages of joining a Yellowstone Forever (formerly Yellowstone Association) field trip is the opportunity to be led to special places those in the know would otherwise keep quiet. Examples include a remote site with century-old Shoshone lodgepoles, ancient junipers, remnant elk boneyards, and abandoned wolf dens. Check out the bookstore in a small cabin; if it's locked, a member of the staff will gladly open up if they're not too busy. The cabins behind the store are only available to participants in Yellowstone Forever courses.

AFTER BISON NUMBERS WERE REDUCED FROM 30 TO 60 MILLION TO A MERE FEW DOZEN, INCLUDING THIS ONE SHOWN IN 1906, THEIR POPULATIONS WERE REBUILT IN CORRALS AT THE LAMAR BUFFALO RANCH   NPS

West of the institute, the valley broadens into another extraordinary wildlife

BEARTOOTH HIGHWAY: A SCENIC AND ENGINEERING WONDER

Entering the twentieth century, Yellowstone National Park was becoming an international tourist destination. Gateway communities such as West Yellowstone, Gardiner, Cody, and Bozeman were riding a wave of economic success once automobiles were legally allowed into the park early in the twentieth century. Though separated from Yellowstone by some of the region's most forbidding terrain, Red Lodge nevertheless wanted a piece of the action—especially after a nearby coal mine closed in 1924.

A road over the rocky Beartooth Plateau, city fathers surmised, would give tourists direct access to the park's Northeast Entrance and also enable businesses in Cooke City to tap a mother lode of gold in the New World Mining District. They weren't the first to consider travel over the Beartooth—Native peoples had been doing it for thousands of years—but the task was daunting nonetheless. The grandiose vision was to punch a road into Rock Creek Canyon, carve switchbacks out of the side of a 4,000-foot mountain, lay pavement across the plateau's fragile tundra and 3-billion-year-old rocks, then etch a serpentine route down the boulder-strewn and forested back side in Wyoming to Cooke City. It took years of planning.

In 1931, as the darkness of the Great Depression enveloped a nation, work began on a road whose difficulty would match the Going-to-the-Sun Road effort then still underway in Glacier National Park a decade after it began. Remarkably, construction of the Beartooth Highway took only five years and it opened to great fanfare in 1936. The gold mining at New World never panned out, but by the late 1970s the highway had earned national acclaim for its scenery. Answering a letter from a fan inquiring about the most beautiful drive in America, the folksy CBS newsman renowned for his regular "On the Road with Charles Kuralt" features responded, "US 212." While atop the plateau, on the tundra above the timberline, it feels as if you can literally reach out and touch the clouds or stars. You can also see many of the nearly 1,000 Beartooth lakes that glisten like jewels.

Not surprisingly, keeping the Beartooth Highway open and maintained is a chore. Wicked weather heaves and chews the road, requiring regular upgrades. In 2005, a mudslide kept it closed all summer, much to the chagrin of businesses in Red Lodge.

area. Bison and coyote are almost always visible here, and the distant foothills frequently have herds of elk keeping an eye out for wolves and grizzlies. Continuing west, the road slips through the Lamar River Canyon, where giant boulders as much as 2.7 billion years old have been exposed by the roiling river waters. The canyon is less than a mile long and positively rages in the spring. After the canyon, you'll enter an open area marked by the turnoff for Slough Creek Campground and Trail. Next to the pit toilet is a seemingly out-of-place mailbox. Believe it or not, mail is actually delivered to Silver Tip Ranch, which sits on the outside edge of the park's northern boundary. Though the 1913 ranch now has an airstrip, guests often still arrive and depart via wagon or horseback along Slough Creek Road. Slough Creek itself is a terrific little fly-fishing stream, and the Park Service encourages keeping nonnative rainbow and brown trout as it seeks to restore native cutthroat. As you're looking down the gravel road from the turnoff, the little sage hill just to the right is Dave's Hill, whose top is worn bare by legions of wolf watchers. Across the creek valley, in a draw with several dead aspen, is where the Junction Butte wolf pack denned in 2018.

Crossing the new Lamar River Bridge, you will see a sign on the south side of the road that simply says TRAILHEAD. In Yellowstone, these unnamed and unmaintained routes are called "social trails." The conspicuous path upward is the most direct and

The road officially opens Memorial Day and closes after Labor Day, though often it's possible to drive the route into October. Don't be surprised if you run into snow, even in July. A 90-degree summer day in the valleys below translates to about 65 degrees on the plateau.

WHEN COMPLETED IN THE 1930S, THE BEARTOOTH HIGHWAY WAS CONSIDERED AN ENGINEERING MARVEL

steepest route to Specimen Ridge, famed for entombed trees from several Yellowstone eras. You'll see breadfruit, avocado, sycamore, maple, and other specimens, but the most stunning are the calcified stumps of giant redwoods. The views on top are extraordinary, too.

Just beyond the wide parking lot, on the north side of the road, is an area called Little America Flats. A Civilian Conservation Corps camp was constructed here in the 1930s and christened in honor of a similarly named settlement on Antarctica, reputedly because the weather was bitterly similar. About 3 miles later is the Yellowstone Picnic Area, in a shaded area with several glacial "erratic" rocks. Take a few minutes for the short hike above the picnic area to a trail that goes along the rim of the lower end of the Grand Canyon of the Yellowstone. Look for osprey, hawks, and peregrine falcons swooping into the canyon, bighorn sheep on rocky outcroppings, and possibly even the elusive mountain lion. Black bears are common here.

Rising out of the Yellowstone River Canyon, the road comes to a T at Tower Junction. You'll find a gas station, ranger station, and the rustic Roosevelt Lodge, famed for its tiny cabins, Western cookouts, and rocking chairs on the front porch. The right fork leads past the gas station toward Mammoth, the left heads over Dunraven Pass to Canyon Village—the last road in the park to be cleared of snow each spring.

RETURN OF THE WOLF: A QUARTER-CENTURY ON THE LANDSCAPE

Park naturalist James Halfpenny, a noted author on wolves, called it "the greatest ecological experiment of our time." After years of study and contentious debate, 14 gray wolves were brought to Yellowstone from Alberta in 1995 after a seven-decade absence, and another 17 came from British Columbia in 1996; 35 were released in Idaho over those two years. From those first 66, now about 1,900 in more than 280 packs roam the Northern Rockies, and a profound impact has been evident ever since. It is without question the most divisive animal in the region.

IN THE WINTER, WOLVES OFTEN TAKE THE ROAD MORE TRAVELED JACOB W. FRANK / NPS

Thousands of visitors come to Yellowstone each year simply to see wolves, especially in the winter, when they are more visible. Communities such as Gardiner, West Yellowstone, and Cooke City have savored a winter economic boon. As noted earlier, some scientists also believe the wolves are having a major positive impact on the health of the ecosystem.

Nevertheless, the wolf continues to fight for tolerance, acceptance, and appreciation. Hunters and outfitters blame the wolf for declines in elk and moose populations in some areas. Ranchers fear predation of their cattle and sheep. Thanks in large part to images of frothing killers in fairy tales, some people simply loathe wolves.

Tensions in the region over wolves have eased since Endangered Species Act protections were lifted in 2011. State management has given ranchers and hunters a sense they have more control when predation occurs.

THE YELLOWSTONE PICNIC AREA, FREQUENTED BY MANY CRITTERS, ALSO SERVES AS A TRAILHEAD

TOWER JUNCTION TO CANYON (19 MILES)

The gradual climb toward Tower Fall, popular among cross-country skiers for up to six months, rises through a forest to the first breathtaking view, just under 2 miles later, at Calcite Springs Overlook. The overlook provides a glimpse at the part of the canyon called the Narrows and a series of springs famous for their yellowish moonscape appearance. This is a significant place in Yellowstone's history: Thomas Moran's famous paintings of volcanic upheaval here illustrated the incomparable raw beauty, helping lead to the park's creation.

In Yellowstone, wolf numbers have fluctuated based on available prey, from a high of more than 170 in 2009 to around 100 in a dozen or so packs for the past decade—a number biologists say is just about right. There has never been a documented fatal attack by wolves on humans in the lower 48 states, and only a few times since 1995 have individual animals had to be removed from Yellowstone for being too acclimated to people.

FROSTED TREES ARE AWAKENED BY A MID-WINTER SUNRISE IN THE LAMAR VALLEY JACOB W. FRANK / NPS

Just past Calcite Springs Overlook, the road was once narrow and hugged the sheer columnar basalt en route to 132-foot Tower Fall, one of the most photogenic in the park. Upgrades have made the overlook more accessible and the segment to Tower Fall less anxious for those with acrophobia. At Tower Fall is a small Yellowstone General Store with the usual treats and trinkets, and a short, paved walk to the prime view. This is another locale to possibly spot the once-endangered peregrine falcon, which was restored to the park in the 1980s and has since taken over the best available habitat—typically cliffs.

A few miles past Tower Fall, the road begins a serpentine climb toward Dunraven Pass, at 8,873 feet the highest roaded point in the park. This section, which briefly follows Antelope Creek before opening up to a sweeping vista of Antelope Valley, is one of the park's prettiest. Meadows with wildflowers seem to go forever to the east and northeast until they hit distant mountains and ridges, especially the Beartooths and Absarokas but also Specimen Ridge and Mount Washburn. On a summer evening, the turnout overlooking the valley is a great place to sit with binoculars, waiting for wildlife to emerge; with any luck, you'll see a grizzly or wolf.

SKIERS TAKE IN THE WINTER SPLENDOR IN THE SHADOW OF THE ABSAROKA MOUNTAINS ON THE LAMAR RIVER TRAIL

BULL ELK SHED THEIR MASSIVE ANTLERS EACH WINTER
AND START OVER EACH SPRING ADDING MORE BULK

As you climb toward Dunraven Pass, note the stands of burned timber, remnants of the 1988 fires. Also notice vast swaths of dead and dying whitebark pines, the victims of a pine-bark beetle infestation (see sidebar) enabled by a climate that has warmed about 4 degrees in Yellowstone since World War II.

Mount Washburn, named for the leader of an 1870 exploratory expedition into the region, is accessed from either side of Dunraven Pass. On the north side is the 1.3-mile Chittenden Road, which ends 3 miles from the fire lookout at the summit. On the south side of the pass is the other end of the Mount Washburn Trail, a steep, 2.2-mile jaunt for hikers only. The descent from Dunraven offers another breathtaking view of Mirror Plateau, the Absarokas, and the Grand Canyon of the Yellowstone to the east. Look for steam rising from Washburn Hot Springs. From there begins a routine drive through forests on the approach to Canyon Village.

SLOUGH CREEK IS A DRAW FOR NUMEROUS WATERFOWL SPECIES

✳ To Do

RECREATION IN YNP

BICYCLING The Northeast Entrance Road is open to road and mountain bicyclists, but like every road in the park, it's a safety crapshoot because of its narrowness. Mountain biking opportunities are limited as well, though the 3-mile climb from the Chittenden parking area on **Grand Loop Road** to the summit of Mount Washburn is sure to set quadriceps ablaze; mountain bikes are not allowed on the trail between Mount Washburn and the Dunraven Pass parking area. For a less strenuous endeavor, pedal the 2 miles on **Chittenden Service Road** between Tower Fall Campground and Grand Loop Road just south of Tower Junction. Also suited

A BIGHORN SHEEP STRETCHES FOR THE TASTIEST NIBBLES ON A STEEP SLOPE ABOVE THE LAMAR VALLEY

ANCIENT TREE MAKING ITS LAST STAND

On the highest flanks of Greater Yellowstone are gnarled conifer trees, some more than 2,000 years old. The whitebark pine scarcely caught the attention of anybody but the most rabid botanist until the past two decades, when they began an accelerated die-off. The primary culprit: a tiny insect called the mountain pine beetle. The reason: warming temperatures. The little bug has built-in antifreeze that allows it to survive inside the bark of a tree at temperatures down to minus 30 degrees; anything colder for extended periods kills them. The problem isn't warming per se, it's that winters simply don't get as cold as they once did. The average daytime temperature has risen 3.8 degrees over the past seven decades at Mammoth Hot Springs.

Whitebark pine experts say the tree will soon be functionally extinct in Yellowstone, surviving only in inconsequential pockets in the highest elevations of the Absaroka-Beartooth Front west of Cody. Why consternation over this seemingly innocuous tree? For starters, the nuts in its cones are a primary food source for the grizzly bear, their protein especially critical for reproduction and hibernation. Furthermore, with whitebarks dying in the park's interior and Yellowstone Lake's cutthroat trout still rebounding, bears are pushing outward in search of food, leading to increasing human-bear conflicts. Grizzlies also are predating more on young and vulnerable elk.

Even more alarming: the consequences for river flows. Whitebarks grow at the highest elevations and provide shade for snow. Without the canopies, runoff is earlier and faster, filling rivers downstream quickly and leaving less water for later in the summer. This in turn is reducing habitat for the native cutthroat trout, which is already being pressed into the region's upper

ANCIENT WHITEBARK PINES ARE ONE OF THE MOST VISIBLE VICTIMS OF YELLOWSTONE'S CHANGING CLIMATE

reaches by warming waters—proving once again that everything is interconnected. What to do? Not much. Reforestation plans are underway on some national forests surrounding the parks, but like its cousin, the ancient bristlecone pine, the whitebark grows slowly. Trees won't produce cones for about 50 years. In addition, the parks and surrounding wilderness areas are places where natural processes are allowed to take place. Though some biologists argue that a warming climate is human induced and thus unnatural, many are still reluctant to intervene.

So, as you drive over Dunraven Pass, lament the acre upon acre of brown trees and appreciate the few live ones remaining.

for mountain bikes, the moderate 1-mile **Rose Creek Service Road** climbs behind the Yellowstone Forever Institute at the Buffalo Ranch. Unfortunately, their parking area is now limited to employees and guests, so use a turnout along the main road.

FISHING The **Lamar River** and **Soda Butte Creek** are two of the park's most frequented fishing areas, and it is rare in summer and fall to not see fly anglers casting to trout at the confluence. The fish generally aren't big, though park employees report coaxing an occasional 20-incher from under an overhanging bank. Park officials like seeing fishermen casting in **Slough Creek** to eliminate rainbow and brown trout and to make more room for the native cutthroat. Lakes are few and small in this region, but 12-acre **Trout Lake**'s short-but-steep proximity to Northeast Entrance Road and abundance of large cutthroat and rainbows make it attractive. Easily fished from shore or float tube, Trout Lake, on a bench amid Douglas fir just southwest of Pebble Creek Campground, once served as a hatchery for rainbows. Look for otters to join in the fishing fun when trout migrate up the channel.

SKIING (NORDIC) Thanks to year-round vehicle access, the northeast corner of Yellowstone is a Nordic skier's paradise, and you're likely to have these trails to yourself. **Barronette Ski Trail**, a 3.5-mile trek, parallels the road and Soda Butte Creek at the base of sheer Barronette Peak. The trail, through mostly forest on an old road, has little elevation gain, and snow remains well into the spring. More challenging is the 13-mile **Pebble Creek Trail**, where you're sure to have solitude. Plan on spending the night if you aim to ski the entire loop between the Northeast Entrance and Pebble Creek Campground. In the same vicinity is **Bannock Trail**, a 2-mile jaunt that begins south of the road at the Warm Creek Picnic Area and continues east along Soda Butte Creek through a slice of the North Absaroka Wilderness into Silver Gate. If you want more exertion, continue 3 more miles on the well-groomed back road to Cooke City; expect to have company from snowmobiles and perhaps a moose or two.

Four more trails are in the Tower Junction area: **Tower Fall**, **Chittenden**, **Lost Lake**, and **Blacktail Plateau**. Park at the closed gate for the gradual 2.5-mile climb through conifers from Tower Junction to Tower Fall. Absorb the views of the Yellowstone River far below before embarking on the more challenging Chittenden Trail through Tower Fall Campground to a meeting with Grand Loop Road some 5.3 miles later. Ski back to Tower Junction to complete a long day. The moderate 4-mile Lost Lake Trail starts at the Petrified Tree and finishes at Tower Junction after schussing past and through the lake, forest, and meadows. The Blacktail Plateau Trail presents 8 miles of gradual climbing before a modest 2-mile descent back to the main road.

RECREATION OUTSIDE YNP

FISHING The **Clarks Fork of the Yellowstone River** is a relatively undiscovered treasure with substantial rewards for the trout angler. The Clarks Fork starts near Cooke City, Montana, and makes a wild headlong dash through canyons, forest, and sage in Wyoming before turning northeast for a more sedate run through agricultural lands to the Yellowstone. Some of the best dry-fly fishing around can be had where the Clarks Fork rushes alongside US 212. The river is awash in caddis, drakes, blue-winged olives, pale morning duns, and other insects. Although the river winds through private properties, access isn't difficult. Given the stunning Beartooth Highway and Sunlight Basin drives nearby, it's a wonder more anglers don't spend time in this breathtaking setting. If you plan to scramble down into the canyon, be careful. This is dangerous terrain, though rewards at the bottom are great.

HIKING

The northeast corner isn't as renowned for hiking as other parts of the park, but the trails are spectacular nonetheless. Perhaps the most crowd-pleasing is the dusty and often windy **Specimen Ridge Trail**, a 17-miler that officially begins just east of Tower Junction and treks along Specimen Ridge until it connects with the Lamar River Trail about 1 mile from Northeast Entrance Road at Soda Butte. A more direct way to reach the ridge is to park at the unofficial 1.4-mile **Specimen Fossil Forest Trail** marker southwest of the new bridge over the Lamar River. This so-called "social" trail is well worn, easy to follow, slightly steep, and takes you past many specimens—entombed remains of ancient trees, including a giant redwood stump on the edge of a cliff. Also still visible on this hike are tepee rings and the remnants of an elk trap used until the 1970s either for relocating or slaughtering what was then an over-abundant animal.

The 12-mile **Pebble Creek Trail** is a full-day adventure that circles around the backside of stately Barronette Peak. If you start at the trailhead 2 miles west of the Northeast Entrance it'll be mostly downhill once you reach the creek. The **Garnet Hill Loop** is a dusty 4-mile sojourn that offers a remote Old West portrait of the park, with the Yellowstone River and Yancey's Hole thrown in for good measure. The trail starts less than 100 yards from Tower Junction and cuts through sage and pine forest on the road used for stagecoach cookouts, then follows Elk Creek to the river.

Hellroaring Trail is a well-traveled, 7.5-mile path that veers west from the Garnet Hill Loop at the Yellowstone River. It crosses the river on a suspension bridge, rises to a sage plateau, then drops into the scenic Hellroaring Creek drainage. Watch for wildlife and bring a fly rod to fish the creek's pools, along with extra water. The scenic 4-mile **Lost Lake** walk through the pines rises 300

SNOWSHOEING IS THE BEST WAY TO ACCESS PEBBLE CREEK CA DURING THE WINTER SEASON

RIVER RUNNING Not for the faint of heart or skill, the **Clarks Fork of the Yellowstone River** offers an unforgettable, experts-only stretch of whitewater as it thunders through a narrow canyon in Sunlight Basin. Rapids range from Class IV to virtually impassable Box Canyon; below the canyon more Class IV water is accessible. We don't advise trying this river unless you're an experienced kayaker with a reliable roll. For more moderate splash-and-giggle floats, the Class II–III **Stillwater River** from Absarokee to Columbus, Montana, offers consistent summer floating.

SKIING (ALPINE) **Red Lodge Mountain Resort** (406-446-2610), a family-oriented ski hill at the edge of Montana's Beartooth Mountains, is favored for its modest lift lines. The mountain receives 250 inches of snow on 1,600 acres, with a 2,500-foot vertical.

FOR SEVERAL YEARS, AN ELK "SHED" HAS GREETED HIKERS ALONG ROSE CREEK BEHIND THE LAMAR BUFFALO RANCH

feet from Roosevelt Lodge to a perky little lake where beaver, black bear, and raptors are frequent sights. Continue on to reach the Petrified Tree.

Favored by fly anglers and photographers, Slough Creek Trail rises from one meadow to the next on a wagon road leading to Silver Tip Ranch. Toward Tower, the Yellowstone River Picnic Area is a rarely used way to see a portion of the Grand Canyon. The 3.7-mile round-trip excursion on the east rim provides exceptional views of the river and canyon, and it's not uncommon to see eagles, osprey, and bighorn sheep. Whiffs of sulphur let you know plenty of hot springs are in the area.

Though not an official route, the 1-mile trail behind the Yellowstone Forever Institute along Rose Creek Service Road leads to the remains of a chain-link enclosure where some of the first wolves were kept in 1995 during reintroduction. Trees have fallen on the fence and doghouses-on-steroids are in decay, but the site exudes a strong sense of recent history. Give a wide berth to ornery bull bison that frequent the meadow leading to the enclosure.

The resort touts its Lazy M run, a 2.5-mile descent. Despite its small size, there's an equal amount of terrain for every skill level. The ability to make snow for nearly one-third of the mountain ensures skiing even when Mother Nature is being fickle.

SKIING (NORDIC) About 2 miles west of town is the Beartooth Recreational Trails Association's **Red Lodge Nordic Center** (406-446-1402), with nearly 10 miles of trails suited to a variety of skill sets. Classic and skate skiing lanes are groomed on Sundays and Mondays. The fees are affordable and family friendly.

SNOWMOBILING Though you wouldn't guess it by the steady stream of SUVs and trucks hauling lengthy toy trailers on Northeast Entrance Road through the winter,

IF YOU'RE ATTENTIVE, YOU MIGHT SEE A BADGER OR TWO SURFACE FROM A DEN ALONG A TRAIL JACOB W. FRANK / NPS

snowmobiling is prohibited in this part of the park. Sledders are headed to Cooke City for miles of trails and extreme high-marking on mountainsides just north and south of town. The de facto headquarters for snowmobiling, Cooke City is abuzz during the winter, with two service stations where you can gas up, rent a sled, and stock up on munchies. Some 100 miles of trails connect with the Beartooth system. Sledders also motor this way from a large gravel pit along US 212 at Pilot Creek, 8 miles on unplowed highway to Cooke City.

✳ Lodging

LODGING IN YNP

Tower Junction: Ask any Yellowstone regular or seasonal employee about their favorite place to get away from it all, and the answer, hands down, is ✪ **Roosevelt Lodge Cabins** ($/$$, 307-344-7311, June to September). The lack of upscale amenities probably ensures that your neighbors are like-minded. The two styles of cabins are primitive and more primitive—the Roughrider, which has no bathroom and is heated by a wood-burning stove, and the slightly upgraded Frontier, which comes with shower, sink, and toilet. They are fairly close together

and feel a bit like kids camp, but no matter. Sit back in a log rocker on the lodge porch, put up your feet, and watch nature in play. Book these gems a year in advance, as they fill quickly.

ALTERNATIVE LODGING IN YNP

Yellowstone Forever has bare-bones cabins at ✪ **Lamar Buffalo Ranch** (406-848-2400) for an incomparable year-round experience, but you must be signed up for an educational course or tour. Cabins are heated and lit but require your own bedding. A central communal kitchen allows guests to prepare food if other arrangements haven't been made, and the immaculate community bathhouse has comfy radiant floor heat as a reward for those grudging wee-hour treks in the cold and snow when nature calls. Be on the lookout for bison!

CAMPING The northeast corner of the park has three first-come, first-served campgrounds at $15 per night: **Pebble Creek**, **Slough Creek**, and **Tower Fall**. Coming west from the Northeast Entrance, first up is Pebble Creek (June to September), which is just off the road in a pleasant wooded area with 30 sites that fill early, including some long pull-throughs. Slough Creek (May to October) is at the end of a 2-mile gravel road and also typically fills early. It has 29 sites, including 14 for 30-foot RVs and 14 more for walk-in tenters. Both campgrounds are in prime grizzly country, so observe posted rules. Slough Creek can be an excellent launch spot for wolf watching. Tower Fall, across Grand Loop Road from the general store, has 32 sites—all accommodating up to 30-foot RVs, if you can navigate a modest hairpin curve.

BEST LODGING OUTSIDE YNP

Silver Gate: For our money and sense of solitude, we adore ✪ ☀ **Pine Edge Cabins** ($/$$, 406-838-2371, May to October), though to our chagrin they no longer remain open in the winter. Built in the 1930s but recently revamped, the 25 cabins retain a rustic wilderness character, as mandated by the town's architectural covenants. The seven attached motel rooms are plain and simple. In front of the cabins, **Range Rider Lodge** ($$, 406-848-2371, May to October) now allows guests to stay in its old bordello rooms above the dance hall. When built in 1937, it was the second-largest freestanding log structure in the country, trailing Old Faithful Lodge. Today it serves up an eerie assortment of ghostly tales.

Across the highway from the Range Rider is ☀ ♿ **The Grizzly Lodge** ($$, 406-838-2219, May to October), a motel-like row of 20 rooms across Soda Butte Creek and a prime choice for a restful sleep. Option four in Silver Gate is two prairie-rustic log cabins—Kay's and Ceil's—behind ☀ ❘❘ **Log Cabin Café Bed & Breakfast** ($$, 406-838-2367, May to September), where you can eat, stay, and play. The best part of the deal: made-to-order breakfast for two at the café is included in the modest rate.

Cooke City: Amid a sea of typical small-scale motels, ✪ ☀ **Antlers Lodge** ($$, 406-838-2432) fills quickly during the peak summer (June to September) and winter (December to March) seasons—for good reason. The 18 log cabins and historic (1913) lodge have a mountain feel, down to the stone fireplace and elk racks on the walls. On the main drag, choose from a variety of room styles and sizes at ☀ **Alpine Motel** ($$/$$$, 406-838-2262), known for cleanliness and superior service. ☀ **High Country Motel & Cabins** ($$$, 406-838-2272) is not only a home away from home in updated digs, it serves as check-in for backcountry adventures from Beartooth Powder guides. Their 15 modernized motel rooms and four log cabins exceed expectations. East of town toward Cooke Pass, ☀ **Skyline Guest Ranch** ($$/$$$, 406-838-2380) is a three-story lodge with six guest rooms with private baths, plus a shared living room, game room, deck, and hot tub. A full hot breakfast is included, and dinner is served by reservation in the winter. Family outfitters for 50 years, the Jacksons offer trail riding, backcountry camping and hiking, fishing, and hunting expeditions.

Red Lodge: The signature place to stay is the redbrick-charmer ✪ ♿ ❘❘ **Pollard Hotel** ($$$/$$$$, 406-446-0001), long-ago host to frontier luminaries Buffalo Bill, John "Liver-Eating" Johnston, and Martha Jane Cannary-Burke (a.k.a. Calamity Jane), among other Wild West celebs. It's a classy hotel with a fitness center, dining room, and English pub.

☀ ♿ **Beartooth Hideaway Inn & Cabins** ($$, 406-446-2288) is one of the larger properties in town and most known for an indoor swimming pool (frequented by locals). Bavarian garnished inside and out, ☀ ♿ **Yodeler Motel** ($/$$, 406-446-1435) fills the niche for charming character and is easy on the wallet. Reserve a room with a spa tub for soaking tired muscles after hitting the slopes, hiking mountain trails, or pedaling Beartooth Pass. The outwardly stylish but unpretentious ☀ ♿ **Rock Creek Resort** ($$$/$$$$, 406-446-1111), 5 miles south of Red Lodge at the mouth of the mountains, has townhouses, condos, and standard rooms in decors ranging from Montanan to Guatemalan.

If a bed & breakfast is your preference, **Gallagher's Irish Rose B&B** ($$/$$$, 406-446-0303), a century-old home with three themed rooms decorated with original artwork by Leah Gallagher, will fit the bill. More Western-themed and rustic-luxe is **Inn on the Beartooth** ($$$, 406-446-1768) bed & breakfast just off US 212, with six rooms—five of them suites. An outdoor hot tub and short walk to tumbling Rock Creek sweeten the deal. Prefer the country? **Two Bears Inn** ($$/$$$, 406-860-5956), on 20 acres tucked into a conifer draw above the Beartooth Highway, is about 3 miles south of Red Lodge. Two Bears has three rooms, plus a cabin for even more seclusion.

Beartooth Pass: ☀ **Top of the World Resort** ($, 307-587-5368, June to September) on the Beartooth Pass is not a resort by any stretch, but it is a "gotta try it once" kind of place. Believe it or not, the four simple rooms next to the store are often booked well in advance, so make reservations. Top of the World opens as soon as Beartooth Highway is clear of snow, usually around Memorial Day.

BEST ALTERNATIVE LODGING OUTSIDE YNP

Red Lodge: About 19 miles from Red Lodge near little Luther are ♿ **Blue Sky**

Cabins ($$$, 406-446-0186). On the other end of rustic, five distinctive and privacy-spaced cabins constitute the retreat, each affording high-end pampering. Stellar mountain views, abundant wildlife, and access to the Beartooth's most rugged canyons provide additional appeal.

Crandall: In a region where dude ranches are king, ☀ **Hunter Peak Ranch** ($$/$$$$, 307-587-3711, May to November) is intimate and understated on neatly manicured grounds in the pretty Clarks Fork of the Yellowstone River Valley. Meals are priced separately and by reservation only. Equally picturesque, ☀ **K Bar Z Guest Ranch & Outfitters** ($$, 307-587-4410) offers nightly and all-inclusive lodging in seven rustic log cabins built in the 1940s at the foot of the Cathedral Cliffs. Family sit-down meals are the norm, along with horseback riding, fishing, and hiking.

As Forest Service cabin rentals go, none can match the 1936 ◎ **Sunlight Ranger Cabin** ($$, 307-527-6241, May to September). Sunlight sets the bar high with electricity, range, fridge, shower, and washer and dryer. The peaceful Absaroka setting, complete with wolf and grizzly tracks, is magical.

Cooke City: Owner Ben Zavora has carved out two special backcountry places, one south of US 212 and the other north: **Woody Creek Cabin** ($$$$, 406-838-2097) and **Mount Zimmer Yurt** ($$$$, 406-838-2097). Woody Creek is on a 40-acre Gallatin National Forest inholding and Mount Zimmer on the edge of the Absaroka-Beartooth Wilderness. Zavora built the cabin himself, hauling all materials on his back except for the timbers. To stay in his yurt you must ski or snowmobile 7 miles.

CAMPING *Red Lodge:* ☀ **Perry's RV Park and Campground** ($, 406-446-2722, May to October) doesn't look like much from the road, but once you descend through the trees and Rock Creek comes

SCRATCHING AN ITCH AT THE HITCHING POST TURNOUT

into view you'll see why this oasis is prime-time camping. Perry's has 10 tent and 20 RV sites, many on the banks of the roaring creek, which drowns out sounds from your neighbors or twigs snapping from an occasional deer or black bear wandering through.

Forest Service Campgrounds: The Beartooth Plateau has six Shoshone National Forest campgrounds at high elevations on the Wyoming side most of the way up Beartooth Pass. There are seven more on the Montana side, managed by the consolidated Gallatin-Custer National Forest. The 13 campgrounds have a combined 226 sites, all within reach of the highway.

In Wyoming, there are three along the Clarks Fork of the Yellowstone River, and in Montana there are three—**Soda Butte**, **Colter**, and **Chief Joseph**—just outside Cooke City near Cooke Pass. Expect chilly nights—the higher the elevation, the chillier. Of the three near Cooke City, the closest and most appealing is Soda Butte, which has 20 RV/tent sites amid

conifers near Soda Butte Creek. Because of grizzly bears, only hard-sided campers are allowed in these three campgrounds, and it's especially important to be bear aware.

Heading south from Red Lodge, first is the 29-site **Basin** campground, and 4 miles farther up the gravel road and more secluded amid pines is the 35-site **Cascade**. Both are on the West Fork Road. Cascade is convenient to several trailheads and fishing on the West Fork; trailers up to 32 feet are OK in either of the two loops. In Rock Creek Canyon, go past **Limber Pine** and **Parkside**—where the paved parking aprons and closeness to the highway entice more people—and settle in at the primitive **M-K Campground**, about 3 miles on gravel off US 212. M-K has 10 intimate sites on a pretty spot overlooking Rock Creek. **Beartooth Lake** on the plateau is a one-of-a-kind experience. At 9,000 feet, you'll feel as if you can touch the stars from each of the 21 sites. The campground, typically open by July 1, has three loops on Beartooth Lake and provides access to trails into the Absa-roka-Beartooth Wilderness.

✳ Where to Eat

DINING IN YNP

Tower Junction: Put on your wide-brimmed hat, boots, and spurs for dining at the **Roosevelt Lodge Dining Room** ($/$$$, 307-344-7311, B/L/D, June to September). Start with a rustic log lodge, toss in two stone fireplaces and a corral for aesthetics, and you've got yourself one of the more memorable Old West–themed dining spots in the park. Scrambled eggs du jour, cowboy burritos, and huevos carnitas will make you think of the ol' chuckwagon. Lunch will have you singing over elk sliders and Wyoming cheesesteak (gluten free available). Hold your horses—there's a smokin' dinner menu as well: applewood-smoked baby back ribs, wild game Bolognese, or smoked bison bratwurst all sided by the signature "Rosie" beans. For a bootful of authenticity, try Roosevelt Lodge's **Old West Dinner Cookout** ($$$$, 307-344-7311, D, June to September), which will take you by horseback on one- or two-hour rides or in a covered wagon directly to a full-meal deal of steak and classic Western fixin's in picturesque Yancey's Hole. Chances are a fiddlin' or singin' cowboy will come along for the ride. Cookouts—save room for the cobbler—are offered late afternoons in the summer, and reservations are required; the lodge doesn't accept dining reservations, so come early or late or be prepared to wait.

BEST DINING OUTSIDE YNP

Silver Gate: The only restaurant, ✪ **Log Cabin Café and B&B** ($$, 406-838-2367, B/L/D, May through September), is a good one for Idaho trout (breakfast, lunch, or dinner), Montana grass-fed beef burgers, and legendary pumpkin bread

drizzled in honey—in fact, get an extra piece for the road.

Cooke City: To catch the best gossip, hang out at **Beartooth Cafe** ($/$$, 406-838-2475, L/D, May to September) for traditional Western (half-pound garlic burger, bison rib eye) or slightly exotic (lamb gyros, Mandarin steak salad) and even vegetarian options; brew lovers have over 130 beers from which to choose. Gourmet French/American sophistication at **Bistro** ($$/$$$, 406-838-2160, B/L/D) includes well-prepared breakfasts, house-made soup, and signature rack of lamb, and their wine selection is the best around. After hiking, Nordic skiing, or a day in the park, **Prospector Restaurant and Saloon** ($$, 406-838-2251, B/L/D) is a good prospect for above-average homestyle cooking and views of towering peaks. The **Miners Saloon** ($$/$$$, 406-838-2214, L/D), an Old West museum dressed up as a saloon and eatery, touts the "dopest food" in the state. Handmade pizzas, fish tacos, and creative dinner specials pair well with pool, sports on TV, or just rehashing the day's events.

Red Lodge: You may want to plan on dining in Red Lodge more than once because outstanding choices abound. Begin your day at **Café Regis** ($, 406-446-1941, B/L), a former grocery store that still looks as if caught in a 1940s-era time warp, where new owners continue to nourish fellow health-food fans while adding their touches. The café serves breakfast until close—omelets, oatmeal, scrambles, and such—with ingredients often picked from the organic garden out back. **Honey's Café** ($/$$, 406-446-1600, B/L) offers a mellow hipster vibe for espresso, teas, and smoothies to go with other café fare that's local, hormone free, and antibiotic free. Likewise, **The Wild Table** ($/$$, 406-446-0226, B/L/Br), home to breakfasts, gourmet lunches, and all things freshly baked, will satisfy your wild side with ebleskivers, quiche, and spanakopita. **Prindy's Place** ($, 406-446-0225, B/L) opens early (6 a.m.) and is your place for classic American fare with a few twists, such as sweet cream pancakes.

More casually appealing for late lunch/early dinner or a chips-salsa-margarita break is **Bogart's** ($$, 406-446-1784, L/D), an always-crowded Mexican and pizza watering hole with a rustic Western feel accentuated by a large back bar. **Mas Taco** ($, 406-446-3636, L/D), another hot spot, customizes tacos, burritos, and quesadillas in six styles, everything prepared to order and right before your eyes. Meals at **Red Lodge Café** ($$, 406-446-1619, B/L/D Wednesday to Saturday), with its life-sized historical murals, log furniture, and retro neon tepee sign, are more about tradition and history, but their food certainly is serviceable. Eco-conscious **Sam's Tap Room & Kitchen** ($/$$, 406-446-0243, L/D), on the Red Lodge Ales Brewing Company property, has relaxing indoor and outdoor seating for sipping suds and nibbling on paninis, baked sammies, and entrée salads. On the south end of town, cool off with a cone full of soft ice cream or enjoy made-to-order burgers creekside at Red Lodge's oldest joint, ✪ **The Red Box Car** ($, 406-446-2152, L/D), housed in a century-old—you guessed it—boxcar.

For casual evening dining in classic elegance, the landmark ✪ **Pollard Hotel Dining Room** ($$/$$$, 406-446-0001, B/D) delivers with a seasonally changing menu, extensive wine list, and stately ornamentation. Through a side door is the side-kickin' **Pub at the Pollard** ($/$$, 406-446-0001, D), a rare opportunity in the Northern Rockies to savor English pub food. **Red Lodge Pizza Co.** ($/$$, 406-446-3333, L/D), the choice pie place in town, has more in the oven—calzones, meatball marinara, and chicken Parmesan, all paired with a wide array of draft beers and wines by the glass. If you're returning late from the park or ski hill, **Foster & Logans Pub & Grill** ($/$$, 406-446-9080, L/D), called "F&L" by locals, is a night spot open daily that fosters surprising diversity in its menu. Representing old Red Lodge is **Carbon County Steakhouse** ($$/$$$, 406-446-4025, D), with a notch-above "cowboy cuisine" of hormone-free beef, bison, elk, "not from the ranch" seafood, and fresh mussels flown in from the Pacific Northwest.

Gateway Community: Cody

✳ Overview

Everything you ever imagined the mythical Old West to be—cowboys riding the open range or bucking broncs on dusty rodeo grounds, iconic ranches extending to the distant horizon and beyond, gunfighters and outlaws terrorizing stagecoaches and robbing trains, lonely outposts with creaky saloons and bustling mercantiles—is manifest in Wyoming's Bighorn Basin.

A FORMER WAY OF LIFE COMES TO LIFE IN CODY

In this thirsty region, the legend of America's most famous cowboy entrepreneur, Buffalo Bill Cody, was birthed and nurtured. John "Liver-Eating" Johnston, the chiseled character on which the Robert Redford movie *Jeremiah Johnson* is based, is buried in Cody. Rodeos are staged everywhere from Florida to Oregon, but none capture the essence like the down-home Cody Nite Rodeo. Also, your first whiff—literally—of the geothermal fury awaiting 50 miles to the west is here in aptly named Colter's Hell in the Shoshone River Canyon. The thermal activity emits periodic sulphuric odors that rodeo spectators can't miss if a westerly wind is blowing. On the cultural front, the five-in-one Buffalo Bill Center of the West evokes differing aspects of the Wild West in each of its compelling museums. And there's always the admittedly hokey yet entertaining nightly gunfight in front of the Irma Hotel, built by Buffalo Bill and named after one of his daughters.

All these activities, combined with a persisting frontier persona and pioneer spirit, make Cody the consummate

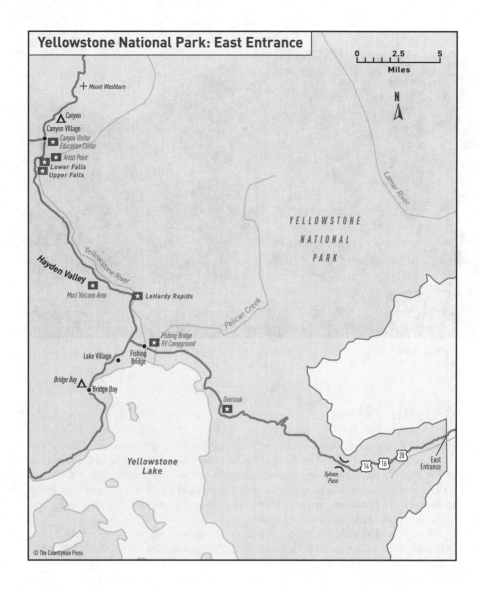

Yellowstone National Park: East Entrance

Mount Washburn

Canyon
Canyon Village
Canyon Visitor
Education Center
Artist Point
Lower Falls
Upper Falls

Yellowstone River

Lamar River

YELLOWSTONE

NATIONAL

PARK

Hayden Valley

Mucl Volcano Area

LeHardy Rapids

Pelican Creek

Fishing Bridge
RV Campground

Lake Village   Fishing
Bridge

Bridge Bay

Bridge Bay

Overlook

Yellowstone
Lake

Sylvan
Pass

14 16 20

East
Entrance

© The Countryman Press

prelude for the wild country evident in the Absaroka Mountains rising abruptly from the badlands immediately west of town.

The winding road along the North Fork of the Shoshone River to the East Entrance is simply spectacular. But the curtain isn't truly pulled back on the majesty of Yellowstone until you reach the summit of 8,530-foot Sylvan Pass, about 7 miles inside the gate. The beautiful blue waters of Yellowstone Lake, an endless horizon of dense forest, and the distant Teton Range lie before your eyes like a Thomas Moran painting. All of Yellowstone's wonders are compressed into this section of road: thermal features along the lake's shore just inside the caldera, wandering bison, a heightened awareness you're in grizzly country, the historic Fishing Bridge area with its popular campground, and the riveting Upper and Lower Falls in the Grand Canyon of the Yellowstone River.

SULFURIC FUMES OFTEN WAFT FROM THE "COLTER'S HELL" SECTION OF THE SHOSHONE RIVER IN CODY

✳ Getting Here

Theodore Roosevelt once called the route through the Wapiti Valley west of Cody "the most beautiful 52 miles in America." US 14/16/20's gradual ascent from Cody begins on the dry side of Yellowstone, where stark cliffs and red-rock outcroppings are especially striking. As the highway hugs the tumbling North Fork of the Shoshone River and enters the Shoshone National Forest, high desert gives way to pine and fir, and frothing creeks arrive from remote drainages.

US 14, 16, and 20 all lead to Cody. The three east-to-west routes join at Greybull after converging from Dayton, Buffalo, and Casper. US 14 and 16 cross the Bighorn Mountains directly to the east—the first Rocky Mountain range many people reared east of the Mississippi River see, as well as the first dramatic hint of what lies ahead.

US 14 drivers have typically peeled off I-90 coming south from Montana after crossing North Dakota on I-94. US 16 is for folks exiting I-90 after the long haul across South Dakota. And US 20 is the turn for visitors heading to Cody after driving west on I-80 across Nebraska or even I-70 through Kansas and into Colorado. If you've driven US 20 from the east, consider exiting onto WY 120 at the desert hot springs town of Thermopolis and stopping for a soak. From there continue northwest along the edge of the Absaroka-Beartooth Front through the little ranching outpost of Meeteetse—home of cowboy chocolatier Tim Kellogg—and on to Cody.

If driving the dry, dusty, and windy Bighorn Basin to Yellowstone's East Entrance isn't your thing, flying is an alternative. Cody's Yellowstone Regional Airport (COD) is served by United Express from Denver and SkyWest airlines out of Salt Lake City. As noted earlier, flying into Cody can be uncertain due to the airport's lack of a radar system.

✳ Along the Way

The 52 miles of US 14/16/20 that connect Cody with YNP split some of the last great and otherwise roadless territory in the lower 48 states. The mountains and drainages, containing the largest population of grizzly bears outside of national parks, are dotted with dude and guest ranches that emphasize the experience with cookouts, trail rides, and backcountry adventures.

Once you squeeze through the gap between Cedar and Rattlesnake Mountains along the raging Shoshone River, the landscape opens to Buffalo Bill Reservoir—a favorite for boaters. On a rocky landscape about 30 miles west of Cody, look south to "The House on the Hill"—a Swiss Family Robinson meets mine shaft structure officially known as Smith Mansion. What began as a family cabin in the 1970s grew into something much more imaginative. Check the website for tours.

If fly-fishing is your gig, the North Fork, paralleling the highway to a rustic resort called Pahaska Tepee near the park entrance, is one of Wyoming's finest trout streams. Be aware of Wyoming's landowner-favorable stream-access laws, which are less welcoming than in Montana and Idaho.

THE LOWER FALLS OF THE YELLOWSTONE RIVER IS PERHAPS THE PARK'S MOST DRAMATIC VISTA

The little outpost on the highway called Wapiti has a popular steakhouse worth the wait and the oldest continuously manned ranger station in the country—fitting for America's first national forest, the Shoshone. You'll note a high fence surrounding the elementary school. Yes, it's to keep out grizzly bears. By the way, *wapiti* is the Indian word for "elk."

The final speck of civilization is Pahaska Tepee, 2 miles from the East Entrance. Goods, gear, and groceries are available, and it's the last place to fuel up before Fishing Bridge 42 miles up and then down the road.

✳ Gateway Communities

CODY, WYOMING

Colonel William "Buffalo Bill" Cody first came to northwest Wyoming in the 1870s with a professor from Yale University. He quickly became enamored with its development possibilities and vowed to return. A decade later he did and began constructing

BEFORE YOU WERE HERE

If there is one Indian tribe most closely associated with the Yellowstone region, it's the Shoshone. Others came and went, but a band of Shoshone called the Tutudika—labeled "Sheep Eaters" by Anglos because they pursued migrating bighorns—actually lived part time in large portions of what is now YNP. Other Shoshone, derisively dubbed "Fish Eaters" by the Blackfeet and Crow for their dietary choices, presided over the eastern and southern edges of Yellowstone.

The Shoshone were not highly regarded by other tribes in part because they were smaller in stature. Some research suggests that when Anglos first arrived the Shoshone were impoverished, their resources scarce, and hunting regions limited by stronger tribes.

Instead of riding horses, the Shoshone moved from camp to camp using dogs to pull travois, a frame used to drag possessions. They frequently left their travois and tepee lodgepoles for the next group of Shoshone passing through. When the park was still young in the 1870s, it wasn't unusual for tourists to see Shoshone moving through in this manner. You can still find stashes of wickiup poles leaning against trees, generally in the northern section of the park between Mammoth and the Lamar Valley.

In earlier days, the role of Indians in the region was largely ignored. But in 1925, the Shoshone of southeast Idaho were invited to ceremonies marking the opening of the West Entrance. Along with Crow Indians, they wore traditional garb and participated in a bison roundup.

The Eastern Shoshone tribe now is largely confined to the Wind River Reservation near Riverton, Wyoming. Northern Shoshone are on the Fort Hall Reservation of southeast Idaho.

More information about the Shoshone is available at the Shoshone-Bannock Tribal Museum in Pocatello, Idaho. Also check out the Wind River Virtual Museum at www.windrivervm.org.

the town on the east end of the Shoshone River Canyon. The town was later moved to the present-day west-end location.

Cody built the town's first hotel and saloon, the Irma. He also coaxed the Burlington Railroad to punch a spur to his new community, persuaded good friend Teddy Roosevelt to build a federal dam (creating Buffalo Bill Reservoir), orchestrated construction of the scenic road to Yellowstone's East Entrance, and founded the town's newspaper, the *Enterprise*, which still serves the city. Small wonder in 1895 the town's fathers voted to name the new settlement Cody.

Buffalo Bill's influence didn't stop at the town's edge. Through Roosevelt, he helped establish the Shoshone National Forest and the Wapiti Ranger Station, both firsts in the nation. Though known as a proud frontiersman on horseback, Buffalo Bill was an early champion of Indian rights, the woman's suffrage movement, and environmental causes.

Cody's name lives on through buildings and landmarks, including the Cody Nite Rodeo, which began in 1938. Some of the town's charm has waned with the arrival of big-box stores and chain restaurants and motels, but a river walk, amphitheater, and trolley tour have added new dimensions.

Among gateway communities, Cody's few downsides are the 52-mile distance from Yellowstone and high lodging costs even by summer standards. On the flip side, you can usually count on pleasant weather. Even the notorious winds have a benefit: They scour the region of snow, opening up wildlife viewing in April and May, when other country is still buried in snow. For a good chance at seeing animals in the spring, take the paved roads along the North and South Fork of the Shoshone or travel 25 miles south to Meeteetse and follow the Greybull River on gravel through the famed Pitch-fork Ranch to the eastern edge of the Absaroka-Beartooth Front. Another fascinating place for exploration is the badlands of the McCullough Peaks directly to the east, home to a highly cherished herd of wild horses.

✳ Hitting the Road

EAST ENTRANCE TO FISHING BRIDGE AND LAKE AREA (30 MILES)

By the time you've arrived at the East Entrance, it's possible you've already seen bison, bighorn sheep, or even a grizzly bear. This reflects the wildness of a route bisecting the North Absaroka and Washakie Wilderness Areas. But if you haven't, don't fret! Wildlife and sensational scenery await.

Most of the road from Cody is gradual uphill, but the ascent becomes even more pronounced after the entrance gate. On the left side of the road, farther and farther below, is meandering Middle Creek. Stop at a pullout for a few minutes, especially in early morning or near dusk, and see if you can spot moose or bear foraging in the lush environs. About 0.5 mile before Sylvan Pass is the overlook for what remains of the innovative Corkscrew Bridge, built a century ago on the original East Entrance Road.

Sylvan Pass is the park's second highest, behind Dunraven, and most challenging to keep open in the winter and spring due to the persistent threat of an avalanche. Look up the scree on your left to see a shack and cannon. The howitzer is used to dislodge snow so snowmobilers can access the park during the winter. If you're hiking trails around Sylvan Pass and happen to see unexploded ordnance—yes, it happens—stay away and report it to park authorities. Just below the pass is Sylvan Lake, one of the last roadside bodies of water to be free of ice each summer.

CORKSCREW BRIDGE BETWEEN THE EAST ENTRANCE AND SYLVAN PASS WAS INNOVATIVE FOR ITS TIME IN 1906. REMNANTS CAN STILL BE SEEN ON THE SOUTH SIDE OF THE ROAD NPS

YELLOWSTONE LAKE EXTENDS ALMOST AS FAR AS THE EYE CAN SEE FROM THE LAKE BUTTE OVERLOOK

Slow down for a 20-mph curve that bends around Cub Creek and look for the turnoff to Lake Butte. The overlook is a great place to watch the sun set behind Yellowstone Lake and Frank Island as well as 10,308-foot Mount Sheridan in the foreground and the Tetons some 60 miles in the distance. It's less than a mile through burned timber to the parking area.

Back on East Entrance Road, you'll quickly arrive at Sedge Bay, named for the nutritious and hardy sedge grass preferred by elk, deer, and bison. Beyond the boat ramp at Sedge Bay, it's 1.5 miles to Steamboat Point and two geothermal features above the lake.

The waters of 132-square-mile Yellowstone Lake might look inviting, but even in the dog days of summer they're a polar plunge. At 38 to 42 degrees, they'll send an instant chill through you, so settle for a little toe dabbing. The lake is so vast—the largest above 7,000 feet in North America—waves lap the shore as if it were an ocean or one of the Great Lakes. Canoeists and kayakers should keep an eye on weather and always stay within 100 yards of shore; a spill here could easily be lethal due to the quick onset of hypothermia.

About 3 miles before Fishing Bridge is the Pelican Creek delta. Look for a wide variety of waterfowl, including geese, ducks, sandhill cranes, and, naturally, the white pelican. Pelican Valley is one of the most extraordinary landscapes in Yellowstone. It has so much grizzly activity it's closed to humans until July 4, and then hiking is only allowed from 9 a.m. to 7 p.m. Have your bear spray handy and hike in groups of four or more.

Pelican Valley is also home to Mollie's wolf pack, descendants of the original Crystal Creek pack and named for the late former head of the US Fish & Wildlife Service,

THE THOROFARE REGION: YELLOWSTONE'S LONELY CORNER

Few parts of Greater Yellowstone elicit more reverence among wilderness purists than the Thorofare in Yellowstone's southeast corner. The Thorofare Ranger Station is the farthest inhabited dwelling from a road in the continental United States. Eagle Peak, at 11,358 feet the highest point in the park, is rarely scaled. Grizzlies, wolves, moose, mountain lions, and other critters roam without intrusion from humans, save for the occasional backcountry hiker. A highlight of the Thorofare is Two Ocean Pass, 18 miles from the closest trailhead. At Two Ocean, waters of a high-altitude marsh part ways, some headed for the Atlantic and some for the Pacific; fish actually cross the Continental Divide here. The Thorofare has 15 backcountry campsites, including a platform at the ranger station. A backcountry permit is required for all overnight stays, and it's crucial to observe rules regarding food storage. Anyone who explores this remarkable and remote country will not soon forget it.

THE REMOTE THOROFARE REGION OF YELLOWSTONE IS PRIME GRIZZLY BEAR HABITAT AND HOME TO EAGLE PEAK, THE PARK'S HIGHEST MOUNTAIN NPS

Mollie Beatty, an ardent proponent of restoring the creature to Yellowstone. The valley's winter climate is too harsh for elk, leaving only the hardy bison. The Mollie's pack initially adapted to bringing down this bigger, stronger, and faster foe. Even then, it can take the pack up to eight hours to kill a single bison, at considerable risk to their own health.

After Pelican Creek, the road straightens and enters forest for the short run into the historic settlement of Fishing Bridge. The place was named for a bridge built in 1902 (replaced in 1937) where the Yellowstone River emerges after its invisible southeast-to-northwest journey through the depths of Yellowstone Lake. Fishermen would stand shoulder-to-shoulder to catch large, migrating Yellowstone cutthroat trout, resulting in a predictable mix of large catches and tangled lines. Today, fishing is prohibited

The largest wolf ever collared in the park was a Delta pack male weighing in at 147 pounds. When it was shot with a tranquilizer dart and weighed in 2011, the Deltas had the three largest wolves since restoration. The majority of the park's largest wolves have been the Deltas and the nearby Mollie's. Both packs roam the mountains and valleys of the park's southeast territory.

from the bridge, and you'll have to be content with scanning crystal-clear water for dwindling numbers of cutthroat.

Fishing Bridge is also a fulcrum for the evolution of grizzly bear management in the park. When open garbage dumps were eliminated cold turkey, removing a prime food source, the great bear was forced to look elsewhere. Campgrounds became a first stop, especially in Fishing Bridge, already familiar to hungry griz. They also congregated around Yellowstone Lake's tributaries to gorge on the same migrating cutthroats favored by fishermen. Inevitably this led to conflicts resulting in frightened humans and dead bears. Today, the expanding grizzly population has adjusted to appropriate food sources, and the Park Service has limited conflicts by closing one campground, eliminating some cabins, instituting bear-awareness programs, and requiring hard-sided campers in the remaining camping area north of East Entrance Road.

Fishing Bridge is the consummate park setting, with rustic stone and dark-wood buildings blending with lush lodgepole forest. The stone Fishing Bridge Museum and Visitor Center, built in 1931, is on the National Register of Historic Places. The general store is classic Yellowstone parkitecture and a good place to regroup or grab a bite to eat.

Nearly 3 miles past Fishing Bridge, now on Grand Loop Road headed toward West Thumb and Grant Village, is Lake Village, site of the immense Lake Hotel, Lake Lodge and Cabins, general store, and 1923 ranger station also listed on the National Register.

FISHING IS NO LONGER ALLOWED ON FISHING BRIDGE, WHERE ANGLERS ONCE STOOD SHOULDER-TO-SHOULDER IN PURSUIT OF CUTTHROAT TROUT

FISHING BRIDGE TO CANYON (16 MILES)

Few routes in Yellowstone pack more punch than this lovely drive along the Yellowstone River through the wildlife-rich Hayden Valley. And in a park blessed with spectacular scenery, there is no more mesmerizing sight than the Grand Canyon of the Yellowstone River. Along the way, brief stops worth a peek include Mud Volcano, Sulphur Caldron, and LeHardy Rapids, spelled "LeHardys" on some maps.

LeHardy Rapids, named for a topographer whose raft capsized there in 1873, is slightly less than 3 forested miles from Fishing Bridge junction. It's considered the official northern boundary of Yellowstone Lake because it's the first place the river drops discernibly. A boardwalk was constructed in 1984 to enable viewers to watch trout leap the rapids, like salmon, as they return to the lake. The path is closed in the spring mating season of resident harlequin ducks.

Below LeHardy, the Yellowstone again turns into a broad, lazy river that's building a debt it'll pay with vengeance downstream. It's idyllic for fly-fishing, though anglers should note the short no-fishing stretch in the channel next to the road. Keep an eye out for wandering bull bison as you follow the river to the next attraction, Mud Volcano. Once volatile, Mud Volcano is relatively tame but still fascinates with bubbling and gurgling pots that sound like grits on the stove. While you're in this area prone to small earthquakes, you might notice the hissing of Dragon's Mouth Spring and rumbling of Black Dragon's Caldron. The latter released its fury sometime in the late 1940s with such force that mature trees were flattened. Equally engrossing is Sulphur Caldron, albeit from a safe distance. Sulphur, just north of Mud Volcano and across the road, is more acidic (1.3 pH) than battery acid, according to park literature that cautions visitors about getting too close.

Less than 0.5-mile past the caldron, the world opens up to the Hayden Valley, announced by an ominous white sign with red lettering warning against approaching

A YELLOWSTONE NATIVE'S FIGHT FOR SURVIVAL

Until the mid-1990s, Yellowstone Lake was one of the finest and most important cutthroat trout habitats in the world. As a native—unlike the more coveted rainbow, brown, and brook trout, which were imported to enhance fishing opportunities—it is a symbol of ecosystem health.

In the summer of 1994, that picture literally changed overnight when a fisherman reeled in a lake trout, or mackinaw, another nonnative fish that had been introduced years earlier to nearby Shoshone, Lewis, and Heart Lakes. The appearance of that single fish sent a shudder through biologists who knew what that moment foretold for native cutthroat. Yellowstone Lake, for thousands of years a safety-deposit box for a gleaming fish with the telltale red slits below its gills, was sounding its death knell.

How did the lake trout get there? The prevailing sentiment at the time was that a so-called "bucket biologist" caught a few lake

A NATIVE CUTTHROAT LEAPS LEHARDY RAPIDS EN ROUTE TO YELLOWSTONE LAKE
NPS

dangerous wildlife. The sign is more eyesore than helpful reminder, and it's curious why the wildlife-rich Lamar Valley isn't similarly marked. At any rate, the Hayden is unique in that the soil is too thick for trees to root, and serene flows of the Yellowstone River along with Trout and Elk Antler Creeks form a water wonderland. This in turn provides a wildlife-watching bonanza for tourists who routinely see a huge variety of bird and mammal life from elevated perches overlooking the placid river. They don't call one of the viewing sights Grizzly Overlook for nothing.

The road undulates for slightly more than 4 miles across the valley, reentering the forest at Alum Creek. It's another 3 miles to the turnoff across Chittenden Bridge—frequently used by wolves and other wildlife as an easy river crossing—to Artist Point and the south rim of the Grand Canyon of the Yellowstone. For 10,000 years, the river has been carving a yawning chasm in the geothermally weakened rhyolite walls, creating a 1,000-foot-deep canyon that's 20 miles long and as much as 4,000 feet wide.

BRUINS ARE KNOWN TO STOP TRAFFIC AND CREATE "BEAR JAMS" IN HAYDEN VALLEY ERIC JOHNSTON / NPS

trout in Lewis Lake in the late 1980s and decided to start a population in Yellowstone Lake. Superintendent Bob Barbee decried it as "an appalling act of environmental vandalism." Another theory, generally discredited, is that helicopters scooping buckets of water to fight the 1988 fires unwittingly dumped mackinaw in the lake.

In 2018, yet another idea emerged, from park fisheries biologist Todd Koel: Lake trout were washed down the dam spillway at Jackson Lake in Grand Teton National Park and swam 40 miles up Pacific Creek to a meeting with North Two Ocean Creek. From there, they eventually reached the "Parting of the Waters" at Two Ocean Pass, where they descended in Atlantic Creek to an eventual arrival at the Yellowstone River upstream from the lake.

Regardless of how it came about, the discovery was ominous. The lake trout is a voracious eater, a single fish consuming more than 40 of the smaller cutthroat each year. They're also prolific breeders. In the quarter century since their introduction, probably at West Thumb, the lake trout took over Yellowstone Lake.

As is always the case in nature, fallout hasn't been limited to the trout. Wildlife long reliant on cutthroat spawning in the lake's tributaries have been impacted. Large numbers of grizzlies, osprey, eagles, otters, and more than 40 other species have left the lake area in search of food. Another recently observed impact: Bald eagles have turned on other bird species for food, threatening their existence in the park.

What to do? More than a decade ago the Park Service began an all-out effort, hiring a gillnetting crew from the Great Lakes to catch several hundred thousand lake trout each year. In addition, scientists began implanting radio telemetry in "Judas fish" that lead them to mackinaw spawning beds deep in the lake, inaccessible to predators. In doing so, they have achieved 100 percent mortality of the eggs by smothering them with carcasses of lake trout caught in gillnets. By 2012, biologists reported an increase in juvenile Yellowstone cutthroat trout for the first time, and in 2018 the number of lake trout killed reached 1.5 million, signaling the collapse of the population. The battle remains far from over, and anglers are still encouraged to pursue lake trout. In fact, if you catch one you're required to keep it or kill it.

People stare in awe at the rich hues of sheer orange, pink, tan, and yellow canyon walls, viewed from many different angles.

How such a dramatic landscape occurred on a river that mostly meanders isn't entirely clear. Scientists speculate that when glaciers retreated some 11,000 years ago, they left ice dams at the mouth of Yellowstone Lake. Melting of the ice was like pulling a cork, sending mountains of water northward and scouring the canyon at the weakest points in the rock. Chances are, more than one such catastrophic flood was caused by the melting of glaciers.

Today, the river continues to work its erosive magic, digging the canyon deeper for future civilizations. If time permits only one stop at Grand Canyon, make it Artist Point. You and your shoulder-to-shoulder fellow gazers will recognize the view of the 308-foot Lower Falls and eye-popping sheer drop to the raging river below. If you're lucky, the falls will sport a photogenic rainbow.

✳ To Do

ATTRACTIONS

Buffalo Bill Center of the West is an impressive collection of Western artifac
museums under one 300,000-square-foot roof: the Buffalo Bill Museum, Pl
ans Museum, Cody Firearms Museum, Whitney Gallery of Western Art,
Museum of Natural History. It began a century ago as the Buffalo Bill Mu

IN THE WINTER, THE LOWER FALLS OF THE YELLOWSTONE RIVER ARE ACCESSIBLE VIA SNOWCOACH, SNOWSHOE, OR NORDIC SKIS JIM PEACO / NPS

the street, in a log cabin that has since become the Chamber of Commerce offices. Volunteers and docents are especially helpful and friendly. Nearly 250,000 visitors annually pass through a facility sometimes called "The Smithsonian of the West," named *True West*'s top Western museum in 2017. **Harry Jackson Studios** (307-587-5508) once had regular hours, but now viewing times are limited and you need an appointment to see his gallery. Jackson was 14 years old when he left his Al Capone–ruled mafia family in Chicago for a new life in the West. His work ranges from World War II paintings to sculptures of Sacajawea. Jackson split his time between Cody and Italy until his death in 2011.

For a glimpse at a relatively recent slice of regrettable American history, **Heart Mountain Interpretive Center** (307-754-8000), 14 miles northeast of town on the way to Powell, is the remnants of an internment camp where 14,000 Japanese American citizens were relocated for three years during World War II. The site, marked by a red chimney with a haunting concentration-camp aura, opened as a full-on interpretive center and museum in 2011.

CALLED THE SMITHSONIAN OF THE WEST, BUFFALO BILL CENTER IS FIVE EXTENSIVE MUSEUMS IN ONE LOCATION

Fans of the frontier mystique will want to save time for **Old Trail Town/Museum of the Old West** (307-587-5302, May to September) near the Cody Nite Rodeo grounds. On the grounds is a collection of 26 Old West buildings dating as far back as 1879 and as recent as 1901. You can see horse-drawn carriages, Indian artifacts, and other frontier memorabilia, including a cabin once inhabited by Butch Cassidy and the Sundance Kid. The small cemetery out back is the resting place of many Western luminaries. People have varying opinions about dams, but either way **Buffalo Bill Dam & Visitor Center** (307-527-6076, May to October) on the west edge of town is instructive. Originally called the Shoshone Dam and renamed in 1946, 325-foot Buffalo Bill was the tallest dam in the world upon completion in 1910 and was one of the first such concrete structures in the United States.

RECREATION OUTSIDE YNP

FISHING No longer on any best-kept secrets list, the **North Fork of the Shoshone River** continues to be an extraordinary place to wet a line. Where else can an angler find elbow room on a blue-ribbon trout stream that flows alongside a major highway? Many visitors are in such a hurry to get to the park that they neglect 50 miles of free-flowing river teeming with native browns, rainbows, and cutthroats averaging about 16 inches. The best fishing, especially with dry flies, is right after runoff ends in early July and again in the autumn. Expect smaller fish in August and early September. Study your maps. This is a dude-ranch corridor, and much of the North Fork flows through private land, which includes river bottoms in Wyoming.

AN UPGRADED PATHWAY LEADS TO INSPIRATION POINT AT THE GRAND CANYON OF THE YELLOWSTONE
JIM PEACO / NPS

HIKING

Canyon Village Area: Some of the most spectacular vistas in Yellowstone are from the north and south rims of the Grand Canyon of the Yellowstone River, where eight overlooks are connected by 5 miles of trails. Substantive rehabilitation work has been completed in the area in recent years to make foot traffic safer. On the south rim, visitors will recognize the view from **Artist Point** from numerous paintings and photographs—a view known to move people to tears. The more adventurous can take **Uncle Tom's Trail**, a 500-foot descent on 328 steps leading to the Lower Falls. The trail reopened in the fall of 2018 after extensive restoration. If you're curious about the name, this was the location in the early 1900s where H. K. "Uncle Tom" Richardson took folks into the canyon using steps and rope ladders. He would ferry them across the river to a landing above the canyon. The **Brink of Upper Falls Trail** is slated for renovation, with plans to reopen by 2020. On the north rim, if a little vertigo doesn't bother you, hike the paved switchbacks to the **Brink of the Lower Falls**, where you can peek over the railing at the lip of the thundering 308-foot drop and steam from hot springs downstream. A more soothing but no less inspiring view is from recently rehabilitated **Inspiration Point**, probably the second-most-attended tourist stop. **Grandview Point** is another overlook worth your time, as is the 0.5-mile descent to **Red Rock Point**, where mist from the Lower Falls provides relief on rare hot summer days. Note: Red Rock Point and Brink of the Lower Falls observation points are scheduled for closure due to renovation beginning in 2020.

About 1.5 miles north of Canyon heading toward Dunraven Pass is the breezy **Cascade Lake Trail**, a jaunt through forests, wildflower-laced meadows, and along small creeks to a pretty lake at the end. About 3.5 miles west of Canyon, the moderate 3-mile **Grebe Lake Trail** leads to a lake known for the increasingly rare Arctic grayling, a prized fish that requires the coldest and cleanest of waters for survival. Much of the trail winds through charred 1988 fire remnants.

The longest trail in the park is the 150-mile **Howard Eaton Trail**, a series of well-worn paths that roughly parallel the Grand Loop. It includes a moderate 12-mile stretch that hits several small lakes while connecting Canyon and Norris. Due to marshy conditions, it's often inaccessible until July, and while certainly hike-worthy, it has been a while since the Park Ser-

BULL ELK GROW SPIKE ANTLERS AT AGE TWO, AND TINES BEGIN BRANCHING INTO RACKS AT AGE THREE. THE LARGER THE RACK, THE HEALTHIER THE BULL
ERIC JOHNSTON / NPS

ICE CLIMBING One of Greater Yellowstone's ice-climbing meccas is on the **South Fork of the Shoshone River** west of Cody. Climbers from around the world come to test their mettle on 15 named routes on frozen waterfalls about 45 minutes from town.

RIVER RUNNING Sun-kissed trips through Red Rock Canyon and Lower Canyon range from scenic floats to tumultuous whitewater on the **Shoshone River** near Cody. The rapids are a cushy Class I–II. Guided trips through the canyon are available, but we suggest renting a raft or inflatable kayak and trying your own hand at entry-level whitewater. The popular float starts at DeMaris Street west of Cody and goes for 7 to 13 miles, ranging from 1.5 to 3 hours. For more action with

vice maintained it. South of Canyon Village, in Hayden Valley, a trailhead starts the moderate hike to Mary Mountain on the Central Plateau. Look for bison and elk, and keep an eye open for signs of grizzlies as well. If there's one don't-miss hike in this region, it's Mount Washburn, weather permitting. Views of Yellowstone's mountains are astounding and extend to the Tetons on clear days. Two moderately strenuous routes, each 3 miles long, lead to the 10,243-foot summit. Bring a jacket, even if it's warm in the parking lot. Winds howl across the summit, where a fire lookout offers telescopes, water, and a break from sudden squalls. The south trail accessed from Dunraven Pass typically has less traffic and is slightly more interesting because it's an actual trail. Go in the morning, before the winds blow and thunderstorms arrive.

Observation Peak is a challenging 3-mile hike from Cascade Lake to the top of a 9,397-foot mountain that offers views of the Absarokas to the east, Central Plateau to the south, Prospect Peak to the north, and the Gallatins to the northwest. A terrific 6- to 8-hour adventure for fit hikers who want to get off the beaten path is Seven Mile Hole. It's a strenuous 11-mile trek that leaves the south rim of the Grand Canyon near Inspiration Point, sneaks past Silver Cord Cascade, and quickly drops 1,400 feet to the Yellowstone River. It's the only true trail that takes you to the bottom of the canyon. Watch for dormant and active hot springs. Though not a secret among diehard fishermen, strap a fly-rod to your back for exceptional angling. There are three campsites at the bottom, all requiring a backcountry-use permit.

Yellowstone Lake Area: Avalanche Peak is a strenuous 5-mile round-trip climb that's worth the effort once you see the stunning views of the lake and mountains. The switchback trail gains 1,800 feet through forest, whitebark pine, and open scree. Elephant Back Mountain is a moderately strenuous 3-miler that climbs 800 feet through lodgepole pine to views of the northwest corner of Yellowstone Lake. Pelican Creek is a leisurely 1-mile loop through forest on the lakeshore and a small marsh where bison and birds like to hang out. For views of the lake and its neighboring wildlife, take the easy 2.3-mile Storm Point Loop. The route goes through forest to a rocky promontory that juts into the lake. Check the Fishing Bridge Visitor Center for possible closure due to grizzly activity, and keep your eyes out for the curious yellow-bellied marmots.

a similar pace, at least until water flows are too low in July, put in on the **North Fork of the Shoshone River** for a half-day float. Expert kayakers will find the highly technical Class IV action on the Shoshone between Buffalo Bill Dam and DeMaris Springs a thrill. No fewer than five companies offer guided trips and/or equipment.

SKIING (NORDIC) The **North Fork Nordic Trails** (307-587-3125) are 25 kilometers of groomed trails near Pahaska Tepee and the Sleeping Giant Ski Area between Cody and the East Entrance, on the Shoshone National Forest. The trails, supported by the Park County Nordic Ski Association, follow the North Fork of the Shoshone River and are suitable for classic and skate skiing. Rentals are available at Pahaska. For pure solitude, head south to Meeteetse and then another 30 minutes to **Wood River Ski Park** (307-868-2603), which has 25 kilometers of classic and skate skiing. A warming hut at the trailhead makes for sweet après-ski moments, but to make the most of your memories, rent the fully stocked cabin ($30 donation) from the Meeteetse Recreation District.

SNOWMOBILING The Cody County Snowmobile Association has 70 miles of groomed trails in the area, though most riders in this neck of the woods prefer Cooke City and the Beartooth Plateau in Montana. A handful of snowmobilers head up the North Fork of the Shoshone and ride over Sylvan Pass to Fishing Bridge, but the area is avalanche prone and openings are unpredictable. Rentals are available at Roger's Sports Center, Mountain Valley Motorsports, and Cody Custom Cycle, to name a few.

✳ Lodging

LODGING IN YNP

Lake Village: The sunny yellow ❂ ♿ ¶ **Lake Yellowstone Hotel ($$$$) and Cabins** ($$$, 307-344-7311, May to September), Yellowstone's oldest surviving hotel (1891) and now the second-largest wood-frame building in North America, looks as if it was plucked from a plantation in the Deep South. Its look was created in 1903 by Robert C. Reamer and renovations have continued through the years, including a major interior reconstruction completed in 2014 that enhanced the 158-room hotel's Southern Colonial persona. Lake views are superb from the Sun Room, where music from a grand piano serves as a backdrop for a game of chess or a good book and glass of wine. Accommodations have modern furnishings, from the Presidential Suite once occupied by Calvin Coolidge to more basic rooms with one or two beds. For the more economically inclined, the refurbished **Lake Yellowstone Hotel Annex** lacks views but compensates with tasteful environs. ♿ ¶ **Lake Lodge and Cabins** ($$/$$$, 307-344-7901, June to September) contrast the grand hotel with log beam interiors, modest furnishings, and rocking chair views from the porch. The basic 1920s cabins come in three flavors: primitive and economical Pioneer, more traditional log-and-plank and renovated Lake (formerly Frontier), and the slightly more spacious Western modules of four and six units. Lake Lodge and Cabins do offer solitude yet are a short walk from the more vibrant hotel happenings.

Canyon Village: If you haven't been to Canyon in a while, you won't recognize much of it. What was once a visually unappealing compound spread among the conifers has become the poster child for eco-consciousness. In the process, ♿ **Canyon Lodge and Cabins ($$/$$$,** 307-344-7901, June to September) became the largest property in the park while condensing its footprint. No longer is a stay at Canyon akin to drawing a short Yellowstone straw. Five new three-story lodges have opened with a combined 409 rooms. Still standing are 100 module-style, Mission 66–era Western cabins—down from 540—and two smaller motel-style lodges: Cascade and Dunraven. Four of the new accommodations are Gold-level LEED certified, the fifth Silver. The new bunking meets all budget needs, from small with no bath to two-room suites with balconies.

ALTERNATIVE LODGING IN YNP

CAMPING All three Yellowstone campgrounds listed in this section take reservations through Yellowstone National Park Lodges. **Fishing Bridge RV Park** ($, 307-344-7311, May to September), longtime hub for the home-on-wheels crowd, is one of the few offering coin showers, laundry, and dump station. Because it's in busy grizzly country, only hard-sided campers are allowed. Note: The RV park was to be closed all of 2019 to redesign the 325 sites and to improve comfort stations and the camper-services building.

More than 400 sites compose **Bridge Bay Campground** ($, 307-344-7311, June to September), a virtual tent city—no surprise given its proximity to Yellowstone Lake's only marina. A picnic table at each site, flush toilets, dishwashing stations, a store, and ranger presentations provide everything a camper could need or want. Tent-only loops include food-storage boxes to limit bear temptations. Some loops are closed in early summer due to bear activity.

Preferred for its central location and forested grounds, ♿ **Canyon Campground** ($, 307-344-7311, June to September) has 250 tent and RV sites (no hook-ups) with picnic tables and fire grates, coin showers, laundry, an amphitheater, and separate sites for hikers and cyclists. Serious bear-safety rules are provided at check-in, and bear boxes are located in densely treed areas to ensure food and odorous supplies are properly stored.

BEST LODGING OUTSIDE YNP

Cody: At ⊘ ❅ ♿ **Green Gables Inn** ($/$$, 307-587-6886, May to October), Linda Cody, widow of Buffalo Bill's great-grandson Kit Carson Cody, has 15 well-managed, simple rooms with two queen beds and log furniture in each; hanging flower baskets add a homey splash of color. The only motel with a resident cockatoo greeter ⊘ ❅ ♿, **Carter Mountain Motel** ($$$, 307-587-4295) is a small, no-frills, reasonably priced set of 29 rooms. The second-floor deck has dynamite views of the sun dropping behind Carter Mountain. More value lodging includes ❅ ♿ **Big Bear Motel** ($$, 307-587-3117), with 64 rooms—32 recently updated—and an outdoor heated swimming pool on 4 acres with horseshoes, playground, and pony rides, all within walking distance of the Cody Nite Rodeo. **Buffalo Bill's Antlers Inn** ($$, 307-587-2084, May to October) has two floors of 40 Western-style rooms adorned with Thomas Molesworth–style burl wood furniture made by the previous owner.

If your style tends more toward pampering, you'll like ♿ **Cody Legacy Inn & Suites'** ($$$, 307-587-6472) modern Western-motif rooms, fitness room, swimming pool, hot tub, and antler-clad lobby accentuated by a huge stone fireplace and black-and-white photos of the town's more famous figures. Among chain hotels, Cody boasts one of the more appealing **AmericInn Lodge & Suites** ($$, 307-587-7716). Parents will like the hot breakfast buffet and fitness center; kids will love the indoor pool.

Leaning more to historic and rustic, the ⊘ ❙❙ **Irma Hotel** ($$/$$$, 307-587-4221) was the first building constructed in this frontier town. Rooms on the bottom floor are furnished much the same as in Bill's day, minus the TV and Internet access but plus a friendly ghost or two. A newer addition features more contemporary fixtures. We admittedly are quite smitten with ⊘ ♿ **Chamberlin Inn** ($$$, 307-587-0202). Ev and Susan Diehl put a ton of sweat and love into restoring this dreamy 21-unit charmer. The hotel's guest registry includes names such as Marshall Fields and Ernest Hemingway, who stayed in Room 18 in 1932. Reputedly, he finished his *Death in the Afternoon* manuscript, went to fish the Clarks Fork, returned to mail the manuscript, and then downed a few at the Irma Bar before again wetting a line. The Diehls also offer lodging in Cody's original courthouse, consisting of a garden cottage, apartment, and loft apartment.

If you're looking for a more traditional upscale experience, ❅ ♿ **The Cody Hotel** ($$$$, 307-587-5915) fancies itself the town's first true luxury hotel, and the extra touches back up the claim even if the exterior is fairly basic. Lodging ranges from standard to deluxe king and queen rooms with balconies, and luxury suites with fireplaces. Also marketing to those who prefer creature comforts is the ♿ ❙❙ **Best Western Premier Ivy Inn & Suites** ($$$$, 307-527-2572), towering above the last turn on Cody's main drag as it veers west toward the rodeo grounds. The property has an extensive fitness center, indoor pool, cocktail lounge, and a restaurant favored by Cody-ites. Head wrangler Jerry and first cowgirl Bette Kinkade's ⊘ **K3 Guest Ranch** ($$$, 307-587-2080) was once listed by NBC-TV as one of the four most unique bed & breakfasts anywhere. Mold-breaking accommodations abound, such as bunking in an authentic chuck, hay, or sheepherder wagon, glamping in a canvas tent, and comingling with veggies in the greenhouse. And there's plenty to do on the ranch after your hearty breakfast cooked outdoors and served family style.

Cody has many fine B&Bs, starting with **Salsbury Avenue Inn Bed & Breakfast** ($, 307-587-1226), a 1914 home starring four fancy rooms—a king, two queens, and a room with two twins—three blocks from downtown. Another nesting space, 🐾 **Robin's Nest** ($$/$$$, 307-527-7208) has Western curb appeal expressed in log furnishings along with a quiet neighborhood location and willingness to accept pets with advance notice. "You've never had so much fun in a church" is Barbara and Robert Kelley's motto for their converted **Angels' Keep Bed & Breakfast** ($$, 307-587-6205). The three comfortable rooms with private baths will keep your spirits up, and the gourmet breakfast is downright heavenly. For adults only, **Buffalo Bill's Cody House** ($$, 307-587-6169, June to December) was built by Buffalo Bill in 1902 for Irma Hotel employees and moved to its present location in 1972 to avoid demolition. All rooms are upstairs and themed after famous frontier alums, including Buffalo Bill himself.

BEST ALTERNATIVE LODGING OUTSIDE YNP

The alternative to motel living mostly comes in the form of guest ranches or bringing your own home and "roughing it." An abundance of dude and guest ranches are tucked into rugged creek drainages between Cody and the East Entrance, a.k.a. Dude Ranch Alley. We have listed, starting from Cody, standouts for longevity, reputation, hospitality, and superior setting. Many facilities do not have TVs, phones, or Internet, and cell coverage is spotty.

Shoshone River Valley: Pretty-as-a-postcard ⏾ **Absaroka Mountain Lodge** ($$$/$$$$, 307-587-3963, May to September) was once owned by Buffalo Bill's grandson and still sports many of his wildlife mounts. Cradled in Gunbarrel Canyon, the 1910 lodge has 16 cabins and a restaurant open to the public for

breakfast and dinner. ⊘ ⏾ **Shoshone Lodge & Guest Ranch** ($$/$$$$, 307-587-4044, May to October) is a collection of 18 distinct golden-pine log cabins tucked into a sweet forest draw. The log-and-wood dining hall serves homestyle breakfast and dinner for an extraordinarily low price. Horseback riding and fishing can be arranged on the Shoshone River and Grinnell Creek; porch sitting requires no advance planning. The family-run, -owned, and -oriented ⏾ **Creekside Lodge at Yellowstone** ($$/$$$, 307-587-9795, May to October) has 10 compact cabins in a mountain setting sided by postcard-pretty Goff Creek, and 2.5 million acres of Shoshone National Forest in its backyard. On-site are a full-service restaurant serving breakfast, lunch, and dinner, a full bar, and general store.

🐾 ⏾ **Elephant Head Lodge** ($$$/$$$$, 307-587-3980, May to October) is a tight half-circle of 15 cabins sleeping from 2 to 15 under the watchful eye of a rock outcropping shaped like—you guessed it—an elephant head. No minimum stay is required and meals are separately charged, both unusual for a guest ranch. Open to nonguests are the dining room, lounge, and family room in a snug lodge listed on the National Register of Historic Places because it was built by Buffalo Bill Cody's niece, Josephine Thurston. At ♿ ⏾ **Bill Cody Ranch** ($$/$$$, 307-587-2097, May to September), one-night stays are OK, making for flexible vacationing. The ranch has 17 one- and two-bedroom log cabin duplexes, a few stand-alones, a restaurant, and a saloon at the base of Ptarmigan Mountain along Nameit Creek. Campfires are every night, and chuckwagon cookouts are staged on Wednesday and Saturday.

CAMPING

Shoshone River Valley: ⊘ 🐾 ⏾ **Yellowstone Valley Inn and RV** ($$/$$$, 307-587-3961, May to September) consists of 10 nifty duplex log cabins totaling 20 rooms with modern amenities, including WiFi, and 15 motel rooms, most with views of the Shoshone River. Also at the friendly complex are a heated pool, indoor hot tub, banquet room, and karaoke dance hall. The treeless RV section has 57 sites—19 with full hook-ups, 38 with electric and water—and there's a grassy shaded area for tents. We suggest at least one dinner at the surprisingly high-quality and fun restaurant/saloon.

☗ **Green Creek Inn and RV Park** ($$/$$$, 307-587-5004, May to September) is a tidy complex just off the highway, with nine RV sites, cabins, and 15 motel rooms adorned with log furniture. Horseshoe pits, picnic tables, and a playground add to the kid appeal, as does Internet access. The ☗ **Cody KOA** ($$, 307-587-2369, May to October) is spendy compared to similar franchises, reflecting the high summer demand. Located on the eastern edge of town, the village has various camping cabins with and without bathrooms, a tepee that sleeps five, full hook-up RV slots, tent sites, a swimming pool, free pancake breakfast, and shuttle to the Cody Nite Rodeo.

National Forest Campgrounds: America's first national forest has 12 primitive campgrounds in the North Fork of the Shoshone River Valley, all with varying levels of proximity to the park and fantastic fishing. Generally speaking, the closer you are to the park, the more picturesque, forested, and quiet the setting. Three campgrounds—**Wapiti**, **Eagle Creek**, and **Three Mile**—are notable in that no soft-sided tents or pop-up campers are allowed because of grizzly bear activity. Precaution, preparation, and heightened awareness are critical.

✳ Where to Eat

DINING IN YNP

Lake Village: The crème de la crème of Yellowstone restaurants is the **Lake** **Hotel Dining Room** ($$$, 307-344-7311, B/L/D, May to October), notable not just for mesmerizing views of the lake and classic Southern charm but also for sustainable cuisine and an extensive list of domestic and imported wines. The spacious dining room provides a sense of privacy even when crowded. Reservations are required for dinner in summer; breakfast and lunch are first-come, first-served.

There's no getting around the fact that **Lake Lodge Cafeteria** ($$, 307-344-7311, B/L/D, June to September) is a load-your-tray kind of place, but it does have advantages: no reservations required, no need for a 20 percent tip, and typically no waiting. Tables are cleared quickly to make room for the next wave of hungry customers. The rotating menu considers kids (chicken nuggets, Nathan's hot dogs), vegetarians (spinach pie, mushroom stroganoff), and omnivores (trout amandine, bison chili), and it's as tasty as it is a good value. We appreciate that you can bring your own wine or beer. The front porch is made for absorbing nature's finest work from the seat of a high-back rocker while sipping a refreshment from the corner lobby bar.

Canyon Village: As part of Yellowstone National Park Lodge's massive eco-friendly reconstruction at Canyon, the four refueling spots were re-created to provide a sustainable model while retaining the offbeat Mission 66 style. **Canyon Lodge M66 Bar & Grill** ($/$$$, 307-344-7311, B/ D, May to October) is the centerpiece, along with its neighboring lounge. The chef gets creative with bison, trout, and chicken; beers are regional and wine is on tap. **Canyon Lodge Eatery** ($/$$, 307-344-7901, B/L/D, May to October) is innovative by park standards, with healthy "Fresh Wok" and "Slow Food Fast" plates, bowls, and stews. **Canyon Lodge Falls Café** ($/$$, B/L/D, May to October) is all about simple grab-and-go sandwiches, flatbreads, salads, and other snacks. Finally, **Canyon Lodge Ice**

Creamery ($, May to September) doesn't have just any ice cream—it's Montana's own Big Dipper scooped into cones, cups, waffle cones, or create-your-own sundaes. Just need a quick morning snack or shot of espresso? **Washburn Lookout** ($, May to October) in the Washburn Lodge has your pick-me-up.

BEST DINING OUTSIDE YNP

Cody: Naturally, you won't have trouble finding a Wyoming-sized steak or burger—beef or bison—in Cody. Though not to be confused with Jackson, options aren't limited to cowboy cuisine. Italian, Mexican, Chinese, and even a Japanese restaurant mix it up, and though there's nothing fancy, you should find just about anything a palate desires.

First thing, get your beta on at **Beta Coffeehouse** ($, 307-587-7707, B/L), a sporty and snug hole-in-the-wall owned by accomplished rock climbers, with a Beta burrito, exceptionally good coffee, smoothies, house-made chai, and a dose of local info. Another happening hub is **Our Place** ($, 307-527-4420, B/L), known for solid food at solid prices and liked by the horse and iron-horse crowd as well as visitors in the know. Biscuits 'n' gravy, platter-sized hotcakes, and overflowing omelets are served to tables squeezed into every possible nook; coffee drinkers will appreciate the ongoing tradition of the 25-cent bottomless cup. For a quieter and more laid-back, late-morning meal, **Heritage Bakery, Bistro & Coffee Roaster** ($, 307-587-2622, B/L, Tuesday to Friday) in the front room of a home in a residential area caters to business folk. Baked goods, soups, sandwiches, and coffee are the mainstays.

Midday munchies begin with **Breadboard** ($, 307- 527-5788, L) and sandwiches put together the way you want, much like the chain sub shop but way tastier—especially when layered on their sunflower bread. A trendier choice, **Rocky Mountain MoJoe** ($, 307-578-8295, B/L) believes in catering to the customer with lattes and the like, gourmet oatmeal (banana pecan), bistro-style paninis on Parmesan bread, and the Wrangler Joe (tri-tip beef dip).

Your south-of-the-border cravings are readily satisfied in Cody. If you're not in a hurry, family-run **El Vaquero** ($, 307-271-1212, L/D) has that certain hole-in-the-wall feel. They're off the beaten path and their exterior isn't much, but they prove it's what's on the inside that counts with authentic, made-from-scratch comida. **Tacos El Taconazos** ($, 307-578-8530, L/D), whose owners hail from Guadalajara, moved in above the Wyoming Buffalo Company. They've been favored as an authentic alternative to Tex-Mex. A staple since 1994, unpretentious **Zapata's** ($, 307-527-7181, L/D) main claim to fame is made-from-scratch red and green salsas—also sold separately. On the go? **Rosa's & Ruben's** ($, 209-329-9086) taco truck up the hill on the way to Meeteetse has tacos, tortes, enchiladas, and plenty more to appease your *hambre*. Cohabitating with the cowboy culture in Cody for well over a decade, **Shiki Japanese Restaurant** ($$, 307-527-7116, L [Monday to Saturday]/D), is a welcome course change from meat 'n' taters.

For at least one dinner during your stay, you'll want to round 'em up and move 'em out for a steakhouse supper. Cody doesn't disappoint in the beef's-for-dinner category. Opened in 1922, **Cassie's Supper Club** ($$, 307-527-5500, L/D; Br [Sunday]) was originally a dining hall and dance club run by the determined and business-savvy Cassie Walker, who needed steady income after her husband died. A dark labyrinth leads to three bars, rooms for dining, a huge dance floor, pool tables, and a virtual museum hanging from the walls. Live music on weekends adds to the charm or chaos, however you see it. If you're itchin' to extend your rodeo experience, get your dusty boots on over to **Proud Cut Saloon & Steakhouse** ($$/$$$, 307-527-6905, L/D). Rodeo photos and memorabilia set the mood while hand-cut steaks, chicken, seafood, and entrée salads easily make the cut. At the **Wyoming Rib & Chop House** ($$/$$$, 307-527-7731, L [weekdays]/D/Br [Sunday]), award-winning ribs, Angus steak, fresh seafood flown in, soups, and sauces made in-house mark a few differences for this regional chain. Sunday brunch is sensational, and if you have a designated driver, enjoy the legendary 26-ounce margarita. The **Irma Hotel Bar Restaurant and Grill** ($/$$, 307-587-4221, B/L/D) is true-blue Western, open early and semi-late, and sports a serviceable kids menu. The expansive breakfast and lunch buffets are good grub for greenhorns. Seven steaks, four cuts of specialty prime rib, and Rocky Mountain oysters highlight the dinner docket.

More of a date-night place, **8th Street at the Ivy** ($$/$$$, 307-587-2572, B/L/D) in the Best Western Premier hotel invites you to gussy up and branch out from the steak 'n' taters scene. The vibe is Western casual, their meats hand-cut and locally purveyed, the ingredients organic, and bread, soups, and desserts homemade. Another exceptional option if you're in the mood to dress up: **Il Padrino** ($$/$$$, 307-527-7320, L/D), the latest and most promising attempt at an Italian-themed restaurant in an elegant setting where owners and hosts are so committed they "personally guarantee your experience." Pasta, ravioli, and lasagna accommodate your inner Italian;

locally produced beef for steaks sate the more traditional palate. Switching European flags, **Gasthaus Cardi** ($$, 307-578-8202, L/D)—in the old La Comida quarters—brings central Germany to the frontier with schnitzel, kartoffelpuffer (potato pancakes), rouladen (a beef-wrapped meat dish), and beef sauerbraten. Order beer and wine with dinner or choose a bar stool at Bierstube Chuck to imbibe.

If small plates with wine, whiskey, or a cocktail are enough to satisfy, **Juniper Bar + Market + Bistro** ($, 307-527-4472, L/D) is the place to try. By customer request, Michele and Ruffin Prevost moved and grew their business that began as a bottle shop with a small wine bar in back. Sip and nip at the bar/lounge, on the patio, or in the ventilated cigar room. Two "funky but functional" lofts above the bar offer a place to toss your cowboy hat and rest your head. **The Local at Whole Foods Trading Co.** ($/$$, 307-586-4262, B/L/D) is the place to go for folks with a strong eye for healthy, locally produced, seasonal foods.

DIY Get your picnic supplies, snacks, beverages, or nutritional supplements at **Whole Foods Trading Co.** (307-587-3213, closed Sunday) in back of The Local. Their shelves are stocked with products that emphasize sustainable, organic, GMO-free, and purveyors who treat livestock humanely.

SOUTH ENTRANCE

*South Entrance to West Thumb / West Thumb
to Lake Village & Fishing Bridge /
Grassy Lake Road*

Gateway Community: Flagg Ranch

❋ Overview

If there's an entrance where you're most likely to be stuck behind a truck trailering a boat, it's the South. This is the gateway to Yellowstone's lake region, starring America's largest high-elevation lake: the clear, cold, and deep Yellowstone Lake. The impressive cast includes Lewis Lake and its sister, Shoshone, the largest lake in the country without road access. Also here is Heart Lake, requiring a 7-mile hike but yielding plenty of rewards.

On either side of the highway is some of the least-traveled country in the park. To the west is the immense Pitchstone Plateau, a 2,000-foot-high lava mound birthing numerous streams tumbling westward toward Cascade Corner. To the east, through territory split by the headwaters of the Snake River, are Two Ocean Plateau, the Trident, and the Thorofare.

This region has fewer facilities and activities than any stretch of road in the park. For 20 miles between the entrance and Grant Village, there is but one campground and picnic area. They are both at the boat launch for Lewis Lake about 11 miles inside the park. This route certainly has its bounty of beauty, though. The highway follows a deep gorge carved by the Lewis River as it pours from the caldera near the south end of Lewis Lake. Also notable in this section are the only three Continental Divide crossings in Yellowstone.

❋ Getting Here

The South Entrance is often part of a double feature: tours of both Yellowstone and Grand Teton National Parks. It's also a common arrival point for tourists driving diagonally across Wyoming on I-80 or I-70 (See Chapter 7 for routes from Jackson). The other choice is via US 26/287 through Dubois, Wyoming. To take this badlands approach, leave I-80 at Rawlins on US 287/WY 789 and head across the vast Red Desert and Great Divide Basin to Lander. From there, the road angles to the northwest along the ever-narrowing Wind River Valley past vermillion hills to Dubois—once called "Never Sweat" because even the hardest of workers never broke a sweat in the dry air and unceasing winds.

Eventually you'll ascend Togwotee Pass, descend into Moran Junction, and slice across a corner of Grand Teton National Park. The John D. Rockefeller Memorial

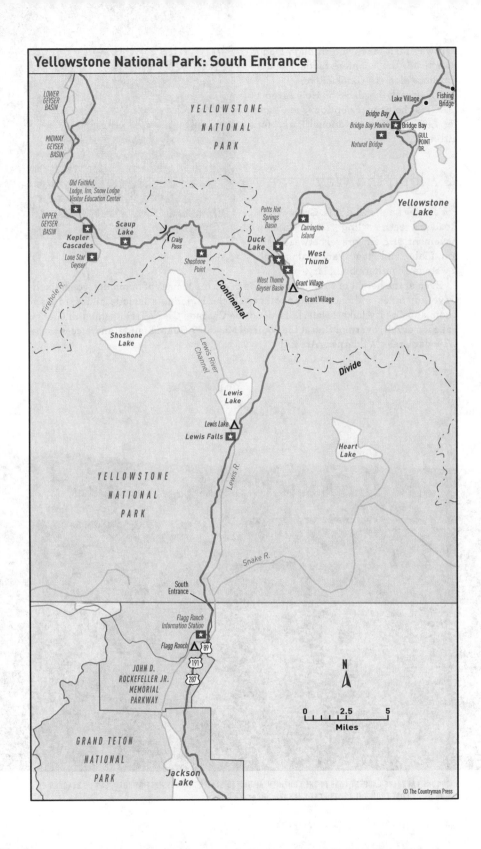

Yellowstone National Park: South Entrance

LOWER GEYSER BASIN

YELLOWSTONE

NATIONAL

PARK

MIDWAY GEYSER BASIN

Lake Village

Fishing Bridge

Bridge Bay

Bridge Bay Marina

Bridge Bay

GULL POINT DR.

Natural Bridge

Old Faithful, Lodge, Inn, Snow Lodge Visitor Education Center

UPPER GEYSER BASIN

Scaup Lake

Kepler Cascades

Lone Star Geyser

Craig Pass

Shoshone Point

Potts Hot Springs Basin

Carrington Island

Duck Lake

West Thumb

Yellowstone Lake

West Thumb Geyser Basin

Grant Village

Grant Village

Continental

Firehole R.

Shoshone Lake

Lewis River Channel

Divide

Lewis Lake

Heart Lake

Lewis Lake

Lewis Falls

YELLOWSTONE

NATIONAL

PARK

Lewis R.

Snake R.

South Entrance

Flagg Ranch Information Station

Flagg Ranch

89

191

287

JOHN D. ROCKEFELLER JR. MEMORIAL PARKWAY

N

0   2.5   5

Miles

GRAND TETON

NATIONAL

PARK

Jackson Lake

© The Countryman Press

Parkway then takes you through Flagg Ranch to the conifer-studded South Entrance along the Snake River.

If you're flying, Jackson Hole Airport (JAC) is the primary option (see Chapter 7, "Grand Teton National Park," for airlines).

✳ Along the Way

For a drive on the wild side, Grassy Lake Road is a teeth-rattling 52-mile jaunt on pavement, dirt, and gravel between Ashton, Idaho, and Flagg Ranch, along Yellowstone's southern boundary.

Even at the height of summer, when the parks are a mass of humanity, you'll likely travel for miles without seeing another vehicle. Highlights include hiking to Fish, Loon, and Grassy Lakes; waterfalls along the Cascade Creek Trail; fishing in Grassy Lake Reservoir; overnighting at the Squirrel Meadows Guard Station; and access to the Winegar Creek Wilderness Area.

SHOSHONE LAKE, THE LARGEST LAKE IN THE CONTINENTAL UNITED STATES INACCESSIBLE BY ROAD, CAN BE REACHED BY HIKING OR BY BOAT FROM THE LEWIS LAKE CHANNEL JIM PEACO / NPS

Grassy Lake Road also is fancied by snowmobilers, generally from December to March. Between April 1 and June 1 the road is closed because of grizzly bear activity. This is true backcountry with no services, and you might as well shut off your cell phone. Plan on driving 15 to 25 mph for a minimum of 90 minutes, probably longer, depending on how recently the road has been graded. Standard sedans can usually negotiate it, but four-wheel-drive or high-clearance vehicles are recommended.

✲ Gateway Communities

FLAGG RANCH, WYOMING

Flagg Ranch isn't a community per se; it's more of a resort village akin to Colter Bay in Grand Teton National Park. It does have the amenities of a gateway community, just a little scaled back: lodging, dining, fuel, some groceries, a gift shop, and a campground. Flagg Ranch is the hub of the 8-mile John D. Rockefeller Memorial Highway between the parks and part of 24,000 acres dedicated to the philanthropist in 1972 for his devotion to conservation and role in creating Grand Teton National Park. The forested area was a traditional camping site for Indians and then trappers because of its relative flatness and access to hunting and fishing.

The military moved into the region after Yellowstone was established to protect it from poaching, squatting, and vandalism. With its proximity to Jackson Hole and newly settled parts of southeast Idaho, Yellowstone's southern boundary was particularly vulnerable. For many years after the military left, what became Flagg Ranch was much like it is today—a place for travelers to rest, eat, and refuel. For trivia buffs, it was once owned by a mafia don who valued the security of isolation.

LAKE HOTEL STAFF SHOW OFF A STRING OF CUTTHROAT TROUT, A NATIVE FISH NO LONGER IN SUCH ABUNDANCE NPS

BEFORE YOU WERE HERE

The Bannock Indians of southeast Idaho's upper Snake River Plain reputedly were deathly afraid of evil spirits they believed lived amid the roiling geothermal regions of Yellowstone. But they were even more afraid of the Blackfeet and the Crow Indians.

So, every summer, instead of skirting what became the park's northern and southern boundaries to reach still-fertile buffalo hunting grounds, they braved the belching fumaroles and spitting geysers. Their annual migration had become a necessity because once-abundant buffalo of the Snake River country had been wiped out.

Their route, used for about four decades and known as the Bannock Trail, was frequented by other tribes. The Nez Perce Indians used it in their flight from the US Army in their fateful summer of 1877. Like the Blackfeet, Crow, and Sioux, the Bannock were nomadic and used horses to travel. The tribe spun off from the Northern Paiute once they acquired horses in the 1700s. They remain classified as Great Basin indigenous peoples, a reference to the basin and range landscape that extends from northern Mexico into southern Oregon and Idaho.

The Bannock lived peacefully alongside the poorer Shoshone, fishing the Snake River for salmon in the summer, hunting bison the rest of the year, making pottery, and trading with other tribes. They now share the Fort Hall Reservation with the Northern Shoshone in southeast Idaho, between Pocatello and Idaho Falls.

Today, Flagg Ranch remains the oldest continuously operating resort in the northern part of Jackson Hole, and its future seems assured. Grand Teton Lodge Company, which operates Jenny Lake and Jackson Lake Lodges, now manages the resort.

✳ Hitting the Road

SOUTH ENTRANCE TO WEST THUMB (22 MILES)

The Rockefeller Parkway cuts through wild country all the way to the entrance. Look for moose in marshes along the Snake and Lewis Rivers. Less than 2 miles inside the boundary and a 1-mile hike from the road, the waters of Moose Falls on Crawfish Creek roar toward a meeting with the Lewis River. Other trails lead into the invisible, toward country infrequently seen by human eyes.

SPRING SHOWS ITS MANY TEXTURES, INCLUDING VELVET ON A HEALTHY BUCK

After 4 miles of driving through pine and fir, you'll reach the southern end of Lewis River Canyon. Everything begins to look starker here due to the jagged volcanic rocks and lodgepole spires from the '88 fires. Just before the 7-mile marker is an interpretive sign describing those fires and the aftermath; it's worth a stop for information as well as for views of the canyon. About 1 mile upstream, the river mellows and becomes marshy again just below photogenic Lewis Falls' 30-foot

DOWNSTREAM FROM LEWIS LAKE, THE LEWIS RIVER OFFERS SOLID TROUT FISHING AS IT FLOWS TOWARD A MEETING WITH THE SNAKE RIVER JACOB W. FRANK / NPS

plunge. The river's right bend is so sharp it seems as if the falls must be on a tributary. Another mile ahead is the turnoff for Lewis Lake Campground, picnic area, and boat launch.

The highway hugs the east shore of Lewis Lake for a couple of miles before continuing through forest to the lowest of three Continental Divide crossings (7,988 feet). From here, it's about 2 miles to Grant Village, a collective of lodging, campground, picnic area, eateries, gas station, two Yellowstone General Stores, Yellowstone Forever bookstore, and visitor center/backcountry office.

Grant Village was once the most controversial of Yellowstone's settlements. The idea behind the Park Service's national Mission 66 plan was to create a busy hub for a growing number of people coming by car, relieving pressure at Old Faithful, Fishing Bridge, and other crowded centers. In theory, a one-size-fits-all site would eliminate the need for facilities elsewhere. Part of the original concept called for the removal of the buildings at Fishing Bridge because of impacts on grizzly bears. Trouble was, Grant Village, also in prime grizzly habitat, would dramatically impact five cutthroat-trout spawning migrations important to bear sustenance. Over two decades, plenty of folks found plenty of reasons to halt the project, but the Park Service persisted, and Mission 66 went forward in the early 1960s.

Once-mundane lodging has received a facelift and is more appealing. Another perk: It's the closest Yellowstone accommodation to Grand Teton National Park. About 2 miles beyond Grant Village is West Thumb, with smallish West Thumb Geyser Basin perched at the edge of Yellowstone Lake. A bookstore and information station remain, but other services were moved to Grant Village by late 1980.

West Thumb Geyser Basin, once known as Hot Springs Camp, has a short circular boardwalk through colorful pools and geysers. Jutting from the lake is Fishing Cone, where anglers reputedly could catch cutthroat trout and cook them at the same time. These days, high water typically submerges much of the cone. Also view-worthy: Abyss Pool. The park's deepest at 53 feet, it was one of the most colorful until coins and other junk altered the rich green hues. For more detail about all of the thermal features, grab a brochure at the information station.

WEST THUMB TO OLD FAITHFUL (17 MILES)

Two crossings of the Continental Divide, the lone roadside glimpse of Shoshone Lake, and Lone Star Geyser are the highlights of this comparatively ho-hum section of road connecting lake country with geyser country. Leaving West Thumb, take a last glimpse of the Absaroka Mountains rising above Yellowstone Lake in the distance and the rich blue hues of tiny Duck Lake in the foreground. The road soon disappears into the forest while making its initial ascent to the first Continental Divide crossing at 8,391 feet. A picnic area and plenty of room to pull over for photos mark the third-highest paved spot in the park.

INDIAN PAINTBRUSH IS AMONG THE FIRST VEGETATION TO RETURN AFTER A FIRE ED AUSTIN & HERB JONES / NPS

About 4 miles beyond the first divide is Shoshone Point and a fleeting look at Shoshone Lake to the distant southwest. It's the only place where the park's second-largest lake is visible from pavement. Less than a mile past the point are 8,262-foot Craig Pass and Isa Lake, also known as Two Ocean Lake because waters seeping out of each end of the lily pad–dotted pond flow toward different oceans. How is this possible? The divide is so flat, water can accumulate without entirely draining off. The DeLacy Creek picnic area and trailhead are also here.

The next 3 miles feature more forest, two trailheads, Spring Creek picnic area, diminutive Congress Lake, and eventually Scaup Lake, named for a duck species. Another 2 miles brings the turnoff to the parking lot for Lone Star Geyser, formerly Solitary Geyser. A 2.5-mile walk or mountain bike ride on an abandoned service road along the Firehole River is required to reach the 10-foot, cone-shaped geyser, but it's definitely worth the effort. Lone Star erupts about every three hours, lasts roughly 30 minutes, and reaches heights of 45 feet.

Just downstream of the Lone Star Geyser parking area is Kepler Cascades, the beginning of a rugged gorge on the Firehole. The cascades drop 150 feet in all, including one 50-foot plunge. From Kepler, it's a breezy 4-mile drive into the congestion at Old Faithful.

WEST THUMB TO LAKE VILLAGE AND FISHING BRIDGE (19 MILES)

For nearly all of this stretch, you'll be hugging the west shore of Yellowstone Lake, predominantly along the so-called West Thumb. Bison frequent these reaches and are not remorseful about plodding along at their own leisurely pace down the center of the road. About 2 miles into the drive is Potts Hot Springs Basin, originally considered West Thumb's Upper Group of thermal features. This is an extremely active locale that could include as many as 40 geysers. The area is unmarked and closed to the public but visible from the road. In another 2 miles, you'll notice a solitary pine tree growing out of a rock reef near the lake's shore. This is Carrington Island, named after a zoologist who was said to be the first to sail on Yellowstone Lake. The shallows surrounding the island have been a primary focus of lake-trout suppression efforts.

Continuing along the shoreline, you'll arrive 2.5 miles later at a picnic area called Hard Road to Travel. If you have snacks and drinks, continue another mile to Park Point picnic grounds and take in sweeping views of the lake and 10,305-foot Mount Sheridan to the south. A third picnic area, Spruce Point, is nearly 2 miles past and also serves up superior lake views. Yet another picnic spot before Bridge Bay is a mile down the pike and has interpretive signage explaining the conifer forest.

A mile from Bridge Bay is paved Gull Point Drive, a 2-mile detour that hugs the shore before returning to Grand Loop Road. This is a good place to fish from the bank. You might also be treated to a good glimpse of Stevenson Island, the second-largest island in Yellowstone Lake.

Just before the entrance to Bridge Bay Marina is the turnoff to Natural Bridge, a 1-mile walk or mountain bike ride to an arch created by rushing Bridge Creek. The arch is also accessible from the parking area at Bridge Bay, where boats operated by Yellowstone National Park Lodges are available to rent. A ranger station assists with boat rentals, and a small store services fishing needs. One-hour scenic cruises on the *Lake Queen* leave the dock periodically each day. It's OK to use smaller craft such as kayaks and canoes here, but heed the sign on the bridge pointing out the dangers of paddling these frigid waters. It is best to use smaller craft in the morning before winds kick up, and it's always wise to stay within 100 yards of shore in nonmotorized craft.

✳ To Do

RECREATION IN YNP

FISHING The granddaddy of 'em all is **Yellowstone Lake**, an imposing, 87,000-acre body of darn cold water. Boaters caught off guard by an afternoon thunderstorm could pay the ultimate price. If pitched into the 40-degree lake, you can figure on lasting about 20 minutes before hypothermia sets in. The lake has long been known as a repository for the Yellowstone cutthroat trout, which can grow to the size of a rugby ball, but it is strictly catch and release. Anglers are encouraged to fish for invasive lake trout and required to either keep or kill them to help restore the struggling native cutthroat population. To catch cutthroat, cast closer to the shore in a float tube or boat. You'll have the best luck early in the morning at Gull Point in Bridge Bay.

The second-largest body of water is secluded 80,000-acre **Shoshone Lake**, perhaps the No. 1 destination of the angling crowd in part because of the effort required to access America's largest lake without road access. Famed for big brown and rainbow trout, with some scrappy cutthroats and decent-sized brook trout, it also serves up lake trout. It's fishable throughout the summer but best in fall, when big fish move into the Lewis River channel. The Shoshone can be fished from trails or by boat, with access from the Lewis Lake ramp. Lewis is prized for browns as well as for the occasional brook and lake trout, all considered exotic species because they were introduced long ago.

Also in the backcountry but no less a secret than Shoshone Lake is **Heart Lake**. The heart-shaped gem is just far enough off the beaten path to provide isolation and offers terrific fishing for trophy lake trout, cutthroats, and whitefish. An 8-mile hike is required on Heart Lake Trail, which starts just north of Lewis Lake. Despite the effort,

HIKING

West Thumb/Grant Village Area: For those seeking a short leg-stretcher, Duck Lake is a 1-miler sporting views of Yellowstone and Duck Lakes. An even breezier stretch is on the 0.5-mile boardwalk at West Thumb Geyser Basin, highlighted by hot springs and dormant geysers on the shores of Yellowstone Lake. For more exertion, the Lewis River Channel/Shoshone Lake/Dogshead Loop provides two choices: a moderate 11-mile round-trip that takes in Shoshone and Lewis Lakes as well as the channel connecting the two, or a shorter forested hike with a return on the 4-mile Dogshead Trail. Bring a fly-rod in the fall because big browns and cutthroats move into the channel to spawn. Riddle Lake is a moderate 2-mile trek through meadows and marshes to the Continental Divide and a sweet, petite lake. Whenever you're in willowy marshes, there's a chance to run into an obstinate moose. And the special bear-management area means trail closure from April until mid-July.

The Shoshone Lake/DeLacy Creek Trail is an easy to moderate 6 miles through meadows rife with wildflowers and wildlife possibilities, including sandhill cranes and moose. Hiking the entire circumference clocks in at 28 miles. The Yellowstone Lake Overlook walk from West Thumb Geyser Basin parking is a 2-mile trail with lake and Absaroka Mountains views.

don't expect to have the place to yourself. About 40 percent of Yellowstone's backcountry trips target Heart Lake as a destination.

South of Bridge Bay is a fun spot for catch-and-release native cutthroats, **Riddle Lake**. For those who prefer stream angling, the **Lewis River** has a mellow 2-mile section below Lewis Falls for brown trout. Farther below, the canyon run might look inviting because of limited pressure, but it's slippery navigation, and those who've tried report mediocre fishing at best.

HEART LAKE IS POPULAR AMONG ANGLERS, EVEN THOUGH IT REQUIRES EFFORT TO GET THERE   JEREMY SCHMIDT / NPS

RECREATION OUTSIDE YNP

HIKING *Flagg Ranch Area:* Two decidedly different hikes leave from the ranch. The 5-mile **Flagg Canyon** hoof showcases the Snake River as it carves the canyon before spilling out to the south in Jackson Hole. The 2.3-mile **Polecat Creek Loop Trail** encompasses lodgepole forests and marshlands resplendent with wildlife, especially birds, and leads to Huckleberry and Polecat Hot Springs. Both once were popular with soakers but are closed due to environmental damage and health risks from the waters.

SNOWMOBILING Outside West Yellowstone, the South Entrance is a busy hub for snowmobilers and an important contributor to Jackson's winter economy. Guided trips can be arranged from Flagg Ranch as well as from outfitters in Jackson. Preferred destinations are Yellowstone Lake, Canyon Village, and Old Faithful.

✳ Lodging

LODGING IN YNP

Grant Village: As park lodging goes, perhaps the most unparklike is ♿ **Grant Village** ($$/$$$, 307-344-7311, May to September), a massive commercial endeavor carved out of the trees. The 300 rooms are evenly distributed between 6 two-story structures. Premium lodge rooms were remodeled in 2015, and Internet service is available for a fee. Given how quickly park lodging fills in the summer, "Grant Central Station" still provides a serviceable base to explore Yellowstone, Shoshone, and Lewis Lakes as well as the Old Faithful area. It also has the best proximity to Grand Teton National Park.

ALTERNATIVE LODGING IN YNP

CAMPING With 400-plus woodsy campsites, **Grant Village** is a nonstop buzz of activity and has all the accompanying amenities, including showers, laundry, and store. Generators are allowed to run until 8 p.m. For quieter (no generators allowed) environs, our choice is the 85-site **Lewis Lake** campground on a hill overlooking the lake. Access, seclusion, and pretty sunsets seal the deal. Because reservations aren't accepted, try to get there early. But if you're coming in late and you've been shut out elsewhere, Lewis Lake is often your last best chance.

BEST LODGING OUTSIDE YNP

At 2 miles from Yellowstone's southern boundary, 🐾 ♿ 🍴 **Headwaters Lodge & Cabins at Flagg Ranch** ($$$/$$$$, 307-543-2861, June to October) is between Yellowstone and Grand Teton on flat, forested grounds. Just about everything is fairly new. Cabin choices are Deluxe and Premium, the difference being a mini-fridge and microwave in the Premiums. A gift shop, deli, and Sheffield's Restaurant & Bar are connected to the main lodge and the only choice for dinner and amenities without a drive. While Flagg Ranch makes a handy jumping-off point for both parks, it might be too isolated for some.

BEST ALTERNATIVE LODGING OUTSIDE YNP

CAMPING *Flagg Ranch:* 🐾 **Flagg Ranch Campground** ($, 307-543-2861, June to October and December to March), in the pines and near the Snake River, has 100 pull-through RV sites, 75 tent sites, and 40 camping cabins. They aren't cheap and perhaps not as desirable as other spots, but reservations are nevertheless recommended because the location does fill up. The campground is cramped, but what it lacks in scenery it compensates for in access to both parks.

Forest Service Cabins: One of the few rentable Forest Service cabins in the region, 🐾 **Squirrel Meadows Guard Station** (208-652-7442, May to March) is on Grassy Lake Road, about 24 miles east of Ashton, Idaho, and 28 miles west of Flagg Ranch. The 1934 two-bedroom cabin is only $40 a night and sleeps up to eight. As with most USFS rentals, propane cooking facilities, bunk beds, and mattresses are provided, but you're on your own for sheets, sleeping bags, pillows, dishes, etc. Restroom facilities are in a framed outhouse, and drinking water comes from an outdoor hand pump. Winter access is via snowmobile, skis, or snowshoes.

✳ Where to Eat

DINING IN YNP

The **Grant Village Dining Room** ($$, 307-242-3499, B/L/D, May to September) serves breakfast and lunch on a first-come, first-served basis. Breakfast can be ordered off the menu or self-served with a trip (or two) through the buffet.

Though cavernous open seating feels nonpersonal, it still ranks high in the ambiance category because of the piney views of Yellowstone Lake. Reservations are required for dinner. While you wait, cool your heels on one of seven bar stools at **Seven Stool Saloon.** For up-close and personal lakeside dining, the **Grant Village Lake House** ($/$$$, 307-344-7311, B/L/D, June to September) is a short walk through the woods to what was once a marina. Banks of tables lining the windows are preferred seating, but you can see the West Thumb of the lake from most any table. Once offering standard park fare, the menu now highlights sustainable purveyors. Breakfast is buffet only and all you can eat. Reservations are not accepted, so if you're looking for certainty, consider the **Old Faithful Inn Dining Room**, which accepts reservations.

BEST DINING OUTSIDE YNP

Flagg Ranch: **Sheffield's at Headwaters Lodge** ($$/$$$, 307-543-2861, B/L/D, June to September) has undergone

DINING AT GRANT VILLAGE INCLUDES A VIEWSCAPE OF YELLOWSTONE LAKE   JIM PEACO / NPS

an upgrade since Grand Teton Lodge Company took over operations. The solidly Western ambiance, highlighted by elk-antler chandeliers and log furniture, is much the same, but the menu a step up. As with other Yellowstone entities, Sheffield's puts emphasis on healthy and sustainable cuisine—what it calls "Appetite for Life"—that includes vegetarian and gluten-free selections. Regionally influenced offerings are the norm, starting with breakfast (Seattle's Best Coffee, Mountain Man trout and eggs), continuing through lunch (Teddy Roosevelt's Western chili, bison taco salad), and peaking at dinner (Grand Prismatic salad, Wyoming prime rib, seared local trout). Finish with tempting desserts such as the S'more Skillet. Got lucky? The kitchen will prepare your catch of the day with advance notice. Also here is the less-formal **Bistro and Saloon**, which opens at the crack of dawn. Sheffield's full menus are available during lunch and dinner hours, but choices are limited before and after.

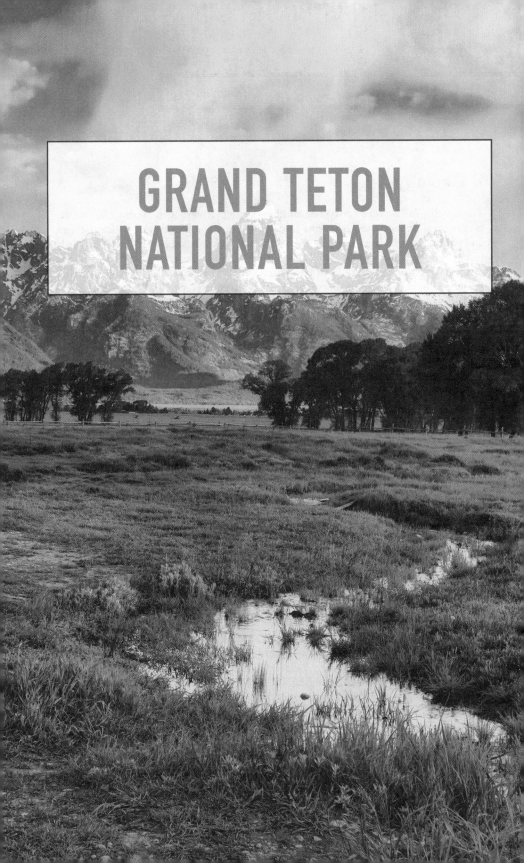

GRAND TETON NATIONAL PARK

A PRIMER

✳ Geology

The Greater Yellowstone Ecosystem contains some of America's most dramatic mountain ranges. Though each is unique in its splendor, none has captured imaginations and photographers' lenses like the Tetons. These "granite cathedrals" tower abruptly from the floor of Jackson Hole in a description-defying display of glacier-carved rock and ice. It's fitting that Grand Teton National Park is 57 years younger than the world's first national park just to the north, because in geological terms it's a mere baby.

The youngest of the Rocky Mountains was born in a geological nanosecond some 9 million to 13 million years ago, when the east and west sides of a 40-mile north–south fault decided, mostly via earthquakes and other released tensions, to go their separate ways—up on the west, down even more dramatically on the east. Imagine what a photographer's nirvana it would have been then. By the time the fault blocking and glacial carving had concluded, Grand Teton had risen from 6 miles underground to more than 5 miles above what would eventually be Jackson Hole.

Ever since, the limestone peaks of Grand Teton, Middle Teton, Owen, and Moran have eroded considerably. Much of the sediment has filled in Jackson Hole, signaling a likely reunion. Grand Teton has slipped to a mere 13,770 feet above sea level, less than 1.5 miles above the rising town of Jackson. Along the way, glaciers carved the jagged ridges and outcroppings that left the Tetons with unique contours once the last ice floe retreated about 13,000 years ago. Today, the Tetons are one of the world's premier visual wonders, especially from the east, where the fault-blocked rise and fall left few foothills to mar the views for photographers such as Ansel Adams and William Henry Jackson.

Every few thousand years or so, the gap between the valley floor and the top of the Tetons increases by a few feet due to a gentle temblor. But eventually Jackson Hole will rise and meet the tips of the Tetons—until the next great quake separates them again.

✳ People

One look at the toothy peaks of Grand Teton, Middle Teton, and Mount Moran would seem sufficient evidence to instantly declare the awe-inspiring area south of Yellowstone a national park. In fact, early Yellowstone superintendents and Wyoming politicians periodically proposed expanding YNP's boundaries southward. The US House of Representatives even approved setting aside the rock and ice of the Teton Range plus eight glacial lakes as a national park in 1929.

That was the easy part.

More than 75 years of controversy, political wrangling, and compromise would pass after the establishment of Yellowstone before an increasing tide of tourists empowered Washington in 1950 to create the Grand Teton National Park we know today.

SCAN FOR WILDLIFE AT WILLOW FLATS BETWEEN MESMERIZING GLANCES AT JACKSON LAKE AND THE TETONS
NPS

As much as wilderness purists sometimes blanch at the growth and unaffordability of Jackson, they would've cringed at what Jackson Hole had become at the beginning of the twentieth century. A utilitarian vision for the region south of Yellowstone began in 1910 with the construction of 70-foot-high Jackson Lake Dam on the Snake River. The dam enlarged an existing lake, flooding 7,200 acres of pines and backing up water to supply potato and beet farmers on the other side of the mountains in Idaho. The dam actually might've planted the seed for the park's creation half a century later. An ugly shanty town for construction workers sprang up overnight. Dead trees poked through the surface of Jackson Lake. The image quickly sparked an emotional preservation-versus-development debate.

Like those who appreciated Yellowstone's marvels, some entrepreneurs gazed at the grandeur of the Tetons and envisioned multitudes coming west to escape life's workaday pressures. The vacation dude ranches so prevalent today actually had their genesis at the time the dam was built. Their owners saw the benefit of preserving the scenic value of the area and began the long, winding, and bumpy road to protection.

In 1926, a visit by millionaire John D. Rockefeller, at the behest of Yellowstone superintendent Horace Albright and a coalition of dude ranchers, cattlemen, and others who feared exploitation of the valley, spurred action beyond protecting just the

JACKSON RESIDENTS CELEBRATE THE DEDICATION OF GRAND TETON NATIONAL PARK IN 1929. PARK BOUNDARIES WERE EXPANDED IN 1950 NPS

mountains as a national park. Rockefeller purchased 35,000 acres of delinquent ranches with the intent of donating the land to the newly created Park Service to add to the existing park. Knowing a giveaway to the federal government wouldn't sit well with ranchers who used the rocky valley as a cattle thoroughfare between summer and winter grazing lands, he bought the land covertly under a company name that implied his group would operate as a ranch.

The deal was complete in 1930 before locals knew what hit them, and many politicians and ranchers were furious. After Rockefeller's end run, opposition to further protection intensified. The ire was so fierce that the feds wouldn't even accept his donated land. Park opponents opined that expanding the boundaries would "lock up" land from development and put ranches out of business. For 13 years, they had their way with Congress.

In 1943, with the country distracted by World War II, President Franklin D. Roosevelt used his popularity to override Congress and accept Rockefeller's donation. Roosevelt took another 130,000 acres of Forest Service land and created the Jackson Hole National Monument, again with a predictable reaction. Wyoming politicians repeatedly introduced legislation to overturn the monument, only to be rebuked in Washington.

Ultimately, tourists saved a valley now challenged by their very passion for it. The money they brought during a celebratory post–World War II travel boom eased economic fears. In a move that would aid in the creation of future national parks and wilderness areas, the federal government compromised by "grandfathering" in the right of ranching families to run cattle and of hunters to pursue elk within certain parts of the new park boundaries. On September 14, 1950, Rockefeller's donated land and the national monument both were incorporated, bringing Grand Teton National Park to its present size.

Today nobody is more thankful than the residents of northwest Wyoming. No region in the state has a more consistently vibrant economy. Tourism flourishes at unprecedented levels. Though sprawl is evident, the park boundary, mountains, and the National Elk Refuge to the north limit Jackson's growth. And even that old eyesore, Jackson Lake Dam, was rebuilt in the late 1980s so that it's a better fit for the landscape. Above the dam, visitors to Jackson Lake Lodge now gaze over Willow Flats and shimmering lake waters to towering mountains that form arguably the most breathtaking backdrop in America.

✳ Wildlife

Grand Teton National Park doesn't take a backseat in this department, especially if your goal is to see a moose, grizzly bear, or the lovable little pika. You just have to know where to look.

GRIZZLIES ARE SO ROUTINELY VIEWED IN GRAND TETON THAT THE PARK NOW REQUIRES VEHICLES TO STAY AT LEAST 100 YARDS AWAY NPS

BIGHORN SHEEP The National Elk Refuge isn't just for elk. Rising on the east side is Miller Butte, where bighorns routinely are seen from the road in the winter. The rest of the year, they're in the mountains and you'll probably need to be on a trail.

BISON Take a drive through the sage in Antelope Flats, especially around Mormon Row. They're also visible from US 89, typically on the east side of the highway. In the winter, they're often at the National Elk Refuge, where food is readily available. Unlike Yellowstone's genetically pure bison, Grand Teton's are hybridized with cattle.

BEAR (BLACK) Black bears cover much of Grand Teton, though stream corridors and brushy areas with food sources are far more fertile than the open sagebrush plains. Keep your eyes focused as you drive slowly along Moose-Wilson Road, especially near hillsides with berry bushes.

BEAR (GRIZZLY) Grand Teton is home to the most popular and photographed wild grizzly bears in the world—22-year-old (in 2018) Grizzly Bear No. 399 and her 16 offspring. The family often is spotted along Moose-Wilson Road in the south to Pilgrim Creek on the north, but the hub seems to be around Jackson Lake Lodge and the dam. Because the crowd-pleasing bears often create traffic jams, vehicles must remain at least 100 yards from grizzlies in Grand Teton.

EAGLE Thermals created by the Tetons plus an abundance of prey make the park an ideal home for bald and golden eagles. Look for the larger, darker, gold-hued, and equally majestic goldens soaring at elevations above 10,000 feet. For the tow-headed bald eagles, the best viewing is along rivers or lakes.

ELK Wapiti are guaranteed in the winter and spring when they congregate by the thousands for alfalfa pellets served by the National Elk Refuge. In the summers, most

FOR A SHOW OF BRUTE STRENGTH, IT'S HARD TO TOP SPARRING BULL MOOSE NPS

elk disperse into high country, though they are seen amid the sage and aspen in the park. In the summer, grab binoculars and a huckleberry margarita, then hunker down at the Willow Flats overlook at Jackson Lake Lodge. During the spring and fall, migrating elk are in Antelope Flats and along Moose-Wilson Road.

MOOSE Sightings of this rangy behemoth remain relatively common despite its recent woes, including along and near Flat Creek in Jackson. The Gros Ventre River drainage on the northern edge of the National Elk Refuge is another prime location. Ditto for the ponds and soggy landscapes along Moose-Wilson Road, Willow Flats, and Oxbow Bend along the Snake River.

MULE DEER This stately ungulate made big news when it was discovered that it had eclipsed the pronghorn for longest overland mammal migration in the continental United States. Each year they disperse from GTNP and move southeast in the Wind River Range to the deserts of southern Wyoming. Mule deer are visible in much of the park.

PIKA One of the more personable creatures to watch is the pika, which inhabits rocky areas on mountainous slopes. The cherubic little mouse-like creature often performs for hikers on the Cascade Canyon Trail above Jenny Lake. It is also highly vulnerable to a changing climate: Pikas can overheat and die at temperatures above 78 degrees.

PRONGHORN (ANTELOPE) You're certain to see these speedsters in either Antelope Flats or Elk Ranch Flats, wandering amid the sagebrush. Timbered Ridge southeast of Jenny Lake is another safe bet. In the fall and spring, these creatures undertake an overland migration from the park to and from the Red Desert, some 180 miles to the south.

WOLF Truth is, if you want to see wolves, you're better off heading north. In the winter, wolves are occasionally seen on the fringes of the Elk Refuge, looking for a vulnerable elk or bison. Typically, the densest populations are south and east of GTNP, along Gros Ventre Road, where the pack of the same name roams. Most are concentrated in the forests and mountains on the east side of the valley and difficult to see.

PIKAS ARE FRISKY LITTLE CRITTERS THAT LOVE GRAND TETON'S ROCKY SLOPES NPS

WHAT'S WHERE IN GRAND TETON

Practical Information for Your Visit

LICENSES/PERMITS

Backcountry: Walk-in permits are $35 and available at recreation.gov; reservations are accepted at one-third of campsites, the remainder are first-come, first-served. Garnet Canyon permits must be picked up at Jenny Lake Ranger Station, along with backcountry permits involving mountaineering or technical climbing. Grand Teton has 16 backcountry camping "zones" that require a $25 nonrefundable deposit for reservations (307-739-3309). They are strongly recommended and usually necessary due to the popularity of backcountry camping.

Boating: Motorized craft are allowed only on Jackson and Jenny Lakes. The permit is $40 and there is a 10-horsepower maximum on Jenny Lake. Water-skiers, surfers, and sailboats are allowed only on Jackson Lake. Nonmotorized craft—canoes, kayaks, driftboats, and stand-up paddleboards—are $12 and allowed on Phelps, Emma Matilda, Two Ocean, Taggart, Bradley, Bearpaw, Leigh, and String Lakes. Wyoming also requires aquatic invasive species decals and inspections: $5 for Wyoming owners and $15 for out-of-state owners.

Fishing: The park is fully within Wyoming and subject to state fishing regulations. Nonresident daily tags are $14 and five-day tags are $56; fees are $6 and $27 for residents. Anything longer than a one-day tag also requires a Conservation Stamp. Unlike Yellowstone, GTNP does not have a park license.

Hunting: A half-price autumn elk hunt is conducted in a portion of the park to help reduce numbers spilling from the adjacent National Elk Refuge. A $15.50 Elk Special Management Permit and proof of hunter-safety certification is required. Only one elk may be taken.

SPECIAL PROGRAMS Ranger-led activities start in late spring and continue into late fall. Activities take place at Colter Bay, Jackson Lake Lodge, Gros Ventre Campground, Signal Mountain Lodge, Lizard Creek Campground, and Flagg Ranch. Guided hikes are organized at Jenny Lake and Colter Bay. Junior Ranger Programs offer outings for kids of all ages. **Teton Science School** (307-733-4765) is a longstanding program that has its original campus in Kelly and a 900-acre campus between Jackson and Wilson. Learn about nearly every aspect of the natural processes taking place in the Greater Yellowstone Ecosystem. Classes are geared to kids and college-age adults. Seminars ranging from one to five days are offered during the summer tourist season, and simple lectures are available for a nominal fee. A part of the science schools is the Murie Ranch, located a stone's throw from park headquarters at Moose. Tours and "Front Porch Conversations" take place throughout the summer.

VISITOR CENTERS **Craig Thomas Discovery and Visitor Center** (307-739-3399) at Moose is open from 8 a.m. to 7 p.m. in the summer and from 8 a.m. to 5 p.m. in spring, fall, and winter. This palatial, innovative, and high-tech center is a worthwhile first stop. It is home to exhibits, including one that takes a close look at the area's endangered species, a relief map of the park, and videos running full time on the floor. The only day the center closes is Christmas.

Jenny Lake (307-739-3343) is open May to September. It stays open from 8 a.m. to 7 p.m. in June, July, and August, then from 8 a.m. to 5 p.m. in May and September. It's 8 miles north of Moose at the junction of Teton Park Road and is also the location of a ranger station.

Colter Bay (307-739-3594) opens from 8 a.m. to 7 p.m. during peak season from early May to early September, and changes from 8 a.m. to 5 p.m. in late spring and early fall. Demonstrations, tours, and crafts are exhibited much of the summer.

Flagg Ranch (307-543-2372) is open from 9 a.m. to 5:30 p.m. from June to August and has irregular hours from mid-December to mid-March. It's between the two parks, off the John D. Rockefeller Memorial Parkway, 16 miles north of Colter Bay.

Laurence S. Rockefeller Preserve Center (307-739-3654) is open from 9 a.m. to 5 p.m. from the end of May until the third week of September. At this education center you'll get a glimpse of why conservation has mattered to generations of Rockefellers. The land on which the preserve is located was donated by the Rockefeller family to the park.

GRAND TETON NATIONAL PARK

*North Entrance to Jackson Lake Junction /
Jackson Lake Junction to Moran / Jackson Lake
Junction to Moose / Moran to Moose / Moose to
Gros Ventre Junction / Gros Ventre Junction to
Jackson / Antelope Flats Road / Gros Ventre
Road / Moose-Wilson Road*

Gateway Communities: Jackson, Victor, and Driggs

✳ Overview

If Yellowstone is a living, breathing example of an intact ecosystem, Grand Teton is its visual alter ego. The park certainly has a wild flavor, too, but the primary draw here is obvious: magnificent views of the most mesmerizing mountains in the lower 48 states from nearly every road in the valley.

First, some definition: Most of Grand Teton National Park is part of a larger area known as Jackson Hole. One of the best places to appreciate how and why this high-altitude valley got its name is atop Teton Pass. At just above 6,000 feet, the southwest corner of Jackson Hole is its lowest part. Though the "hole" appears to be table-flat, the northern end is actually about 700 feet higher. It isn't unusual in late spring to be amid patches of snow at Moran Junction and in blossoming wildflowers around Jackson. Another important component of Jackson Hole is the National Elk Refuge on the northern fringe of Jackson.

The appeal of Jackson Hole partially explains why Teton County consistently flirts with having the most expensive real estate in the nation. A major factor: Only 3 percent of the county's roughly 2.7 million acres is in private hands, with the remaining 97 percent owned by the public in the form of the park, elk refuge, Forest Service, Bureau of Land Management, and state lands. South of the park, spectacular trophy homes, resorts, dude ranches, and even a few working ranches dominate or mesh with a landscape that has become a destination for the rich and famous as well as for the young and active. Ski areas, golf courses, and high-end shopping, lodging, and dining reflect the county's exclusivity. Indeed, to Wyomingites from any other county, the telltale "22" on Teton County license plates is tantamount to out of state.

✳ Getting Here

Few airports offer a more rewarding arrival than Jackson Hole Airport (JAC)—the only commercial airport in America completely within the confines of a national park.

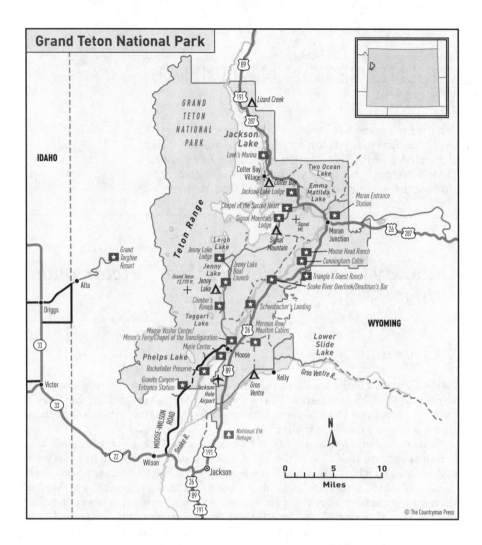

Landings are always north to south, with the approach from the east, so book a window seat on the right side of the aircraft for a bird's-eye view of the Tetons and Jackson Lake. Of course, that means takeoffs are south to north and the left side is most coveted. Seasonal service is provided most prolifically by United from Denver, with up to six flights daily during busy seasons. Delta and SkyWest serve Jackson Hole from Atlanta, Minneapolis, Salt Lake City, Seattle, Los Angeles, and New York. American is Dallas/Fort Worth, Los Angeles, Chicago, and Phoenix. Frontier comes from Denver, and United has service from Chicago, Houston, San Francisco, and Los Angeles. United also connects with Newark during the ski season. Saturdays are the busiest days in the summer; be sure to check the airport's website for parking updates because the lot fills.

Once on the ground, it's 7 miles via taxi or rental car south on US 26/89/191 into Jackson. No fewer than 10 taxi and nine rental car agencies plus Uber serve the airport.

MOULTON BARN ON MORMON ROW MIGHT BE THE MOST PHOTOGENIC BARN IN AMERICA

✳ Along the Way

For drivers, four US highways converge at Jackson, all from scenic directions. If you're coming south from Yellowstone National Park, the fastest route is US 26/89/191 on the east side of Jackson Hole—be aware of moose, bison, elk, and other wildlife on the road. A more relaxing and awe-inspiring alternative is to turn south at Jackson Lake Junction and take the well-traveled, paved interior road for 10 miles to Moose. For the time being, you won't have to purchase a GTNP pass if you're coming from Yellowstone because there is no entrance station.

If you're arriving from the west, US 26 and ID 31 leave Idaho Falls and eventually fork in different directions. US 26 hugs the South Fork of the Snake River past Palisades Reservoir and the Grand Canyon of the Snake through Hoback Junction. ID 31 arches over a small pass to the junction of ID 33 in the burgeoning little community of Victor.

From here, it's a steep climb to Teton Pass for a panoramic view climaxed by a wood sign declaring, "Howdy, pardner, you're in Jackson Hole!" A winding, 6-mile, 10-percent grade leads to the valley floor at Wilson. Neither drive offers much culturally, though ID 31 passes near the site of the 1976 Teton Dam collapse, which sent 80 billion gallons of water through three towns and killed 11. You can drive to a ruddy overlook, but there isn't much left other than an eerie sense of dread.

From the east, the choice is the Wyoming Centennial Scenic Byway on US 26/287 up the red-rock Wind River Valley, along the base of the towering Wind River Range to Dubois. From there, it's over Togwotee Pass to the first views of the Tetons and Moran Junction. Reserve time for Lander, an outdoor-recreation hub where you'll find the Museum of the American West and photogenic Sinks Canyon State Park. The splashy

BEFORE YOU WERE HERE

Not surprisingly, today's herds of tourists aren't the only people who've gazed in wonder at the Teton Range and felt touched spiritually.

From all accounts, the indigenous peoples who spent their summers in the shadows of the Tetons also revered the towering mountains serving as sentinels to Jackson Hole. The Blackfeet, Crow, Shoshone, Bannock, Nez Perce, and Gros Ventre all hunted and/or fished in the Snake River Valley as they prepared to disperse for slightly warmer winters elsewhere.

Big game was plentiful. So were berries and roots, particularly the camas. The Shoshone are said to have used as many as 125 plant species for food and medicine.

Interestingly, though two prominent natural features are named for the Gros Ventre tribe—a river and mountain range flanking the east side of Jackson Hole—little of their history is recorded on the Grand Teton landscape. The Gros Ventre, literally "big belly" in French, mostly lived a nomadic existence in what is now northern Montana and southern Saskatchewan. They were given that name by the French, who did the same for the Hidatsa band of the Sioux. The Gros Ventre called themselves *A'aninin*, or "White Clay People."

Today the Gros Ventre mostly reside on the Fort Belknap Reservation in northern Montana. The Plains Indians section of Buffalo Bill Center of the West in Cody is a fine place to learn more about the Gros Ventre.

Middle Fork of the Popo Agie River disappears into a limestone cavern and re-emerges at "The Rise" about 350 yards downstream.

And from the south, there are two options, depending on whether you're coming from the east or west on I-80. US 191 heads due north from Rock Springs, and US 189 exits the freeway just east of Evanston. Both knife through the sagebrush desert of the upper Green River Valley to a junction at Daniel, 11 miles west of Pinedale. The highway then eases over a gentle pass near Bondurant and drops along the Wild and Scenic Hoback River to a meeting with the Snake River at Hoback Junction. Pinedale has a beautiful Wind River Range backdrop and beckons with the Museum of the Mountain Man. If you choose US 191, stop at the Farson Mercantile, a.k.a. Home of the Big Cone, for mounds of ice cream, a malted, or a shake.

�֍ Gateway Communities

JACKSON, WYOMING

First things first: Jackson and Jackson Hole are not the same, though both are named after an early surveyor named Davy Jackson. Jackson (population 10,500) is the town, while Jackson Hole encompasses the entire valley. Long ago, indigenous peoples came to Jackson Hole in the summers to hunt the bountiful wildlife. It wasn't until 1807, when John Colter veered south from the Lewis and Clark Expedition on the return trip to St. Louis, that the first Anglos saw the region. Fur trappers soon followed to pursue beaver, and many a mountain man converged to rendezvous in the "hole" between the Teton and Gros Ventre Mountains.

Serious settlement didn't begin until the 1880s, a decade after Yellowstone National Park's birth piqued interest in the region. Jackson was founded in 1894 as a hub for the cattle-ranching industry and destination for wealthy eastern hunters. Remnants of a few original buildings remain in Town Square, where Jackson's famed elk-antler

VIBRANT JACKSON IS A BLEND OF COWBOY CULTURE, URBAN CHIC, AND OUTDOORSY TYPES WITH A DOSE OF OLD-TIME MOM-AND-POP

arches mark the four corners. An early hint this would be no ordinary town came in 1920, a year after women were given the right to vote nationally, when Jackson democratically elected a woman mayor and an all-woman city council—a first for the young nation. A rope tow was installed at Teton Pass in 1937, and Snow King opened a few years later, the first ski area in Wyoming.

The movie industry certainly contributed to Jackson's economy. *Nanette of the North* was filmed in Jackson Hole in 1921, John Wayne's first speaking part was recorded in Jackson in 1932, and *Shane* was produced near Kelly two decades later. Henry Fonda's *Spencer's Mountain* in 1963 also brought the region to the big screen.

Today it's a magnet for artists, writers, photographers, and other creative types as well as high-powered, deep-pocketed folks from around the world. Celebrities flock to Jackson, grateful for relative anonymity and greetings of little more than a nod or shrug. It's part of the Jackson charm, even though real estate values are off the charts. Galleries blend seamlessly with curios shops, cosmopolitan restaurants flourish beside busy BBQ joints, swanky resorts reside by throwback mom-and-pop motels, and the wealthy mingle comfortably with carefree outdoorsy types in a place where expensive jeans now come with holes.

JACKSON LAKE LODGE: A CONTROVERSIAL ICON

Depending on one's perspective, Jackson Lake Lodge is either an icon of modern construction brilliantly designed to highlight the views of Jackson Lake, Willow Flats, and Grand Teton . . . or an architectural abomination that no more belongs in a western national park than a fire lookout in Times Square. When it was completed in 1955, many national park enthusiasts accustomed to the rustic and stately elegance of Yellowstone's Old Faithful Inn and Oregon's Crater Lake Lodge were aghast at architect Gilbert Stanley Underwood's creation. Underwood used massive amounts of concrete, and the buildings are mostly oddly shaped rectangles, leaving some to compare the lodge to a bomb shelter. Nevertheless, first-time and annual visitors alike can't help but stop in their tracks after ascending a flight of stairs into a lobby with giant picture windows framing Willow Flats, the lake, and the Tetons. And the views only improve when you step onto the lengthy back deck at the main lodge. Over the years there have been occasional calls to tear down the sprawling structure, but it's too late now: Jackson Lake Lodge became a National Historic Landmark in 2003.

VICTOR, IDAHO

Once the end of a major railroad spur for cattle and sheep production, Victor is the first town after arriving over Teton Pass from Jackson. For years, Victor was a quiet and affordable option for people who cleaned rooms, waited tables, and ran ski lifts in Jackson Hole. But the tentacles of riches have reached across the pass to what locals call "Wilson West," a comparative reference to the last little community on the Wyoming side. It's still a sweet village with a bicycle shop that moved from Jackson, a Midwest-style soda fountain, two microbreweries, and a well-stocked grocery store with the best meat and deli counter in the region. The town truly knows how to take a second seat with class.

DRIGGS, IDAHO

This predominantly Mormon farming and ranching community in Idaho's seed-potato country is experiencing the benefits and costs of discovery. For that, the town of 1,736 can thank—or blame—the prolific snows at nearby Grand Targhee Ski Resort and spillover from Jackson. Once an affordable outlying area where service workers could live and commute over Teton Pass without busting the bank, Driggs is a recreation haven for the energetic. Victor and Driggs are in a picturesque U-shaped valley framed by the Teton and Big Hole Ranges, with the Teton River flowing through.

✳ Hitting the Road

NORTH ENTRANCE TO JACKSON LAKE JUNCTION (16 MILES)

Think of this as the transition zone beginning 8 miles from Yellowstone's South Entrance. Much of this forested stretch follows the east shore of Jackson Lake, past Colter Bay Village and a marina. This is where the Teton Range comes into view, starting with block-shaped 12,605-foot-high Mount Moran.

You'll get a free ride into Grand Teton coming from this direction because there isn't an entrance station, and park officials say there are no immediate plans for one even though separate fees are now required. Everything you need to know about Grand Teton is available at the Flagg Ranch Information Station and bookstore. About 5 miles past Flagg Ranch, the park's northern border touches the northernmost tip of Jackson Lake. Soon after crossing into the park, you'll see the lake out the passenger side of your vehicle. The first lake access is in another 2.5 miles, at Lizard Creek Campground. In another mile is a lakeside picnic area, followed in short order by Jackson Lake Overlook and

three more picnic sites before the turnoff to Leeks Marina, a must-stop pizzeria with splendid accompanying views from the deck.

Another mile south is Colter Bay Village, a preferred hangout for families wanting an economical vacation. The lakeshore setting has 166 refurbished homestead cabins, a visitor center, store, marina, two restaurants, showers, and a gas station. A number of easy trails through the forest and along several waterways begin at Colter Bay. Back on US 89/191/287, the road makes a sweeping southward bend to the turnoff for Jackson Lake Lodge.

Jackson Lake Lodge has 348 cottages and 37 rooms in the main lodge, a medical clinic, a gas station, corrals for horseback adventures, two restaurants, and our second-favorite lounge deck in Grand Teton (behind Dornan's at Moose). The grounds are the best in the park for wildlife viewing, especially behind the lodge, so bring binoculars or

THOMAS MORAN'S PAINTINGS INSPIRED PEOPLE TO PROTECT WILD LANDSCAPES NPS

a spotting scope. Elk and moose are common in Willow Flats, and it isn't unusual to see a grizzly.

JACKSON LAKE JUNCTION TO MORAN (5 MILES)

This short stretch is best known for proximity to the Snake River downstream from Jackson Lake Dam. Most notable is the Oxbow Bend Turnout, where on a calm day you can see for yourself the often-photographed reflection of Mount Moran in the glassy surface. Look for elk, pelicans, swans, and perhaps Grizzly 399 and her family. About 1 mile before the Moran Entrance Station is a left turn on paved Pacific Creek Road and access to trailheads for Emma Matilda and Two Ocean Lake. The asphalt portion extends to the park's boundary with the Teton Wilderness Area. One gravel road veers north toward Two Ocean Lake; a subsequent dirt road continues about 3 miles, also to the boundary between the park and wilderness area. This is Grand Teton's wildest and most wildlife-rich country and the place where wolves spilling over from Yellowstone first arrived. Though these trails are well traveled, carry bear spray.

JACKSON LAKE JUNCTION TO MOOSE (20 MILES)

Teton Park Road winds through the heart of the park and is famed for viewpoints and access to all things Grand Teton. The road weaves in and out of sagebrush and stands of lodgepole and aspen. Shortly after making the right turn at Jackson Lake Junction, you'll pass through the southern edge of Willow Flats. Look for well-camouflaged wildlife in the willows, especially moose and elk, as you cross the century-old dam. Fishermen congregate below the spillway and also ply the waters of Jackson Lake, known for its state-record lake trout (50 pounds). Past the dam about a mile is the log Chapel of the Sacred Heart, an active Catholic church overlooking the lake where services are conducted on weekends in the summers, along with the occasional wedding.

About 0.5 mile past the chapel is the turn for Signal Mountain Lodge, operated independently from the park's other lodges and the only lakeside resort. Begun in the late 1920s with three cabins and three boats, the hillside spread features modest look-alike cabins, a campground, marina with boat rentals, gift and grocery stores, and fuel. Ownership has been the same since 1984 and enhancements are ongoing.

Signal Mountain Lodge is squeezed between the lake and 7,725-foot Signal Mountain, reached via a winding 4.8-mile paved road to the summit. Signal Mountain rises 800 feet above the valley floor and shows off with views of the Tetons, Jackson Lake, and a sizable chunk of Jackson Hole. The turnoff is a mile south of Signal Mountain Lodge. No large motor homes or trailers are permitted.

South of Signal Mountain Road is the north junction for seldom-used River Road and 15 miles of paradise for a mountain biker or anyone with a four-wheel-drive vehicle. In about 3 miles River Road turns right, but another stretch of gravel continues down to the edge of the Snake River. River Road crosses a sage plain along the west side of the Snake until it rejoins Teton Park Road and is an excellent place to see bison.

JENNY LAKE IS CONSIDERED THE CROWN JEWEL OF GRAND TETON'S WATERS, ESPECIALLY BY PADDLERS

Back on Teton Park Road, nearly 2 miles south of Signal Mountain on the left is the Potholes Turnout, so named for its views of glacial depressions, or kettles, carved from the ground as chunks of ice were covered by glacial outwash. About 0.5 mile later on the right is a pullout for a look at block-shaped Mount Moran, at 12,605 feet probably second only to Grand Teton as the most photographed mountain in the range. After snapping a few shots of the seemingly flat-topped peak beyond the southernmost tip of Jackson Lake, look for a gravel turnoff on the right about 2 miles later. This short cutoff leads to Spalding Bay, with a boat launch and primitive camping where pets are allowed as long as they are restrained.

Up next on Teton Park Road is north Jenny Lake junction, the beginning of a loop that is a slower but more picturesque way to cover the next several miles to the south junction. The road drops to trailheads for Strong and Leigh Lakes for 1.5 miles before becoming one-way. At that point it hugs Jenny Lake's wooded east shore past Jenny Lake Lodge to the Jenny Lake Visitor Center. Jenny Lake is the one attraction in Grand Teton that nobody skips, whether to take the shuttle boat to Cascade Canyon, hike around the lake, or simply marvel at crystal-clear waters. The visitor center, housed in a log cabin once the home of park artist Harrison Crandall, is rich with information and ranger-led programs.

The roads reconnect a short drive from here. Teton Park Road rolls another 8 miles through sage and intermittent forest past several scenic turnouts and trailheads to Moose. Midway through the journey you'll notice the Climbers' Ranch (307-733-7271, June to September) on the right. Run by nonprofit American Alpine Club, the ranch has modestly priced bunking for mountain climbers only.

On the left and close to the Moose Entrance Station are the Menors Ferry Historic District and Chapel of the Transfiguration. The chapel is a 1925 log Episcopal church that remains active, and the view of the Tetons through small windows in the back is exquisite. Here, a homesteader named William D. Menor put down roots and built a cable ferry on the Snake in 1890. For a quarter of a century it was the only way to cross the river for miles. The store Menor built still stands and is a museum of sorts, housing a collection of artifacts left by early settlers. A replica of the ferry still carries folks across the river, conditions permitting.

THE CHAPEL OF THE TRANSFIGURATION WAS BUILT AT MOOSE IN 1925 TO SERVE GUESTS AT AREA DUDE RANCHES NPS

Moose is a cluster of buildings, including park headquarters and an entrance station. The 22,000-square-foot Craig Thomas Discovery and Visitor Center is named after a Wyoming senator who drove legislation to protect nearly 400 miles of the Snake River headwaters just before he died in 2007. The center has an extraordinary collection of displays, videos, and technological innovations that'll keep you occupied. Across the Snake is a busy assortment of commercial endeavors on a private inholding within park boundaries, including Dornan's Spur Ranch Cabins, a restaurant and bar, outdoor adventure shops, a gas station, terrific wine shop, and a few other tourism-related businesses. The site has been owned and operated by the Dornan family for six decades.

MORAN TO MOOSE (18 MILES)

Though less interesting than Teton Park Road, this straight shot on a sagebrush bench on US 26/89/191 above the river is the faster route to Jackson, though not lacking in highlights and vistas. Moran is at the confluence of the braided Buffalo Fork and Snake Rivers. Be on the lookout for moose in the first few miles of wooded and watery roadside. After a short distance, the road elevates away from the Snake into sage and grasslands where cattle and sometimes bison mingle. About 2.5 miles south of Moran Junction is the Elk Ranch Flats Turnout, the first place to absorb the grandeur of the Tetons.

Take a leg stretch 3 miles later at Cunningham Cabin, the sod-roofed log cabin built by John Pierce Cunningham and his wife, Margaret, in 1890. The Cunninghams were early proponents of preserving the area as a national park, though they weren't around to see it to fruition. They also are known for constructing the trademark buck-and-rail fence that has become a fixture in Jackson Hole. A peek inside the abandoned cabin offers a sense of what it was like a century ago; the windows perfectly frame the Tetons. Back across the highway is a 5-mile gravel road that loops back to the main road after circling to the east.

Less than a mile beyond Cunningham Cabin is Triangle X Ranch, the only dude-ranch concession in the country within National Park Service jurisdiction. The ranch was purchased by the Turner family in 1926 and sold a few years later to a company serving as a front for the Rockefeller family's effort to buy land for a proposed national park. Many of the Turners moved to other parts of the valley, but a son, John, continued to operate Triangle X as a dude and hunting ranch outside the initial park boundary. When the boundary expanded in 1950, it included Triangle X, but the property was "grandfathered" in. Third- and fourth-generation Turners operate the ranch today under a Park Service contract through 2025.

About 1.5 miles south of Triangle X is a little treat that doesn't appear on most maps. Hedrick Pond, one of the many glacial kettles found in this area, is the site where Henry Fonda's 1963 movie *Spencer's Mountain*—the basis for the 1970s television show *The Waltons*—was filmed. The occasional trumpeter swan is also fond of the pond.

HISTORIC CUNNINGHAM CABIN OFFERS A PEEK INTO THE PAST AND GLIMPSES OF THE PRESENT

THE TETON RANGE CREATES A RIVETING BACKDROP FOR MANY NEW AND RETURNING VISITORS NPS

The remainder of the drive toward Moose is across Antelope Flats, and on clear days views of the Tetons simply won't quit. About 2 miles past Triangle X is a short gravel descent to Deadman's Bar, a much-used launching ramp for scenic Snake River floats. It's named for an 1886 incident in which three men were killed. The turn is near the Snake River Overlook, made famous by Ansel Adams's brooding 1942 black-and-white photo. Roughly across the highway from the overlook is a gravel road leading toward Shadow Mountain, the upscale Lost Creek Ranch, and some swanky private homes. The ascent to the summit of 8,252-foot Shadow Mountain isn't recommended for RVs or trailers. The Teton backdrop at the summit is nothing short of stunning.

Continuing south on US 26/89/191, you'll pass the Teton Point Turnout and arrive 2 miles later at the turn for Schwabacher's Landing, one of four Snake River boat launches. Even if you don't have a boat, a short walk upstream leads to exceptional photo ops of sunsets behind the mountains. Scan the beaver ponds for wildlife such as pronghorn, deer, and elk. Back on the highway, continue the sensory feast, first at Glacier View Turnout and then at Blacktail Ponds, across from the Antelope Flats Road turn.

MOOSE TO GROS VENTRE JUNCTION (8 MILES)

This stretch is more of the same, with increasing indications you're nearing Jackson. Look for elk and bison on either side of the highway and get your camera ready for the Albright View Turnout, the last stop before reaching the junction for Jackson Hole Airport.

GROS VENTRE JUNCTION TO JACKSON (8 MILES)

As Jackson nears, posh neighborhoods spring up to the west of the highway, where elk and moose often graze on rose bushes and other shrubs. Immediately after Gros Ventre Junction the highway crosses the Gros Ventre River. The large fence you'll see angling along the highway on the east side south of the river epitomizes this meeting of urban and rural. The fence represents the northern and western edge of the National Elk Refuge. If you're passing through in the summer, don't bother looking for elk on the mostly flat, wide-open, empty landscape; they've headed for the high country. In the winter, the wapiti are in easy view. At any time of year, look for moose in the Gros Ventre River bottom and scan for bison on either side of the river.

Beyond the park boundary, on the east side of the highway along Flat Creek, is Jackson National Fish Hatchery (307-733-2510). Some 200,000 Snake River cutthroat trout are produced each year to replenish populations in Wyoming and Idaho. The hatchery's Sleeping Indian Pond is an ideal place for kids to learn casting and to experience the thrill of catching a trout, whether on a worm or a fly. The hatchery is open daily except holidays. About 2 miles later, on the flanks of East Gros Ventre Butte overlooking the elk refuge, the National Museum of Wildlife Art (307-733-5771) is a treasure trove of nature and wildlife art housed in an expansive rock structure that resembles a southwestern kiva. Visitors are treated to sculptures, paintings, photography, and other exhibits that bring the West's wildlife and nature to life.

Entering Jackson, be sure to stop at one of the finest information facilities anywhere: the Jackson Hole & Greater Yellowstone Visitor Center, a cooperative effort among seven government agencies and other groups. The impressive wildlife diorama is a highlight in a place you could spend hours gleaning information about the ecosystem. Be sure to check out the observation deck overlooking the southern end of the elk refuge. To see the refuge from another angle, head east on Pearl Street from downtown and continue several miles. Eventually the road turns to gravel and winds out of the valley toward Curtis Canyon. There are several wonderful viewpoints of the valley floor and Tetons.

ANTELOPE FLATS ROAD (7 MILES)

This flat, paved road heads east near Moose and is the primary route to Mormon Row, where homes and barns of early settlements remain. Mormon settlers from Idaho arrived in the 1890s and created a cluster of 27 homesteads. The six remaining today fell into disrepair until 1990, when the Park Service began preservation. Among them are Moulton Ranch Cabins, once one of the most appealing settings for lodging in Jackson Hole but only for national park staff starting in 2019. North of the road at the Mormon Row intersection is yet another place you'll recognize from numerous photos: the classic Moulton Barn and its Tetons backdrop. Photographers likely will be moving in and out of the sagebrush, looking for the precise spot others have stood to capture the majesty. Bison are common amid the grasses, wildflowers, and sage, and the

THE NATIONAL ELK REFUGE: AN ONGOING DILEMMA

In 1912, an unusually harsh winter settled over Jackson Hole and its rapidly growing hub community, Jackson. Until then, elk had migrated into the valley once the snow flew in search of forage, as they had for thousands of years, and the few hardy souls who wintered in Jackson Hole paid scant attention.

But in 1912, with development having encroached on habitat and snows piling ever deeper, the citizens of Jackson were witnessing an agonizing sight: starving elk stumbling, staggering, and collapsing before their eyes. A well-intentioned citizenry came to the rescue by tossing hay onto the snow. A wildlife refuge and annual tradition were born.

Nearly every winter since, Jackson has fed elk, typically with alfalfa pellets and/or hay dropped from a truck, and in the process the herd has grown to anywhere from 7,000 to 10,000 animals—well above the refuge's stated capacity of 5,000. Results have been mixed. On the one hand, outfitters can promise successful hunts and residents can take visitors on sleigh rides amid wild elk. As long as people remain in the sleighs, the habituated animals barely notice.

On the other hand, the unnatural congregation of so many animals has altered the ecosystem. For instance, the banks of Flat Creek coursing through the refuge feature 100-year-old willows an inch tall, all grazed to the nubs each year. Another challenge is the prevalence of diseases such as brucellosis, scabies, and hoof rot. What has biologists most worried is the arrival of the always-fatal chronic wasting disease (CWD), a brain disorder related to mad cow disease and Creutzfeldt-Jakob disease in humans; CWD was first detected in Grand Teton in a mule deer buck in November 2018. Another consequence of artificial feeding: to keep numbers manageable, GTNP conducts a hunt every autumn—the only national park to allow the activity.

As Jackson commemorated a century of feeding in 2012, the community was divided over whether to continue. Supporters don't want to see elk starve again and risk losing the herd's hefty economic benefits. Detractors envision a natural ecosystem resulting in a healthier herd and the return of other wildlife. Animal experts agreed that the arrival of chronic wasting was inevitable but debate the consequences, with powerful constituents on both sides relying on information that backs their stance.

pavement is a favorite of road cyclists. Antelope Flats Road continues east for nearly 2 miles before making a sharp right turn toward Kelly.

GROS VENTRE ROAD (9 MILES)

This paved stretch follows the river along the edge of the elk refuge to the Bridger-Teton National Forest. Check out the funky little settlement of Kelly along the way; it's known for its unusual dwellings, including yurts. Keep going past Kelly on Gros Ventre Road to a right turn, where once you rise into the aspens you can still see a decaying cabin used in the filming of the movie classic *Shane* in 1951. Outside the park boundary is the Gros Ventre Slide, where the entire mountainside slid about 1.5 miles into the river in 1925 and formed Slide Lake. Learn more about this natural phenomenon on the Gros Ventre Geological Trail, past what is now Lower Slide Lake.

MOOSE-WILSON ROAD (10 MILES)

This favorite is actually two drives in one. From Moose to the tiny Granite Canyon Entrance Station, it is a narrow and sometimes winding, mostly paved road through

The elk refuge is one of 23 such winter feed grounds in western Wyoming and costs state taxpayers over $2 million annually. It's notable that neighboring Montana and Idaho have banned feeding and worry that afflicted animals will bring diseases to their states in the summers. Oddly, Idaho allows fenced game ranches and Wyoming outlaws them, offering the same argument Idaho makes against feeding. Warmer temperatures could resolve the feeding issue, at least at the National Elk Refuge. In the winter of 2017–18, Jackson Hole was warm enough that officials eschewed distributing pellets for the first time in 37 years.

THOUSANDS OF ELK GATHER FOR THE WINTER FEEDINGS AT THE NATIONAL ELK REFUGE, AN ANNUAL RITE THAT BEGAN IN 1912 WHEN NATURAL FORAGE WAS SCARCE

aspen and pine stands, with a mile of washboarded gravel thrown in to keep the traffic and speeds at a minimum. Elk, moose, bear, beaver, and other wildlife frequent the marshes and hillsides. South of the entrance station, the road widens and passes Teton Village, where traffic increases. The road is closed in the winter from the entrance station north.

Almost immediately after turning onto Moose-Wilson Road west of park headquarters, you'll reach the turnoff for the Murie Ranch Historic District. Driving the 0.5 mile of gravel to this collection of cabins is like taking a step back in time, in many ways to the birth of conservation. Free tours are offered from 2:30 to 3:30 p.m. daily from early May to mid-October.

Back on Moose-Wilson Road, the pavement bends left and climbs onto a bench. A parking area on the left is a hopeful place to look for wildlife, especially moose, in the wetlands below. Stops are few as the road winds through aspen and conifer stands to the turn for the Death Canyon Trailhead. Shortly thereafter is the 1,106-acre Laurance S. Rockefeller Preserve, an elegant tribute to wildlands and wildlife on land donated by the family. The property, fully within the park, has 8 miles of immaculate trails, and the 7,500-square-foot building houses a sensory feast of nature that reflects the spirit of the family's conservation bent. Trucks, RVs, and trailers are prohibited on the gravel between Rockefeller Preserve and the Granite Canyon Entrance Station. From the South Entrance to the junction of WY 22 the views of the Tetons return, but the surroundings become increasingly civilized.

✳ To Do

ATTRACTIONS

Jackson: The 2,500-foot **Alpine Slide at Snow King Mountain** (307-201-5667, June to August) starts with a ride up the mountain on a chairlift, followed by 0.5 mile of twists and turns through forest. Speeds are controlled by riders, so it's suitable for all ages. The slide is reached via the Snow King Scenic Chairlift, taking riders to panoramic views of Jackson Hole and the Tetons as well as a network of trails. Nearby **Amaze'n Jackson Hole** (307-734-0455) offers a race against the clock and against your friends in a large maze. Squirt guns are allowed by day and flashlights by night, there's a candy store with shaved ice, and you can play miniature golf. The nonprofit **Jackson Hole Museum** (307-733-9605, May to October) was founded in 1958 and highlights local artifacts dating to the first humans to walk the area. They offer walking tours of Jackson four days a week in the summer. Exhibits at the free **Jackson Hole Historical Society & Museum** (307-733-2414, June to September) range from the history of Plains Indians to the creation of Grand Teton National Park, and there's also a research library. The beautiful **National Museum of Wildlife Art** (307-733-5771) overlooking the National Elk Refuge is 12 galleries with more than 4,000 works of wildlife art, including paintings and sculptures. The stone and wood building was carefully constructed to embody its setting. With rounded corners, it has the feel of a southwestern kiva. To avoid being known only as a tourist stop, the museum allows Jackson residents free admission on Sundays.

Teton Village: Four lifts now carry riders high into the mountains above the village. The **Aerial Tram** (May to October) is a 10-minute, enclosed ride for up to 60 people that rises more than 4,100 feet to Corbet Cabin at the summit of 10,450-foot Rendezvous Mountain. Needless to say, the views are spectacular. Only slightly less riveting and definitely more intimate is the free **Bridger Gondola** (June to September), seating eight and landing at Couloir Restaurant and The Deck @ Piste after climbing 2,784 feet in seven minutes. The third option is geared to mountain bikers who want to feel the wind in their faces as they race downhill: The **Teewinot High-Speed Quad Lift** (307-739-2654, June to September) carries four riders and bicycles from the Bridger Center more than 400 feet in three minutes to six trailheads. The newest high-speed addition is the **Sweetwater Gondola**, which carries eight people per cabin 4,200 feet past a midway stop to its terminus just above Casper Restaurant; it moves roughly 1,600 skiers per hour and replaced two older lifts.

Driggs, Idaho: Do yourself a favor and set aside one evening of your Jackson Hole visit for the **Spud Drive In** (208-354-3727, June to September), a throwback to another era but with some creative twists. Call in your order for food that has a solid local reputation; some people happily pay the entry fee just to have access to the grub. Double features are shown on weekends. Rates are $7 for spec-"tators," $6 for "seasoned tators," $4 for "small fries" (6–12), and free for "tator tots" (5 and under).

RECREATION IN GTNP

BICYCLING *Road Cycling:* Grand Teton has 100 miles of paved roads and tremendous views for the road crowd, including more separated pathways than any national park in America. There isn't much variation in terrain, so don't expect a great workout. The best ride is the 8-mile path along **Teton Park Road** from Moose to Jenny Lake. From Moose, you can pedal the winding Moose-Wilson Road through aspen and pine, watching for wildlife. Expect some teeth rattling on the unpaved portion, but it's usually manageable with thin tires. The 3-mile **Jenny Lake Scenic Drive** is a great side trip, and the **Antelope Flats/Gros Ventre Road** loop has limited traffic and unlimited views.

Mountain Biking: If you're on fat tires, options are limited because hiking trails are off-limits. The 3-mile **Two-Ocean Lake Road** ride and the 15-mile **River Road** along the Snake are outstanding exceptions. For a true muscle-grinder, pedal to the summit of Shadow Mountain, so named because the Tetons shadow it at sunset. Much of the ride is outside the park, but it starts and ends inside the east boundary.

FISHING *Rivers:* Exceptional fishing exists in the heart of Grand Teton National Park on what is technically the **South Fork of the Snake River** but commonly referred to simply as "the Snake" until it reaches Palisades Reservoir at Alpine. Guides are at the ready to lead you to big cutthroats on the entire 80 miles from Jackson Lake to the reservoir. A beautiful tributary of the Snake that receives waters from the highest drainage in the park, the **Buffalo Fork River** in the northeast corner offers great dry-fly trout fishing for those willing to make the effort. The river is braided, flows through grizzly country, and traverses a great deal of private land outside the park, but pressure is light and the cool waters mean the fish are active during the dog days of summer.

Lakes: You name the trout, the deep and cold waters of **Jackson Lake** have it. A state-record 50-pound lake trout (actually a char called a mackinaw) was coaxed from these depths. Cutthroat, brook, and brown trout also inhabit the rich waters, best accessed by boat except in May, when bank anglers have a crack at trophy trout that cruise the shores for bait fish. In the summer, you'll have to drop line as deep as 200 feet. A few coves or inlets can be fished with a fly-rod from float tubes. Jackson Lake is closed in October so mackinaw can spawn undisturbed. **Jenny Lake**, surely the most beautiful body of water in Wyoming, also has its fair share of mackinaws, cutthroats, and browns. Fish from a canoe or kayak around the edges, where the fish will lurk for insects, including a renowned flying black ant "hatch" in late June or early July. Try streamers, woolly buggers, or other submerged flies. Cutthroats will occasionally rise for a dry. Jenny Lake is an excellent choice in October, when Jackson Lake is closed. **Leigh Lake** is a remote lake north of Jenny and String Lakes famed for its views and solitude. Fish it the same as Jenny—with flashy streamers, woolly buggers, or other deep wet flies. A canoe will provide the best serenity. Fish the inlets where waters pour off the flanks of the Tetons.

ROCK CLIMBING/MOUNTAINEERING Few experiences can match the thrill of standing atop 13,770-foot Grand Teton on a cloudless morning, especially on one of those rare windless days. The world stretches forever in every direction. Combined with the different challenges each peak presents, it's no wonder that climbers from around the globe bring their ropes, ice axes, and bolts. More than 4,000 people climb Grand Teton each year, usually in July and early August. Novices can get training and go with guides. Expect to pay anywhere from $1,000 to $3,000.

For less technical climbs, hikers can reach the summits of South and Middle Teton in a day after spending a night at one of four campsites. Mount Moran's isolation from the others often renders it a forgotten peak, but it has several memorable routes to its 12,605-foot summit. Registration isn't necessary to climb any of the Tetons, but overnight camping requires a backcountry-use permit. As with most climbing, it's best to go early, before afternoon winds and frequent lightning storms arrive. By mid-August,

HIKING

Jackson Lake Lodge/Colter Bay Area: **Colter Bay/Hermitage Point** is a leisurely 9.7-mile round-trip walk through lodgepole forest and meadows along streams and past ponds. Several trails branch from the trailhead, including for the 2-mile **Lakeshore Trail** and 3-mile **Heron Pond/San Lake Loop**. They are all in wildlife-rich areas and they return to the same place. Look for waterfowl, moose, and trumpeter swans in marshy areas. The end is Hermitage Point, which juts into Jackson Lake. Jackson Lake Lodge offers two easy hikes: a popular 0.5-mile stroll called **Lunch Tree Hill** that ends at a perch overlooking Jackson Lake, with Willow Flats and the Tetons in the distance, and 3.3-mile round-trip **Christian Pond Loop** through marsh into a forest. At Lunch Tree, interpretive signs are at the top of the hill. Some folks like to drive to the summit of **Signal Mountain**, but you can give your quads a workout with a moderate 6.8-mile roundtrip hike through forest to views of Jackson Lake.

Teton Park Road Area: **Cascade Canyon** is Grand Teton's most popular hiking area, with most visitors taking the Jenny Lake boat ride to the base of the mountains for moderate to strenuous hikes. Nearly everyone hikes the 1.1 miles from the boat dock—it's 4.8 miles roundtrip along the lakeshore—to 200-foot **Hidden Falls**. The majority continue another 1.8 miles to **Inspiration Point**, which features a busy collection of yellow-bellied marmots, an occasional pika, and stirring views of the lake, Jackson Hole, and the Gros Ventre Mountains. From there, the more adventurous folks turn left and continue another 3.4 miles to **Lake Solitude** and the rest of the way to **Hurricane Pass** and views of Schoolroom Glacier, a 19-mile round-trip. The trail forks right toward **Paintbrush Canyon** and Leigh Lake, then back to Jenny Lake. Moose are common in the canyon and black bears are frequently spotted. Self-guiding maps and information are at the trailhead, and there's a fee for the boat trip across the lake.

Another breezy walk is at **Leigh Lake**, where two options are available—an easy 1.8-mile roundtrip walk to the lake along the channel connecting Leigh to String Lake or a 7.4-mile adventure along Leigh's east shore northward past smaller lakes to Bearpaw Lake and **Trapper Lake**. On the latter hike, Mount Moran will constantly be in view across the lake. Mosquitoes can be brutal here and bears of both types are known to frequent the area. Many visitors miss the 3.7-mile hike around skinny **String Lake** because of its proximity to Jenny and Leigh lakes, but locals like it for the solitude. This trail also serves as the starting point for the strenuous **Holly Lake** hike up Paintbrush Canyon, a 12.4-mile round-trip sojourn that encircles the lake and returns. If you're looking for more, keep going on a strenuous **Lake Solitude** trail and a return down Cascade Canyon for an arduous 19.2-mile affair.

Just before Moose, one of the park's most rugged trails is **Lupine Meadows**, which leads to **Garnet Canyon** and Amphitheater Lake. It's 8.4 miles roundtrip to the canyon and another 1.4 miles to a series of glacial lakes on switchbacks. **Taggart Lake** is a popular choice for those wanting to skip the crowds at Jenny Lake. The moderate hike rises on glacial moraines to Taggart and then Bradley lakes, both surrounded by burns from a 1985 fire. Three loop options are available, including along tumbling Beaver Creek. **Chapel of the Configuration** is a gentle 0.3-mile round-trip walk to century-old buildings on the Snake River at Menor's Ferry and

anything is possible with the weather. Check with the Jenny Lake Ranger Station (307-739-3343) from 8 a.m. to 6 p.m. for advice, guidebooks, and information on the availability of campsites. Climbers also have an inexpensive option for lodging before making their assault: the American Alpine Club's **Grand Teton Climbers' Ranch** (307-733-7271) charges $10 per night for bunks in small cabins, cooking facilities, and hot showers. Bring your own bedding and food. Reservations are recommended, and the ranch is limited to climbers only.

a log church built in 1925. Sunday services are conducted in the summer. Other buildings include Bill Menor's old cabin and store.

Moose-Wilson Road Area: At Death Canyon, take your pick between the brisk 1.8-mile round-trip to the Phelps Lake overlook on a glacial moraine or the muscle-wrenching 8-mile trek into the wilderness to Static Peak Divide. From the overlook, it's another fairly steep mile down to the lake—remember that you'll have to return this way—and then 2 strenuous miles up into Death Canyon. Here the trail forks at the Death Canyon Patrol Cabin toward Static Peak Divide on steep switchbacks through whitebark pine. It's a challenging up, down, and up to the cabin built in the 1930s by the Civilian Conservation Corps for trail maintenance. A 0.5-mile distance beyond the cabin is another overlook of Death Canyon. Unlike Cascade and Death canyons, Granite Canyon doesn't have natural stopping points on the way to the Teton Crest. It is 10 strenuous miles along Granite Creek into subalpine meadows at Marion Lake. About 2/3 of the way up, you can backtrack to the south to where the tramway at Jackson Hole Ski Area drops off riders or head down Open Canyon to Phelps Lake. Of course, at any point you can always turn around and return to the trailhead.

Also here is a network of trails at the Laurance S. Rockefeller Preserve, ranging from the easy 3-mile Lake Creek/Woodland Trail Loop along Lake Creek to 5.8-mile (Aspen Ridge/Boulder Ridge Loop) and 6.3-mile (Phelps Lake Trail Loop) moderate treks through boulder fields and aspen to and around Phelps Lake.

Moran Junction Area: In the northeast corner of the park is Two Ocean Lake, where you'll get an entirely different perspective on the park than from any other trails. While most head up canyons into the Tetons, these wrap around Two Ocean and Emma Matilda lakes in the northeast corner of the park, just outside the Teton Wilderness Area. The hikes range from 6.4 miles round-trip to a 13-mile journey that encompasses both lakes. The focus is lakes, forests, and wildflowers, as opposed to mountain views—though Grand View Point between the two lakes offers vistas of Mount Moran and its siblings. Black bears are common here and grizzlies have moved into the area as well.

West Side: Teton Canyon is a rugged, 12-mile round-trip scramble up the back side of the Tetons that begins outside the park at the Teton Canyon Campground southeast of Grand Targhee Ski Resort. The trail rises to within 0.5 mile of the summit, where it becomes talus. Go the extra 0.5 mile for splendid views. Above it all is Teton Crest, the king of all Teton hikes. Plan to spend at least four days to cover the entire 40 miles on the west side of the Tetons. Only a portion of the trail actually enters the park, and once you're on the trail, it's moderately challenging compared to the canyon hikes that intersect the route. The southernmost terminus is Teton Village, and the trail goes to Paintbrush Canyon. Most hikers wanting to walk the entire trail start either at Teton Village in the south or Paintbrush Canyon in the north, though there are numerous entry and exit points. The hike is only accessible from mid-July to mid-September and you'll need a permit, which are available the first Wednesday in January. Walk-up permits are also available daily on a first-come, first-served basis. The permits are necessary to regulate camping at the 11 backcountry sites. Also on the Idaho side is picturesque Alaska Basin, accessed from Driggs. From the Teton Canyon Campground, it's eight miles of varied terrain that includes the Devil's Staircase to wondrous views and alpine meadows.

RECREATION OUTSIDE GTNP

BICYCLING (ROAD CYCLING) Thanks largely to a nonprofit organization called Friends of Pathways, Jackson has an inviting 56-mile system of paths well suited for bicyclists, walkers, horseback riders, and other recreationists. Along with 14 miles in Grand Teton National Park, a path parallels US 26/89/191 from Jackson to Moose—though the segment next to the National Elk Refuge closes November 1 to April 30 because of elk migration. In addition, you will notice a steady stream of cyclists heading west on WY 22 from Jackson through Wilson, where they begin the arduous 10-percent grade—probably more in some spots—6 miles up to Teton Pass. A more sedate but bumpier paved route is to take the parallel 7.3-mile **Old Pass Road** (1,900-feet elevation gain), which was used over the pass until 1969. A breezier ride is to go south from Wilson on Fish Creek Road. If you're looking for a serious day on two wheels, gear up for what locals call **"Around the Block"**: a century-plus loop that ascends and descends Teton Pass and Idaho's Pine Creek Pass, then returns along Palisades Reservoir and the Snake River Canyon. Don't have room for your bike? Hoback Sports in Jackson and Teton Village Sports offer rentals.

BICYCLING (MOUNTAIN BIKING) Jackson Hole is nirvana for the fat-tire crowd. It doesn't have Moab's slickrock, but neither does it have the crowds on its 115 miles of trails. **Black Canyon Creek** is an 11-miler that's either all lactic-burning uphill (3 miles) or a hair-raising descent (8 miles), starting near the top of Teton Pass at Old Pass Road and finishing in Wilson. The views of Jackson Hole are spectacular—if you dare look up long enough from this technical trail. And it's just one of many options north and south of WY 22 at Teton Pass. Down in town, **Cache Creek** is a 23-miler starting at the base of Snow King and winding through aspen and pine high into a meadow, where cyclists are rewarded with a sweet descent toward US 191. Those looking for something more serene will like **Dog Creek**, a relatively flat single-track that starts near Hoback Junction and continues through grasses and spruce to the base of Indian Peak. **Monument Ridge Loop** is one of the area's most popular rides, a 21-miler featuring a heady ascent and screaming descent that's all too short. Catch your breath at the fire lookout at the crest. The climb is on a paved and then gravel Forest Service road about 15 miles south of Hoback Junction; the return descent is mostly on single track. **Phillips Canyon** is an arduous and technical 14.6-miler, mostly on single track with stream crossings and tough turns. For a less strenuous version (i.e., avoiding the ascent), drive to the Phillips Pass parking lot about halfway up Teton Pass. The trailhead is 1 mile up Trail Creek Road from WY 22 at Wilson. If screaming downhill is your gig, the Jackson Hole Bike Park in Teton Village will lift you to the head of six groomed downhill trails geared toward a variety of skill sets.

Across Teton Pass, the old Oregon Short Line railroad spur has become the 30-mile **Ashton-to-Tetonia Trail**, a scenic ride on gravel through seed-potato country, over three breathtaking trestles, with the Tetons rising to the east. The same abandoned line is paved from Driggs to Victor. In all, the old railroad grade from Victor to West Yellowstone adds up to 104 miles.

FISHING Many learned anglers consider the **South Fork of the Snake River** tailwater fishery below Palisades Dam in Idaho, southwest of Jackson, to be the finest for trout in the nation. The water is big, broad, and braided, providing excellent habitat for huge fine-spotted Snake River cutthroat and brown trout, along with a smattering of rainbows. One reason it doesn't receive as much publicity as the Madison and Henry's Fork is that not everyone has access to a raft or driftboat, the only real way to fish the swift and treacherous stream. The river isn't famed for its hatches, though they do occur. The **Gros Ventre River** northeast of Jackson is a pretty freestone stream that enters the Snake just north of town. Most of the best fishing for cutthroat and the occasional rainbow is downstream from Kelly to the confluence. The fish range from about 8 to 15 inches and aren't too fussy, even about dry flies. Though swift, it's suitable for wading and much of the river can be fished from the banks. Floating is not recommended. Only 55 miles long, the Wild and Scenic **Hoback River** south of Jackson nevertheless will produce—and is a solid place for the novice fly angler to experience success. Most of this little freestone river is easily accessed from US 189/191. The Hoback has scrappy cutthroat that'll reach 13 inches, with the occasional larger trout cruising up from the confluence with the Snake. Toss an attractor dry fly and get ready. Be sure to ask permission if you want to bank fish from private property.

HANG GLIDING *Jackson/Wilson:* **Cowboy Up Hang Gliding** (307-413-4164) and **Jackson Hole Paragliding** (307-739-2626) offer opportunities to ride the thermals solo or in tandem with flight instructors over Jackson Hole. There are no fewer than 15 places for this adventure, most notably Rendezvous Mountain. Training is offered for beginners and advanced pilots. Rental equipment also is available and no experience is necessary.

RIVER RUNNING About 25 miles south of Jackson, the Snake River quickens its pulse in a headlong, big-water rush for Idaho. For 8 miles, the river roils and boils in a series of Class III and Class IV drops. The popular journey starts swiftly at West Table Creek Campground with the soon-to-follow Station Creek drop, S-turns, and cutbacks. It mellows in the middle and then collects its debt with the revered Big Kahuna and Lunch Counter plus Rope and Champagne rapids. The river puts on its best show of force in June before becoming more sedate in August. The 3.5-hour trips range from $40 to $85, depending on amenities such as food, and there's no shortage of companies offering trips. Do-it-yourselfers who want isolation might consider the challenging Class III Southgate stretch, where the river leaves Yellowstone and hurries toward Flagg Ranch.

GRAND TARGHEE SKI RESORT IS RENOWNED FOR DEEP POWDER AND A FESTIVE ATMOSPHERE

SKIING (ALPINE) Think Utah has the best deep powder? Try a day at **Grand Targhee Ski Resort** (307-353-2300) on the west side of the Tetons. It's possible to ski in powder up to your eyebrows after a storm rolls in and hits the mountains. Grand Targhee receives more than 500 inches of snow annually on nearly 3,000 acres of terrain on Fred's and Peaked Mountains. And if you're feeling especially adventurous, bushwhack (snow-whack?) up to 9,920-foot Mary's Nipple. Swanky **Jackson Hole Mountain Resort** (307-733-2292) at Teton Village is as known for its 100-passenger aerial tram as its snow, though its 133 runs offer plenty of variety. The resort includes Rendezvous and Après Vous Mountains, with more than 4,100 feet of vertical and access to more than 2,500 acres of terrain. The mountain receives about 450 inches of snow per year and has snowmaking capability. Snowboarding is allowed on all runs. **Snow King Resort** (307-733-5200), a.k.a. "The Town Hill," was Wyoming's first ski area when it opened in 1939. With 1,571 feet of vertical and 32 runs on 400 acres, it's surprisingly steep and challenging. Some 60 percent of the runs are suited for advanced skiers. About a quarter of the terrain is open to night skiing. The resort also has a snow-tubing park.

SKIING (HELI-SKIING) If backcountry adventure is your bag and lift lines aren't, go for the gusto in untracked country with **High Mountain Heli-Skiing** in Teton Village (307-733-3274) and a western base at Teton Springs Resort & Spa (208-787-7235) near Victor, Idaho. This outfit accesses over 300,000 acres of national forest lands in Wyoming and Idaho south of Jackson Hole Mountain Resort with helicopters. Each day features six runs spread between the Snake River, Palisades, Hoback, Gros Ventre, and Teton Ranges. The six runs range from 12,000 to 15,000 vertical feet and are for expert skiers and snowboarders only. A limited number of guests are taken into the Palisades Wilderness Study Area on the Idaho side.

SKIING (NORDIC) **Teton Pines Nordic Center** (307-739-2629), about 4 miles south of Jackson Hole Mountain Resort on Village Road in Teton Village, has 12 miles of mostly flat, professionally groomed track and skating lines. Guided nature trips are offered. Also on Teton Village Road is **Shooting Star Nordic Track**, touting about 12 miles of trail where you can bring your dog. At the bottom of Teton Pass on the Wyoming side is **Trail Creek Nordic Center** (307-733-0296); donations to the Jackson Hole Ski & Snowboard Club for grooming are appreciated. On the other side of Teton Pass, **Grand Targhee** isn't just for downhill skiers—they've got a groomed Nordic track as well.

SLED DOGS/SNOWMOBILES In town, **Jackson Hole Iditarod Sled Dog Tours** (307-733-7388) offers a full-day trip to Granite Hot Springs and a half-day adventure on the same Forest Service Road. On the road toward Dubois, **Togwotee Adventures** (307-733-8800) features full-day treks and half-day snowmobile adventures, with snowmobile/sled-dog combination packages also available. The company offers lodging at Togwotee Mountain Lodge.

SWIMMING **Granite Hot Springs** (307-690-6323) is a glistening mineral pool in a forested valley about 35 miles southeast of Jackson, past Hoback Junction. A maintained gravel road follows Granite Creek to the pool, which has changing rooms and a deck for sunning. Water temperatures typically are in the low 90s in the summer and about 110 in winter. From December to March you'll have to use cross-country skis or snowmobiles to access the pool. You can pitch a tent at the nearby campground and hike into the canyon, where 50-foot Granite Falls is a highlight. Granite Creek also features some primitive hot pools worth checking out.

✳ Lodging

LODGING IN GTNP

Colter Bay: Grand Teton Lodge Company runs the quaint, comfortable, and woodsy 🏕 ♿ ❙❙ **Colter Bay Village** ($$/$$$, 307-543-3100, May to September), a more family-suited alternative to Jackson Lake and Jenny Lake Lodges. This true village of 166 has comfortable homestead cabins brought from Jackson Hole that sleep from two to six. Another distinct experience: Bring your own bedding and rent one of 66 canvas tent structures ($, June to early September). They have two solid log walls, two fabric sides, and a roof; no need to fuss with pitching a tent. For the hard-sided camper, there are 350 sites and 112 RV spaces—103 of which are pull-throughs.

Jackson Lake: On a bluff overlooking Jackson Lake, ⊘ 🏕 ♿ ❙❙ **Jackson Lake Lodge** ($$$/$$$$, 307-543-3100, May to October) greets guests with a picture window framing "the Grand" and her stately mountain sisters across Willow Flats and Jackson Lake. The suites in the lodge are pricey but spectacular. Cottage rooms are motel-ish and generally unspectacular, but it's the setting you're paying for. Views from the deck out back are nearly surreal at sundown. Order a huckleberry margarita at the Blue Heron, gaze at the lake and peaks, and marvel at wildlife foraging in the flats below. The lodge also has a corral, gas station, and medical facilities.

Signal Mountain: 🏕 ❙❙ **Signal Mountain Lodge** ($$$/$$$$, 307-543-2831, May to October) is a collection of rooms, bungalows, cabins, and houses on the south shore of Jackson Lake—the only lakefront accommodations in GTNP. They run the gamut for amenities, nothing extraordinary save for the mountain views, and in keeping with park policy don't have TVs. The remodeled

Lakefront Retreats are snug but afford lake access less than 100 feet away. The Home Away From Home is a welcoming Western-styled, two-bedroom cabin with fireplace. A marina, store, restaurant, bar, and pizza joint complete the package.

Jenny Lake: If you're not put off by the AAA four-diamond rates, ⊘ ♿ ❙❙ **Jenny Lake Lodge** ($$$$, 307-733-4647, May to October) is memorable; costs approach and exceed $700 per night, depending on the accommodations. The 37 rustic Western cabins and suites on the east shore of Jenny Lake provide the consummate Teton vacation and might be the most sought-after lodging in the national park system. The interiors are modest, but it's the little extras that make the difference—most notably remodeled bathrooms and handcrafted comforters. Included in your stay are an exceptional breakfast and five-course dinner. Free bicycling and horseback riding are added perks, and access to Jenny Lake is only a few steps away.

Moose: ❙❙ **Dornan's Spur Ranch Cabins** ($$$/$$$$, 307-733-2522, closed April and November) are part of a 10-acre, self-contained community at Moose with reach-out-and-touch views of Grand Teton. All 12 of Dornan's log cabins—eight one-bedroom and four two-bedroom with lodgepole furniture and modern amenities—are on the wildflowered banks of the Snake River. A restaurant, bar, general store, variety of recreation rentals, and stellar wine shop (which schedules tastings in the winter) are across the parking lot.

ALTERNATIVE LODGING IN GTNP

A number of longstanding guest ranches and operations are technically within park boundaries, grandfathered in as part of the deal in 1950 to create additional lands for the park.

MURIE: THE CONSUMMATE NAME IN CONSERVATION

Few families have done more to protect America's wildlands, from the Northern Rockies to Alaska, than the Muries. Adolph and Louise Murie bought the ranch near Moose in 1945, and they were joined a year later by the more famous Murie duo, Adolph's brother, Olaus, and his wife, Mardy. Olaus served as president of the Wilderness Society, and the family cabins became the first national headquarters for the environmental group. Less than two decades later, the Wilderness Act of 1964 was forged on that very site. Earlier, the couple pushed for preservation of the Arctic National Wildlife Refuge in their other home state, Alaska, where Mardy was the first female graduate of the University of Alaska Fairbanks. The entire Murie Ranch is now a National Historic Landmark, and today the site serves as headquarters for the Murie Center, which promotes science-based understanding of nature and conservation issues through programs that include stays at the ranch.

MURIE RANCH IN MOOSE IS CONSIDERED BY MANY TO BE THE BIRTHPLACE OF AMERICA'S CONSERVATION MOVEMENT

Moose: Chris and Lindsay Davenport now oversee the last privately owned guest ranch completely within Grand Teton National Park, ⫯ **Moose Head Ranch** ($$$$, 307-733-3141, June to August). The family-oriented ranch's 14 log cabins are sprinkled among cottonwood trees, with the Tetons serving as backdrop. Catch-and-release trout ponds are a perk, as are the gourmet meals served three times daily. Although there are no structured programs, activities abound for kids and adults, including pure nature appreciation. The casual and family-owned ♿ ⫯ **Triangle X Ranch** ($$$$, 307-733-2183, May to October and December to March) has 20 log cabins, each containing a story of its own and dating as far back as the late 1800s. The all-inclusive rate includes three meals and two horseback rides per day. Don't be surprised to see elk, fox, pronghorn, moose, or black bear roaming the grounds. Ask about the ranch's history with GTNP; it's a story unto itself.

THE BRAWNY TETONS ARE PROFILED FROM THE PORCH AT JENNY LAKE LODGE

CAMPING Grand Teton's five campgrounds are all first-come, first-served, except for groups of 10 or more. The maximum stay is seven days and most are open from mid-May to mid-September. Group reservations (800-628-9988) may be made at Gros Ventre and Colter Bay. RVs are welcome at all but Jenny Lake. **Colter Bay** ($, 307-543-2811, May to September) is sprawling yet surprisingly quiet. Set amid lodgepole pines, the campground comprises 330 large campsites and 66 canvas camper cabins along with shower and laundry facilities, a grocery store, and service station. A separate RV section has 112 slots and some choice ground for staking a tent.

Another spacious campground is **Gros Ventre** ($, 307-543-2811, May to October), with 318 sites aligning the Gros Ventre River about 11 miles southeast of Moose. Happily for procrastinators, even on the busiest summer day you've got a shot at getting a spot here. **Jenny Lake** ($, 307-543-2811, May to September) has 49 coveted tent-only sites amid forest and glacial boulders next to the shimmering lake. Be there well

before 11 a.m. if you want any chance of nabbing a site. Perhaps the least appreciated and definitely least used are 60 sites at **Lizard Creek** ($, 307-543-2831, June to September), most situated on Jackson Lake north of Colter Bay. Spacious **Signal Mountain** ($, 307-543-2831, May to October) has 81 sites, including 24 with electrical hook-ups at Signal Mountain Lodge; flush toilets take away the "roughing it" aspect.

BEST LODGING OUTSIDE GTNP

Jackson: For your convenience we have separated our suggestions for the numerous Jackson lodging options into six categories: Budget, Economy, Middle of the Road, High End, and Ultraluxury.

In the *Budget* category, **Four Winds Motel** ($/$$$, 307-733-2474) and **Golden Eagle Inn** ($/$$$, 307-733-2042, May to October) are older operations a few blocks from downtown. Both come clean and cozy, with friendly staffs ready to make your stay comfortable. One of Jackson's older motor-court options is the family-owned **Rawhide Motel** ($/$$,

307-733-1216, May to October), a basic 23-room motel on two floors and a fine choice if you're searching for simple, spick-and-span, and a short walk to Town Square.

The quintessential motor court, ❂ **Kudar Motel** ($$, 307-733-2823, May to October) was built in 1938 and designated a historic landmark in 2000. Repeat customers have returned to Joe Kudar's place since the 1950s for the frontier feel of its 14 motel rooms and 17 cabins, all less than three blocks from Town Square. A neon sign and a grassy area with picnic tables under tall cottonwoods in the center of a circle driveway give it that *Happy Days* vibe.

For the *Economy* minded, three Town Square Inns are within easy walking distance of the square. Closest is 🐾 ♿ **Antler Inn** ($/$$$$, 307-733-2535) with its 110 rooms, laundry area, exercise room, and hot tub that'll fit you and 24 of your new buddies. 🐾 ♿ **Cowboy Village Resort** ($$/$$$$, 307-733-3121) brings the country to the city with 82 individual log cabins, all with kitchenettes and sofa sleepers. Decks come with charcoal BBQ grill and picnic table. You'll also get to enjoy a hot tub, swimming pool, guest laundry, and meeting room. Next door is 🐾 ♿ **Elk Country Inn** ($$/$$$$, 307-733-2364), an orderly mix of 90 units, including 25 stand-alone log cabins, hot tub, picnic area with grills, and a playground. Also in the Town Square Inns group is 🐾 ♿ **49er Inn & Suites** ($$/$$$$, 307-733-7550), which has been substantially upgraded with a remodel of 140 rooms and suites, an indoor Roman tub and outdoor hot tub, a swimming pool, fitness room and sauna, conference rooms, and a quality buffet breakfast.

Modestly priced as well is ♿ **Parkway Inn** ($$/$$$$, 307-733-3143), which strays from the area's frontier theme with its early-twentieth-century Victorian decor and American antiques. Ten suites are among the 33 rooms, plus there's a cottage with four suites. Notable amenities: an indoor lap pool, two jetted spa tubs,

and a gym. The affordable ♿ **Ranch Inn** ($/$$$, 307-733-6363) has rooms with balconies facing the Snow King ski area and touts its location as the closest of any lodging to Town Square. If you're a fan of Branson, Missouri, or Pigeon Forge, Tennessee, you'll love the theme-park look and feel of ♿ 🍴 **The Virginian Lodge** ($/$$$, 307-733-2792), a complex of 170 modern Wild West rooms, 20 suites with full kitchens, 103 RV sites (May to October), outdoor heated pool with hot tub, a saloon, liquor store, and hair salon.

Overlooking the National Elk Refuge and away from the buzz of downtown is the 24-room **Elk Refuge Inn** ($$, 307-200-0981), which has 10 balcony rooms with kitchenettes, benches for viewing at the refuge ponds, and grills. **Miller Park Lodge** ($$/$$$, 307-733-4858), less than three blocks from downtown, has a boutique feel to its 15 rooms, some with Jacuzzi tub and fireplace. 🐾 ♿ **Flat Creek Inn & Mart** ($/$$$, 307-733-5276), next to Elk Refuge Inn, is family owned. The 3 two-story buildings with a combined 75 recently rebuilt rooms all face the refuge. It's a bit hectic with a convenience store and gas pump as part of a complex squeezed between the highway and foothills. 🐾 **Pony Express Motel** ($/$$$, 307-733-3835) concedes its 24 basic rooms are "nothing fancy," but they're comfortable and go for about the cost of a dinner for four at many Jackson restaurants.

For *Middle of the Road* lodging, the downtown location of ♿ **The Lexington at Jackson Hole Hotel & Suites** ($$/$$$$, 307-733-2648) plus a hot breakfast buffet give it an edge. The Lexington, started as Trapper Inn a half century ago by the Kudars, has 90 rooms and suites, all tastefully decorated and many completely remodeled in 2012. Formerly a more modestly priced hotel, ♿ 🍴 **The Lodge at Jackson Hole** ($$/$$$$, 307-733-2992) went full-on luxury in 2012 and now has 154 smartly appointed mini-suites. Most units in the two-story log-façade building feature a kitchen, fireplace, and eating area. An indoor heated pool with a retractable glass door to an outside deck, two Jacuzzis, dry sauna, and 24-hour fitness room are a perfect way to finish a day in the park. Once tired and run down, ☀ � ⫪ **Snow King Resort Hotel** ($$/$$$$, 307-733-5200) and accompanying ☀ **Grand View Lodge** ($$$$) have undergone a complete makeover. The 203-room hotel at the base of Snow King Mountain is below the lodge and 85 "classic" and "luxury" condominiums. The rooms are comfortable, and many have views of the Tetons.

Moving into the *High End* bracket, � **Anvil Hotel** ($$/$$$$, 307-733-3668) has undergone changes that retain a rustic feel while adding modern decor that includes custom metal beds, furnishings, and bedding. As small luxury lodges go, ⫪ **Rusty Parrot Lodge & Spa** ($$$/$$$$, 307-733-2000), which has earned AAA's four-diamond rating for two decades running, ranks among the finest. All 32 rooms have comforters and gas fireplaces. Guests receive a full hot breakfast in Wild Sage Restaurant, and the outdoor hot tub overlooking town is a cut above. Body Sage, the first full-service spa in Jackson, can arrange and tailor therapeutic treatments.

The Tudor revival brick-and-stucco ✪ � ⫪ **Wort Hotel** ($$$$, 307-733-2190) is a National Historic Landmark that takes up an entire city block. Evidence of its years as an illegal gambling hall remains throughout, including an original roulette wheel, blackjack table, and historic photos. Greeting visitors is a lobby filled with locally made log furniture, a large rawhide and iron chandelier, and the original staircase and fireplace that survived a fire in 1980. The full-service hotel's 59 classy rooms range from deluxe to the fit-for-a-king Silver Dollar Suite. � ⫪ **Rustic Inn Creekside Resort & Spa** ($$/$$$$, 800-323-9279) is plenty elegant, with its one- and two-bedroom spa suites and cabins, but what sets it apart is its 12 acres flanking Flat Creek and the elk refuge. The heated outdoor pool, sauna, Jacuzzi, lounge, and full bistro and bar with extensive beer and wine selections are great, but here you also get seasonal fishing opportunities on the property's 7-acre nature preserve.

With 22 rooms just three blocks from Town Square, � **Alpine House Lodge & Cottages** ($$$/$$$$, 307-739-1570) feels like a European-style mountain resort, though with more personality and warmth. Amenities include a hot tub amid perennial gardens, Finnish dry sauna and spa, and chef-prepared gourmet breakfast made from locally produced ingredients. Five eco-oriented creekside cottages have full living space and kitchens, and there are two rooms in the lodge. The sprawling ✪ ☽ ⫪ **Bentwood Inn** ($$/$$$$, 307-739-1411) was built with 200-year-old logs left over from the 1988 Yellowstone fires and has five beautiful rooms. Bob and Virginia Schrader's B&B, halfway between downtown Jackson and Teton Village on a wooded 3.5 acres with views of the Tetons, has earned plaudits as one of *National Geographic's* Unique Lodges of the World for its environmental consciousness. Evening hors d'oeuvres and four-course meals served twice weekly in Bentwood's bistro have only upped the ante. Though just three blocks from Town Square, ✪ ☀ **Inn on the Creek** ($$/$$$$, 307-739-1565) feels private and secluded, especially in the rooms overlooking Flat Creek. Down bedding, fireplaces, and private bathrooms are a few of the plusses. ☀ **The Inn at Jackson Hole** ($$/$$$$, 307-733-2311) in Teton Village—once a Best Western—has undergone a major overhaul of its exterior after having the same done earlier with all 83 of its rooms in an effort to match the spectacular surroundings. The 88-room **Hampton Inn Jackson Hole** ($$$$, 307-733-0033) on the south end of town has standard king and queen rooms plus four styles of suites, some with fireplaces. Easy access to WY 22 to Teton Pass is a plus.

For those looking for an ultraluxurious experience and for whom money is barely a consideration, ♿ ❙❙ **Amangani** ($$$$, 307-734-7333) is a posh, 40-suite hotel built mostly from redwood and Oklahoma sandstone atop East Gros Ventre Butte, meaning views of the Tetons are unobstructed. The first of the exclusive Aman resorts to be built in North America is perched on 1,000 acres of wildlife sanctuary, including a migratory route for mule deer and elk between Jackson and Teton Village. A full-service spa, pool, and health center are just a few amenities. The restaurant, the Grill at Amangani, is open to the public and emphasizes local, sustainable, farm-to-fork meals. Neighboring ♿ ❙❙ **Spring Creek Ranch** ($$$/$$$$, 307-733-8833) is luxe-rustic, with its complex of villas, executive homes, condos, and rooms (fourplex cabins). The ranch has naturalists on staff and a Wilderness Adventure Spa featuring in-room or in-tepee hot-stone massage, seaweed body wrap, and private yoga class.

In town, ♿ ❙❙ **Hotel Jackson** ($$$$, 307-733-2200) takes its name from one of Jackson's original five buildings from a century ago and is close to the original location across from Town Square. It offers ultraluxury in 10 styles of rooms, many of them suites. Natural gas fireplaces and a rooftop spa are just a couple of the perks; some rooms have terraces. Like many of Jackson's finer hotels, the Western-themed ♿ ❙❙ **Wyoming Inn of Jackson Hole** ($$/$$$$, 307-734-0035) strives to combine modern luxury with a rustic ambiance. The theme carries into the standard king and queen rooms as well as suites.

Wilson: Formerly the whimsical Teton Tree House, a heavenly hideaway west of town is now named ○ **Jackson Hole Hideout** ($$$/$$$$, 307-733-3233). New owners Greg and Beth McCoy maintained the basic tree-house character while undergoing a significant renovation in 2016. Plush guest rooms with names such as Wrangler and Cowgirl still feature views of the valley and Sleeping Indian Mountain. Sherrie and Ken Jern have created the quintessential B&B at ○ **Wildflower Inn** ($$$/$$$$, 307-733-4710). This gorgeous log home sits on 3 colorful and immaculate acres, with four single rooms and a two-room suite with private decks and bathrooms to match.

Carol and Franz Kessler's family-friendly 🐾 **Teton View Bed & Breakfast** ($$/$$$$, 307-733-7954, May to October) blends mountain hospitality with European flair on the west bank of the Snake River. Choose between a guest room in the house, a two-room suite, a one-bedroom cabin with a kitchen, and a backyard sheep wagon. A full breakfast, outdoor hot tub, and deck come with views of the Tetons and regular visits from neighborhood moose. 🐾 **The Sassy Moose Inn** ($/$$$, 307-413-2995), a 4,800-square-foot log inn of five cowboy-meets-cowgirl rooms in a rural setting west of Jackson, combines Jackson Hole's rustic-luxe with affordability. A stay includes a hearty breakfast, an outdoor hot tub on a large deck that's screened for privacy yet still provides stunning views of the Tetons, and the Sassy Moose Petit Spa for massages and facials.

Teton Village: Teton Village is a compact community at the base and sides of Jackson Hole Mountain Resort. There are lodging choices for all varieties of vacations. The hospitable, traditionally Bavarian 🐾 ❙❙ **Alpenhof Lodge** ($$$/$$$$, 307-733-3242, May to October and December to April) is listed on the National Register of Historic Places and is definitely the most Euro. Forty-two welcoming rooms typically include hot and cold European breakfasts, delivered to your door in the slow season. The outdoor heated pool and hot tub remain open during the winter; an indoor sauna and massage services are always available. Live entertainment often graces the grounds during ski season.

The super-friendly ♿ ❙❙ **Teton Mountain Lodge & Spa** ($$$/$$$$,

ELEGANCE AND BEAUTY ENGULF WILDFLOWER INN, LOCATED IN WILSON

307-201-6066) has 145 rooms and suites that come in various shapes and sizes. The one- and two-bedroom suites have full kitchens, and the three-bedroom and penthouse suites are beyond a home away from home. Other high-lights include the full-service SpaTerre, a fitness center, indoor and outdoor pools, a 22-person rooftop hot tub, and a steam room. The popular Spur Bar & Restaurant offers New West cuisine and ambiance. Another gem on the moun-tainside, &⊪ **Snake River Lodge & Spa** ($$/$$$$, 307-732-6000) offers choices ranging from 125 rooms, three penthouse suites, and 16 two- and three-bedroom residences up to 4,500 square feet to several off-site condominiums. There is an indoor-outdoor heated pool and, as the name implies, a full-service spa to go with a Backcountry Adventure Cen-ter exclusive to guests. The Gamefish

Restaurant (B/L/D) and Fireside Bar serve guests and nonguests, offering a wild game and fish-centric menu. With 🐾 &⊪ **Four Seasons Resort Jackson Hole** ($$$$, 307-732-5000), the name says it all, and the luxury comes in a wide array of room options and packages, including bed and breakfast. A spa, restaurant, two lounges, and ski-in and ski-out access to the mountain are a few of the bonuses. Beagle-sized or smaller dogs are allowed. &⊪ **Hotel Terra Jackson Hole** ($$/$$$$, 307-201-6065) is luxury living with a condo flair, all with large windows and many with neck-arching views of the Tetons. Options range from a standard room all the way up to three-bedroom suites. There are two restaurants, a lounge, infinity pool, and stores. They must be on to something: *Travel + Leisure* chose Terra Jackson Hole as Wyoming's Best Hotel.

Victor, Idaho: **Kasper's Kountryside Inn** ($/$$, 208-787-2726), operated about a mile from Victor by a fourth-generation Teton Valley resident and her husband, consists of two peaceful and private three-room suites on 2.5 acres. Full kitchens, cheery furnishings, and large viewing windows are part of the appeal. ❀ ♿ **Moose Creek Ranch** ($$/$$$, 208-787-6078), tucked at the base of the Teton Range's west side well off the beaten path, has it all: pavilion canvas "glamping" cabins, traditional cabins, a five-bedroom ranch house, a handful of RV sites, and a place to stable your horse, all on the banks of a gurgling creek surrounded by national forest, some of it designated wilderness.

Driggs, Idaho: We mention the lone chain in town— ♿ **Super 8 by Wyndham Driggs** ($/$$, 208-354-8888) simply because sometimes all you need is a bed and pillow or familiarity. Not to mention that year-round lodging options are limited, though increasing, in an area of high tourist activity. Amenities are typical: indoor pool, hot tub, micro-fridge, laundry facility, and continental breakfast. They are serious about their no-pets rule.

John and Nancy Nielson invite you to **Pines Motel Guest Haus** ($/$$, 208-354-2774), a year-round, European-esque hamlet with seven small rooms on an acre that has been in the family for four decades. Each room has a fridge, microwave, and use of the large hot tub; most have their own bathrooms. ✪ ❀ **Teton Valley Cabins** ($/$$, 208-354-8153) are reasonable lodgettes in various sizes and shapes, 20 units in all, including six standard motel-type rooms and seven log duplexes with kitchenettes. You'll also find an enclosed hot tub, laundry, and homey picnic area with horseshoes, volleyball, and a grill.

Alta/Grand Targhee, Wyoming: When we say Alta, we really mean Grand Targhee, the ski area and reason this little community exists. It has no stores,

one restaurant/bar/grill, and limited sleeping options. But you can't beat the location in the undulating pine- and aspen-bathed foothills of the Tetons, about 6 miles east of Driggs, Idaho, barely inside the Wyoming border. ⫪ **Targhee Lodge Resort** (307-353-2300, June to September and November to April) is actually three lodges in one, plus the Tower Suite, with check-in at the same desk and a shared outdoor pool and hot tub. Something else they share: All are ski-in and ski-out to Targhee's lifts. The Targhee ($$) is suited for the budget-conscious, with 15 standard motel rooms. Sioux Lodge ($$$/$$$$) consists of 32 high-end condominiums that come in three styles: studio, loft, and two-bedroom. The newest of the three is Teewinot Lodge ($$$), with 48 spacious rooms and a small lobby fireplace with cushy seating. The Tower Suite ($$), which rises above the main plaza, has two bedrooms, sleeps six, and has a full kitchen. The resort also rents vacation properties off the mountain, and overnight RV parking is allowed in the lot for a modest fee.

BEST ALTERNATIVE LODGING OUTSIDE GTNP

Moran: Brad and Joanne Luton own **Luton's Teton Cabins** ($$$/$$$$, 307-543-2489, May to October), 13 attractive, authentic Western log cabins 4 miles east of Moran, near Grand Teton's North Entrance. The cabins are surrounded by national forest lands and renowned for solitude, location roughly halfway between Jackson and Yellowstone, and views of the northern end of the Teton Range. Horse boarding is available. On Buffalo Valley Road, the sprawling ✪ ⫪ **Heart Six Ranch** ($$/$$$$, 307-543-2477) offers all-inclusive weekly packages and some cabins for nightly stays. The 14 modern, Western cabins come with hundreds of horses and mules for packing on thousands of acres of public lands, much of it wilderness. Buffalo Valley

Cabins at Heart Six are three well-kept, remodeled apartment units on the 1908 homestead site overlooking the Buffalo Fork. Off-season options are more flexible, with reduced rates and meals offered à la carte after August. The dude ranch, one of America's oldest, is designed to get guests outdoors, so there are no phones or TVs. The year-round Buffalo Valley Café (307-543-2062), originally a store-home combo known to be frequented by "scalawags, renegades, discharged soldiers, and pre-destined stinkers," is next to a fly shop. ☀ ♿ ⍟ **Turpin Meadow Ranch** ($$$$, 307-543-2000, June to March) is on 32 acres of seclusion and natural beauty. There are 13 charming log cabins, a lodge, new chalets, and a restaurant that serves three farm-to-fork meals daily. The ranch divides its operations into three seasons: summer, fall (hunting), and winter (snowmobiling packages).

More of a small village, ⍟ **Togwotee Mountain Lodge** ($$/$$$$, 307-543-2847), 16 miles east of the park on the way to Dubois, Wyoming, is a full-service resort with a concession permit from the Bridger-Teton National Forest. There are 28 lodge rooms and 54 roomy, detached log cabins with stocked kitchenettes, front porches, and grills. This is a busy place in the winter with dog sledding, Sno-Cat skiing, and guided snowmobiling tours into Yellowstone plus sledders zigging and zagging all across the forest. Grizzly Grill ($$/$$$, B/L/D) and Red Fox Saloon ($/$$, L/D) are equipped to satisfy your hunger and thirst; even vegetarians are accommodated. A gas station and convenience store complete the village.

Kelly: The remote **Flat Creek Ranch** ($$$$, 307-733-0603, May to September) has been owned since the 1920s by members of the Albright family, descendants of former Yellowstone National Park superintendent Horace Albright. Five small historic guest cabins, total maximum capacity 15, are on 160 acres at the end of a bumpy four-wheel-drive road, remote and surrounded by public lands. Stays can be seven nights beginning on a Friday or Monday, four nights from Monday to Thursday, or a three-night Friday-to-Sunday getaway. Another rod-and-hoof dude ranch, ◗ ⍟ **Gros Ventre River Ranch** ($$$$, 307-733-4138, May to October), surrounded by national forest land, is home to four log cabins and five log lodges along the Gros Ventre River, with 2 miles of private river access and two stocked ponds. Karl and Tina Weber's cabins were brought to the site from the second-oldest dude ranch in the valley and remodeled for a contemporary Western feel. The ranch just missed being buried by the 1925 landslide that created Slide Lake. Weeklong stays are required during peak season, three nights are OK early or late season.

In Kelly, fifth-generation Jackson Hole resident Dawn Kent and hubby Ron Davler own and run **Anne Kent Cabins** ($$/$$$$, 307-733-4773), two decidedly rustic 1930 log buildings—the owners concede they're "not for everyone"—in this tiny, eclectic community. The views are mesmerizing and the cabins difficult to book, but worth the effort for a pleasant alternative stay. Credit cards are not accepted. Supplies plus sandwiches, soft drinks, and beer are available at the small store next door.

Wilson: **Trail Creek Ranch** ($$/$$$, 307-733-2610, June to September) is a working horse ranch hidden away on 270 mountain acres 10 miles from Jackson. Betty Woolsey, captain of the first women's Olympic ski team, bought the land in 1942 for its powdery slope and turned it into a dude ranch four years later. When she died in 1977, her land was placed in a conservation easement to ensure it would remain pristine and wildlife friendly. There are two distinct stand-alone cabins and five rooms in different buildings. Views from the porches, serenity, trail rides, and a heated swimming pool complete the package.

Teton Village: Sleep on the cheap in king, quad, or group bunkrooms in one of the most convenient locations at the resort: ✪ **The Hostel at Jackson Hole** ($/$$, 307-733-3415). Although the rooms are a little dark, they're clean as a whistle and each has its own bathroom/shower/toilet, all atypical of a hostel. There's a large common space filled with books, board games, a pool table, fridge space, tables and chairs, and even a ski-waxing area.

CAMPING *Jackson:* On Moose-Wilson Road, 🐾 **Jackson Hole Campground** ($, 307-732-2267) underwent major upgrades that include 20 identical, ultra-fancy **Fireside Resort** cabins ($$$$). After driving past the cabins, you'll arrive at the RV and camping area amid mature shade trees.

Moran: 🐾 **Fireside Buffalo Valley RV Resort** ($, 307-733-1980), just a few miles east of the junction, shows some age on its 50-amp pull-through RV sites, hot tub, seasonal pool, showers, recreation room, grocery store, and playground, but the staff is friendly and eager to please. Various rental equipment is yours for any outdoor fun you'd like to create.

Hoback Junction: About 13 miles south of Jackson is ✪ 🐾 **Snake River Park KOA** ($$/$$$, 307-733-7078, mid-April to mid-October) on the renowned white-water stretch of the Snake River Canyon. Tent sites are grassy and slightly set apart from the hubbub. The deluxe Kabins ($$$) are super nice, and most have the Snake River in their front yard; you can't beat the sounds of a rushing river for a lullaby. River trips can be arranged through the campground reservation desk.

Victor, Idaho: 🐾 **Teton Valley Resort** (208-787-2647) is as neat and tidy as they come and has full hook-up pull-throughs, wireless Internet, a heated pool, showers, laundry, and a recreation room. A couple of KOA-style camping cabins are on the property but hard to get.

Forest Service Campgrounds: The Bridger-Teton National Forest has 18 campgrounds in the Jackson Hole area, 12 on the Jackson Ranger District and 6 on the Buffalo Ranger District. Coming south from Yellowstone, top choices in the Buffalo district include the intimate nine-site **Hatchet** off US 26/287 about 8 miles east of Moran Junction on the Buffalo Fork River; it's great for fishing and views of the Tetons. Farther south, on the north shore of Lower Slide Lake and at the end of the pavement on Gros Ventre Road, is 20-site **Atherton Creek**. Continuing up the Gros Ventre, **Red Hills** has 10 sites along the river. Up next is **Crystal Creek**, a six-site spot set amid the aspens near Soda Lake and the highest campground along the river, about 25 miles northeast of Jackson. Farther south, after a drive through the National Elk Refuge, is quiet **Curtis Canyon**, a sensational spot to watch hang gliders shove off from Lookout Point; the site has spots for 12 RVs.

✳ Where to Eat

DINING IN GTNP

Most of the dining establishments are under the umbrella of Grand Teton Lodging Company, but that doesn't mean they don't have their own identities and signature dishes.

Colter Bay Village: **The Ranch House** ($$, 307-543-3335, B/L/D, June to September) serves breakfasts (buttermilk pancakes with many topping choices) and lunches that are easy on the pocketbook and a notch above. Dinner is customary Western park fare but evolving as well. The full bar attached has some twists (huckleberry margarita and rhubarb cosmo) and a bar menu from which you can order bits and bites until 10:30 p.m., which is late by park standards.

Jenny Lake: Paradoxically an unpretentious group of cabins surrounding a nothing-fancy log lodge, ✪ **Jenny Lake Lodge** ($$$$, 307-543-3351, B/L/D, May to October) is undoubtedly the most exquisite dining in either park, a place where dinner jackets are recommended and reservations are limited (every quarter hour between 6 and 7 p.m. and 8 and 9 p.m.). They are the most expensive in the area, but you won't be disappointed. Lodging (also on the high end of high) includes breakfast and five-course dinner, but for nonlodge guests, prix fixe pricing is $94 for dinner. If you are watching your wallet, go for lunch, served from noon to 1:30 p.m., when the à la carte menu is more casual but equally memorable. Reservations are a good idea for breakfast and lunch.

Jackson Lake: At Jackson Lake Lodge you'll find three eating establishments, all extensively upgraded in recent years. ✪ **The Mural Room** ($$$/$$$$, 307-543-3463, B/L/D), named for the early-west work of Carl Roters, who was commissioned by John D. Rockefeller Jr. to adorn his "new lodge," starts with ridiculously breathtaking views of Willow Flats and the Tetons through ceiling-to-floor windows. Made-to-order eggs are a highlight of the breakfast buffet. Lunch is modest; if you're going to have one meal here, make it dinner and try to get a window table. The beef, bison, and trout are local, and all meats are prepared in a butcher shop on-site. The breads are freshly baked and the desserts to die for. An American 1950s-style diner, **Pioneer Grill** ($$, 307-543-2811 ext. 3463, B/L/D) is a place to perch on swivel chairs and either look across the U-shaped, snake-like counter at your neighbor's plate or into the long aluminum kitchen. You'll find a surprisingly interesting menu that runs the gamut, a separate kids' menu, and a take-out window for those on the go. There can be a line during prime dining hours because they don't take reservations. We're partial to ordering from the window and taking our meals to the deck. No trip to the park is complete without kicking back with a huckleberry mojito or margarita at ✪ **Blue Heron Lounge** ($$, L/D), the perfect spot to contemplate the grandness of the Tetons, either through the expansive windows or on the deck, mosquitoes permitting. The bar menu provides sandwiches, small plates, and a handful of entrées.

Signal Mountain: We commend and recommend ✪ **Peaks Restaurant** at Signal Mountain Lodge ($$/$$$, 307-543-2831 ext. 220, D, May to October) for showing other restaurants in the park the way with healthy, sustainable, and organic ingredients. Everything on the uniquely diverse menu is laudable, and it changes throughout the season depending on available local ingredients. The views of Mount Moran, Jackson Lake, and the rest of the range aren't bad, either, so best to get reservations. At **Trapper Grill** ($/$$, 307-543-2831, B/L/D), savor casual, good-for-you-and-the-environment meals—including homemade desserts—while sitting on the deck gazing at the Tetons mirrored on Jackson Lake. **Deadman's Bar** ($/$$, L/D) has the same menu as the grill but is more of a hidey-hole, with a fireplace and one of the few TVs in the park—often tuned to sporting events. The claim to fame: blackberry margaritas and the Signal Mountain of Nachos (bean, chicken, or beef). If you're not expecting fine dining or even table service, **Leek's Pizzeria** ($$, 307-543-2494, L/D, May to September) will deliver for the hungry. Located lakeside, you can watch all the boat activity from the deck tables or inside while you imbibe. Leek's gets chaotically busy, so it's sometimes difficult to secure a table. Still, it's worth the wait.

Moose: For pure, unadulterated views of the Tetons, nowhere tops the deck at ✪ **Dornans Pizza Pasta Company** ($$, 307-733-2415 ext. 204, L/D). It's a terrific place to regroup, and the food is quite good, especially after a day hike or a scenic float on the Snake River. Expect

LEEK'S MARINA SERVES PIZZA WITH A SIDE OF LAKE VIEWS

indoor quarters to be cramped and the bar stools full, so head for the upstairs outdoor tables with million-dollar views of the mountains and river. Next door is ✪ **Dornans Wine Shop** (307-733-2415 ext. 202) for a fine bottle with your meal—no corkage fee—and nearly 1,500 selections at what just might be the best wine shop in Jackson Hole. BYOB is also allowed at **Dornans Moose Chuckwagon** (307-733-2415 ext. 203, B/L/D, June to September), where they have been serving Western-style meals from an open-air kitchen since 1948. Locals and visitors like to carbo-load on breakfasts of eggs, meat, all-you-can-eat pancakes, biscuits, and French toast. Lunches are quick and dinners are cooked in Dutch ovens over a campfire, except on Friday and Saturday, when they host private events. For grab-and-go, 15 made-to-order sandwich options are available at **The Deli at Dornans** ($, 307-733-2415) in the store.

BEST DINING OUTSIDE GTNP

Jackson: Does anyone in Jackson Hole have a kitchen? With more than 100 dining choices, a staggering number for a town of less than 10,000—and more than a few that could blend seamlessly into Portland or San Francisco—Jackson/ Victor/Driggs is a foodie's nirvana. The competition is good news for diners. Naturally, Jackson has its share of meat-focused eateries, yet many restaurants will make you forget you're in the land of rodeos, ranches, and wild animals. Because of the prolific number of choices, we've broken them into *Best in Breakfast*; *Midday or Later*; *Best in Dinner*; *Specialty Dining and Steakhouses*; and *Do-It-Yourself (DIY)*. Our picks aren't entirely based on the best food; some are simply must-stops for ambiance, history, and/or local reputation.

In our *Best in Breakfast* class, ✪ **Nora's Fish Creek Inn** ($$/$$$,

307-733-8288, B/L) in Wilson tops everyone's list, including Food Network's Top Places to Eat. The authentic log and cedar plank walls, colorful Tiffany-style lighting, and rock-wall fireplace are the real deal, exuding warmth and bringing cheer to accompany hearty breakfasts that are easy on the wallet. Bonus: They open at 6:30 a.m., enabling adventurers an early start. A go-to for locals and return visitors is **Pearl Street Bagels** ($, 307-739-1218 [Jackson] and 307-739-1261 [Wilson], B/L) for cuppa joe and numerous flavors of bagels with their version of schmeers. Be forewarned: They'll frown if you ask for bagels toasted. Seating is limited at both locations, but in Wilson lovely picnic tables are perched on the banks of Fish Creek.

"Sharing the love" of New York–style bagels and more is **E.leaven Food Co.** ($, 307-733-5600, B/L). Eat in, take out, or choose delivery of their all-day breakfasts, boiled bagels, fresh-ingredient omelets, tempting pastries, refreshing salads, or upscale hot and cold sandwiches served with homemade chips. Also eliciting long wait lines is **Persephone Bakery Cafe** ($, 307-200-6708, B/L/HH), where you can savor delectables from day-of pastries, tarts, and cookies to top-shelf breakfast and lunch entrées (French toast bread pudding, Snake River Farms Cuban sandwich). Day-of bakery selections mean when it's gone, it's truly gone. Tip: Order online for pickup. **Café Genevieve** ($/$$$, 307-732-1910, B/Br/L/HH/D) is as well known for its log cabin environs as for its southern-with-a-twist cuisine. Creative choices such as Pig Candy (slow-baked bacon glazed with sugar 'n' spice) earned them recognition on Food Network's *Diners, Drive-Ins and Dives*. The café's outdoor seating, daily happy hour, and down-home charm will send y'all back for more. ✪ **Cowboy Coffee Co.**'s ($, 307-733-7392, B/L/MD) well-earned reputation for roasted beans is enhanced by its cozy coffee bar with a groovy, welcoming vibe and prime-time view of Town

Square. Check out the "Perfect Cowboy Coffee" campfire recipe on their website.

For *Midday or Later*, ✪ **Snake River Brewery & Restaurant** ($, 307-739-2337, L/D) is highly desirable for premium brews, fun pub grub, and under $10 daily lunch specials—plus they toss a mighty fine pizza. Need Internet access and some bar bites? Look for the wings capital of Jackson Hole, **Eleanor's Again** ($/$$, 307-733-7901, L/HH/D), located inside Plaza Liquor, where "fine dining without the dress code" is the mantra. Philly fans and nonfans alike can chill or cheer at **Cutty's Bar & Grill** ($/$$, 307-201-1079, L/D) while manhandling any number of cheesesteak combos and hand-tossed pizzas. If you're not into the multiscreened sports scene, punt to outside deck seating. Cutty's also scores points with local fans for their generous fundraising efforts. **Hand Fire Pizza** ($/$$, 307-733-7119, L/D) invites you to enjoy skillfully prepared pizza with conversation—no TVs or WiFi on the premises. Aligning with their keep-it-simple and keep-it-good mission is organic flour, sea salt sourced from Utah, hydroponically grown greens, local nitrite-free beef, red-bird chickens from the region—even logoed, organic-cotton T-shirts. **Liberty Burger** ($/$$, 307-200-6071, L/D), a small Texas-based chain, brought its freedom motto, American-grown ingredients, and environmental sensitivity (tree-free napkins) to Jackson Hole in the shape of burgers in many personalities; just reading the menu is entertainment. A local fav for nearly a decade, **Pinky G's Pizzeria** ($/$$, 307-734-7465, D), also seen on *Diners, Drive-Ins and Dives*, fires up specialty pizzas as well as calzones and strombolis, but your sweet tooth won't be able to resist house-crafted cannoli.

Departing to a more global realm, we suggest **Lotus** ($$, 307-734-0882, B/L/D), which describes itself as "a wellness center disguised as a restaurant." Delicious and wholesome dietary diversity comes in vegan, vegetarian, gluten-free, nondairy, organic, and other options. Keeping it weird is **Thai Me Up** ($$, 307-733-0005, L [weekdays]/D), which is part restaurant, part brew pub, part hipster hangout. You will appreciate their full-service bar famed for cocktail concoctions, such as Thai Bloody Mary and Thaigaritta, and 20 craft beers on tap, including their own brew, Melvin's Beer—a big deal locally. ✪ **Pica's Mexican Taqueria** ($$, 307-734-4457, B[Sunday]/L/HH/D) is consistently voted Best Mexican in Jackson for everything handmade: corn and flour tortillas, guacamole, and *muy delicioso* margaritas. **The Merry Piglets Mexican Grill** ($/$$, 307-733-2966, L/D) takes pride in serving authentic scratch comida and bebidas for nearly four decades. Merry homemade salsa, sauces, and Twisted Cowgirl Dip highlight a long list of specialties, along with fish and vegetarian choices. **Hatch Taqueria and Tequilas** ($/$$, 307-203-2780, L/HH/D/Br) is popular with residents and celebrities alike for open-air seating, 10 varieties of fresh tacos, non-GMO tortillas, and a U-shaped, full-service bar backed by spirits fermented in agave: blancos, reposados, anejos, even mescal.

Two decades ago, when Gavin Fine was a mere youngster of 20, he and his ski-bum friends had a mind-set that high-quality dining in their high-brow valley should be available to all. Fine and his partners created the Jackson Fine Dining Group, and today they have nine eateries. In the *Best in Dinner* category, ✪ **Rendezvous Bistro** ($$/$$$, 307-739-1100, HH/D), the JFDG flagship, combines sophisticated cuisine with affordability—$20 or less per plate is the goal—in a casual wrap. Filling a fresh-fish-in-Wyoming void, **The Kitchen** ($$/$$$, 307-734-1633, D) showcases "raw" at their crudo bar with clean, Asian-influenced cuisine. Dinner can be enjoyed in their unique interior or on a spacious exterior deck during the summer. For specialty groceries, including Cream + Sugar artisan ice cream, light

bites, and gathering with friends, try **Bin 22** ($, 307-739-9463, L/D), where you're encouraged to select vino from their bottle shop inventory or simplify and enjoy carefully chosen wines by the glass (Gavin Fine is a sommelier, too) or a Roadhouse Brew (another JFDG project). Order one of everything from their Euro-inspired small plates and don't pass on hand-pulled mozzarella or their version of an ice cream sandwich. If you favor suds over plonk as an afternoon pick-me-up, try a pint of Family Vacation, an American blonde ale, from **Roadhouse Tap Room** (opens at 4 p.m.). Also on tap from JFDG is **Roadhouse Pub & Eatery**, formerly on Moose-Wilson Road and now on East Broadway.

Two passionate-about-food chefs bring you **Trio: An American Bistro** ($$$, 307-734-8038, D) and **Local Restaurant & Bar** ($$$, 307-201-1717, L/HH/D), both in the high-rent district and both believing in keeping it innovative yet relaxed. Trio's uncluttered menu tempts with BLT soup, wood-fired pizza, and grilled elk T-bone. Local's selections run the gamut, from a clever bar menu (hand-cranked while-you-wait sausage) to creative green salads, raw bar options, and high-end meat entrées. Both will have you coming back real soon.

Noodle Kitchen ($$, 307-734-1997, L/D), formerly Ignite, blends urban chic architecture with Asian fusion: Japanese, Thai, Chinese, and Vietnamese dishes. Choose a bottle of wine from their adjoining bottle shop (no corkage) and savor firecracker shrimp, fresh sushi, or a bowl of ramen. Also noteworthy: handcrafted cocktails. Newer to the scene is **FIGS** ($$, 307-733-2200, B/L/D), a sophisticated, intimate (seats 49 overall and 6 at the bar) Lebanese restaurant showcasing entrées made to share ("Mezze"). Feeling intimidated? Order the intro-to-Lebanese prix fixe meal.

The finest of fine *Specialty Dining and Steakhouses* awaits you in Jackson Hole, where renowned and world-class chefs and restaurateurs abound. Topping the list is **Snake River Grill** ($$$$, 307-733-0557, D), an intimate, special occasion restaurant touting an ever-changing, seasonal, and organic menu emphasizing meticulous presentation complemented by an other-worldly wine list. The popular **Blue Lion** ($$$$, 307-733-3912, D) also has a long history in Jackson, excelling in enticing entrées served in a 1930s residential home; save room for the legendary house mud pie. The wildly acclaimed **Wild Sage Restaurant** ($$$/$$$$, 307-733-2000, B/D) in Rusty Parrot Lodge near Town Square is an intimate place favored for regional and exotic cuisine, fresh seafood selections, and a *Wine Spectator* Award of Excellence wine list. With only eight tables and seating for 32, reservations are an obvious must. Speaking of reservations, make one early in your stay and dress smartly casual for the **Grill at Amangani** ($$$$, 307-734-7333, B/L/D). Located in the ultraluxe resort with succulent hilltop views, the regional cuisine is in complete harmony with its surroundings.

In cowboy country there's never a shortage of sizzling slabs of meat, and Jackson is no exception. Our short list begins with the historic **Silver Dollar Bar & Grill** ($$/$$$$, 307-733-2190, B/L/HH/D) in the Wort Hotel, famed for 2,032 uncirculated 1921 silver dollars adorning the bar. Western history depicted in Ray McCarty oil paintings blends with modern amenities, including eight televisions, a 60-inch big-screen, and live entertainment. The grill side is more intimate and family attentive, with a reasonably innovative slate where even a vegetarian can find satisfaction. Not your run-of-the-mill meat lovers eatery, **Million Dollar Cowboy Steakhouse** ($$$$, 307-733-4790, D) has been around longer than anyone can rightly remember. Current owner Kevin Gries and wife Stacy team to make the most of regionally purveyed wild game and beef. Likewise, if you're into old guns, dead-head mounts, and an open-flame mesquite grill in an exceptionally crafted log structure, carnivoristic **Gun Barrel Steak & Game House** ($$$, 307-733-3287, D) will fill your empty barrels. Look for the famous bugling elk atop the building. For a different take on dinner and a show old-timey style, look no further than the **Jackson Hole Playhouse and Hard Rock Saloon** ($$/$$$ 307-733-6994, D, Monday to Saturday seasonally). Gunslinging and song-singing waitstaff serve gourmet chuckwagon grub at their rowdy, mostly PG-rated dinner theater. The saloon, nicknamed the Million Penny Bar, is the place to lift your sore feet and sip some sarsaparilla or suds on a saddle seat at the horseshoe-shaped bar. Buckin' burgers and swingin' sides can be ordered from a singing bartender to boot. For a modest imitation of a Wild West experience, you'll find two choices: **Bar J Chuckwagon Supper & Western Music Show** ($$$$, 307-733-3370, D, May to September, phone reservations only) and **Bar-T-5 Covered Wagon Cookout** ($$$, 307-733-5386, May to September, reservations required). The Bar J is famed for its musical talent from the Bar J Wranglers and an all-you-can-eat chuckwagon buffet—if you don't mind eating on speed dial (500 served in nine minutes is the record). Down the dusty trail a bit, the Bar-T-5 takes guests in horse-drawn wagons 2 miles into Cache Creek Canyon for Dutch-oven chow of chicken, roast beef in special gravy, famed baked beans, salad with ranch (what else?) dressing, corn on the cob, brownies, and musical entertainment from a four-piece cowboy band. On the wagon ride you'll likely encounter Indians, cowboys, and a yarn-spinning mountain man—entertainment suited to families.

GRAB AND GO

You'll find a bounty of healthy choices—sushi, paninis, salads, soups, and smoothies—at **Jackson Whole Grocer & Café** ($, 307-733-0450). The Market Café (in the grocery) also offers a sushi bar, taqueria, pizzeria, and sandwich bar. At

Pearl Street Market ($, 307-733-1300, B/L), your local source for all things yummy, you can BYO (build your own) sandwich of meats—most natural without hormones or additives—imported cheeses, and artisan breads. Three to six house-made soups prepared daily, fresh salad bar, decadent desserts, and hand-crafted baked goods are just a few of the temptations that might jump into your basket. Better yet, preorder and have your goods brought to the door via their ultraconvenient curbside delivery. **The Bunnery Bakery & Restaurant** ($/$$, 307-734-0075, B/L/D), known as a healthy breakfast stop, is also ideal for grab-and-go with its many bakery items made from O.S.M. (oats, sunflower, and millet), including the bread for their thick sandwiches. Finally, **Picnic** ($, 307-264-2956, B/L) in the Albertsons shopping center is a fitting name for goods suitable for just that—a picnic. You can also get a glass of wine or a mimosa.

For chocolate lovers, we'd be remiss not to include **Coco Love** (307-733-3253), a boutique chocolatier with an array of picture-perfect chocolates, pastries, and gelatos created by Oscar Ortega, the first Mexican World Chocolate Master and former coach of the US Pastry Team.

Wilson Area: Historic **Calico Restaurant & Bar** ($$, 307-733-2460, D), a casual, family-welcoming, Italian American establishment, stakes its claim as the oldest restaurant in Jackson Hole, having moved from Mormon Row in 1966. The original building housed a church, hence the stained-glass accents and vestibule bar behind glass windows. Deck dining, a wood-fired oven, specialty cocktails, solid wine list, microbrews, and hearty portions give it a favorable knowing nod from locals. Fans of Steigler's, a longstanding Wilson mainstay, will be happy to learn **Copper Bar** ($$$$, 307-733-1071, D) opened in the same location and is maintaining most of the German and Austrian selections, with some added warmth and a beautiful

hammered-copper bar. Schnitzel, Tafelspitz, and apfelstrudel will not disappoint loyalists or newcomers. **StreetFood @ The Stagecoach** ($, 307-200-6633, L/D), the last eatery on WY 22 before the highway winds up Teton Pass, has long been a popular watering hole. StreetFood's kitchen combines the element of "no-fuss" dining with the passions of chefs whose reach ranges from Mexico to Korea. Sunday nights are extra lively when the Stagecoach Band rocks the rafters.

Teton Village: Located in Terra Hotel, **Il Villagio Osteria** ($$$, 307-739-4100, D) bakes wood-fired pizza in front of diners to convey authentic Italian country environs. A select array of entrées, solid wine list, and cozy seating complete the experience. The umlauts dotting the menu at **Alpenhof's Dietrich's Bar & Bistro** ($/$$, 307-733-3242, L/D) are a clear reflection of the German and Swiss influence, along with house specialties such as cheese and Swiss chocolate fondue. Bavarian ambiance oozes from the wooden cutout shutters and unusually friendly hospitality at this restaurant modeled after a European ski lodge. For fine dining worth the extra euros, make a reservation at **The Alpenrose Restaurant** ($$$, 307-733-3242, B/D). A dramatically different ethnic adventure, **Teton Thai** ($/$$, 307-733-0022, L/D, Monday to Saturday) is perhaps best known for Thai Tea (a vanilla vodka cocktail), Crying Tiger marinated beef, dumplings, and seared green beans.

Mangy Moose Restaurant and Saloon ($$/$$$, 307-733-4913, B/L/D) is a JFDG anchor and favorite hangout, especially on live-music nights. Lunch is typical pub grub, dinner a step up, and summer deck seating with views of village activity a definite lure. **Spur Restaurant & Bar** ($$$, 307-732-6932, B/L/D) at Teton Mountain Lodge claims a spot for reasonably priced nouveau Western cuisine supported by regional ingredients and inside seating or mountainside views of the Gros Ventres from the heated outdoor patio. Dining at altitude (9,000 feet) after a seven-minute ride on the Bridger Gondola punctuated by panoramic views provide the appeal for **Piste Mountain Bistro** ($$$$, 307-732-3177, D, summer/winter). Northern Rockies flavors from mostly regional ingredients create a rarified-air experience. If drinks and shared plates cooked on an outdoor grill are all you need, **The Deck @ Piste** ($/$$, 307-732-3177, D, summer/winter) delivers—no charge for the view.

Victor, Idaho: For a tiny village in what was not so long ago an obscure corner of Idaho, Victor has a remarkable assortment of excellent dining options, though like neighboring Driggs only two establishments have a full liquor license—as of autumn 2018, Knotty Pine Supper Club and the West Side Yard bar across from Big Hole BBQ. **Knotty Pine Supper Club** ($$, 208-787-2866, L/D) is famed not only for Kansas City BBQ and house-smoked meats with heaping sides, but fresh fish, too. The shadowy Western interior makes you feel as if you've stepped into a John Wayne movie, but the black-and-white photos on the walls prove it's the real world, Idaho style. **Big Hole BBQ** ($$, 208-270-9919, L/D), also in Jackson, is the newest big hit in town. The outside upper deck is the perfect summer place to nibble on brisket, sip on brew, and gaze across the upper Teton Valley. At **Spoons Bistro** ($$/$$$, 208-787-2478, D), where Travis and Nicole try to stick to the true definition of bistro, they present creative American/French cuisine in a family-friendly, scribble-on-the-table, deck-dining kind of place with a kids menu. Where's the beef? **Brakeman American Grill** ($$, 208-787-2020, L/D) has it in a dozen or more burly burgers pattied and grilled in their tiny kitchen.

Walk on the wild side at **Wildlife Brewing and Pizza** ($/$$, 208-787-2623, L/D), a pizza joint and much more, notably the respectable microbrews—eight on tap, some canned and ready for the road.

Wildlife is a consistent go-to place for folks trekking the nearby trails. Speaking of wildlife, **Grumpy's Goat Shack** ($, 208-787-2092, L/D) is worth a go, if just for the experience of trying "the biggest weenies in town." Their eats list, most made by hand, has expanded, but it's still cash only. Newer in town, **Butter Cafe** ($, 208-399-2872, B/L/Br) was opened by the folks from StreetFood in Wilson—Victor residents who wanted more breakfast choices. They take butter seriously, as you'll discover in real croissants, cookies, bars, pastries, and more. **Aztec Fusion** ($/$$, 208-787-1209, B/L/D) is Felix Alvorado's first go at his own restaurant. Although they prepare tacos, huevos rancheros, and the like, Alvorado and his Peruvian partner, Susan Tasayco, want you to know they're more than a Mexican restaurant. Thus the diversity: Aztec chicken, quinoa salad, choriqueso appetizer, and burgers and fries.

DIY If we're staying in or need food on the run, we highly recommend ✪ **Victor Valley Market & Cafe** (208-787-2230), open daily year-round and late. They continue to impress with a wide array of DIY sustenance for the oven or grill, a packed deli case, prepared goodies (baked in the back room by valley elves), and an amazingly diverse selection of wine and premium beer. You won't believe how well stocked they are for such limited space.

Driggs, Idaho: Driggs continues to benefit from Jackson spillover. And nowhere is the growth more apparent than in the burgeoning food scene. ✪ **Forage Bistro and Lounge** ($$/$$$, 208-354-2858, HH/D/Br) heads our happy list for eggs Benedict (Sundays) and wonderful wines by the glass. The short menu is long on the unusual, with seasonal changeabouts that accommodate vegans and special diets. If there's no place to park, you know it's going to be good, which is definitely true at ✪ **Royal Wolf** ($/$$, 208-354-8365, L/D). A locals' hangout in a nondescript, modular building a few blocks off the main drag, the quarters are cramped, bar lively, and menu well on the other side of ordinary. They are known for homemade soups, burgers, and hand-cut fries, but equally good are salads made with real greens and humongous, stuffed Idaho baked potatoes. For those who value locally sourced and sustainable food served by friendly staff, give **Three Peaks Dinner Table** ($/$$, 208-354-9463, HH/D) a try. Three Peaks takes pride in regional fare such as Idaho trout and house-made kettle chips plus a selection of fine wines and live music on Fridays. At ❂ **Tatanka Tavern** ($/$$, 208-227-8744, L/D) everything but the salads is baked in a clay oven visible from the bar. Build your own pizza or order cleverly named pies such as Fungus Amongus and Pigs on the Wing, but don't skip on appetizers such as prosciutto-wrapped asparagus. A heavy focus on rotating regional brews, listed on an electronic board above the bar, makes it extremely popular with the outdoors crowd.

Coming off the slopes, try your Irish luck at **O'Rourke's Sports Bar and Grill** ($$, 208-354-8115, B/L/D), which sports a vast menu and nightly drink specials that should satisfy just about everyone in your group. For south-of-the-border cravings, **Hacienda Cuajimalpa** ($, 208-354-0121, L/D) is a solid choice in a town where a prominent Hispanic population means authentic Mexican fare. You can get much the same across the street at **Agave** ($, 208-354-2003, L/D). **Rise Coffee House** ($, 208-354-7473, B/L), in the old red house once occupied by Pendl's Bakery & Café, will satisfy with a quick cuppa good coffee and a pastry or egg sandwich. **Provisions Local Kitchen** ($/$$, 208-354-2333, B/L/D) offers bottomless coffee, a beer bar, and a plethora of homemade specialties, including signature burgers and tacos.

At Driggs-Reed Memorial Airport, you may catch a glimpse of takeoffs and landings from the windows or patio of

Warbirds Café ($$/$$$, 208-354-2550, L/D, Tuesday to Saturday, mid-December to mid-October). A seasonally changing menu highlighted by elk and bison entrées, as well as the chef's skilled prep of fresh fish, a small but thoughtful wine list, and creative cocktails make for a special dining experience. A 2 to 5 p.m. layover menu of apps, salads, and baskets will hold you over until you reach your next destination. Bonus: free admission to the Teton Aviation Warbird Collection of restored and operable military planes.

You'll find everything you need in healthy food at **Barrels & Bins Community Market** (208-354-2307). Smoothies and other nutritious concoctions are available at the Juice Bar, open 9 a.m. to 2 p.m. daily. **Big Hole Bagel & Bistro** ($, 208-354-2245, B/L) will prepare you for adventure with coffee, bagels, or breakfast and lunch sammies.

Alta/Grand Targhee, Wyoming: Alta is home to Grand Targhee Ski Resort, a fun, friendly, laid-back, and modest-sized ski village at 8,000 feet on the western slope

FOLKS MAKE THE DRIVE FROM JACKSON FOR A MEAL AT BADGER CREEK, A HIDDEN GEM IN SLEEPY TETONIA, IDAHO

of the Teton Mountains. The views are fabulous, the powder beyond compare, and eats not too shabby. **Trap Bar & Grill** ($, 307-353-2300 ext. 1360, L/D), "an après institution," is the place to be after lifts close for "Wydaho" nachos, Baja fish tacos, and house-made soup. Rumor has it if you wear your NFL team jersey on Sunday your first "draft" choice is free. Also on the mountain is **Branding Iron Grill** ($$$, 307-353-2300 ext. 1368, B [weekends]/L/D, summer and winter), with a hot breakfast buffet to energize you for a day on the slopes, midday choices for refueling, and enticing dinners to tempt you into lingering longer.

We also appreciate their superior wine service and classic cocktails.

Tetonia, Idaho: A little country blip in the road 8 miles north of Driggs, Tetonia has conspicuously avoided the tentacles of growth from Jackson Hole. Yet, even with so many dining choices in Driggs, Victor, and Jackson, locals will drive over the hill to ✪ **Badger Creek Café** ($, 208-456-2588, B/L [Thursday to Monday]/D [Friday and Saturday]) for home-cooked meals that rise above standard country-café pickings. They even serve wine and cocktails, and mimosas on Sunday.

INDEX